MIDDLE EAST STUDIES
HISTORY, POLITICS, AND LAW

Edited by
Shahrough Akhavi
University of South Carolina

A ROUTLEDGE SERIES

MIDDLE EAST STUDIES: HISTORY, POLITICS, AND LAW
SHAROUGH AKHAVI, *General Editor*

NEW PYTHIAN VOICES
*Women Building Political Capital in
NGOs in the Middle East*
Cathryn S. Magno

ISLAMIC LAW, EPISTEMOLOGY AND
MODERNITY
Legal Philosophy in Contemporary Iran
Ashk P. Dahlén

TURKEY IN GERMANY
THE TRANSNATIONAL SPHERE OF DEUTSCHKEI

Betigül Ercan Argun

Routledge
New York & London

Published in 2003 by
Routledge
711 Third Avenue,
New York, NY 10017

Published in Great Britain by
Routledge
2 Park Square, Milton Park,
Abingdon, Oxfordshire OX14 4RN

First issued in paperback 2014

Routledge is an imprint of the Taylor and Francis Group, an informa business

Copyright © 2003 by Taylor & Francis Books, Inc.

All rights reserved. No part of this book may be reprinted or reproduced or utilized in any form or by any electronic, mechanical, or other means, now known or hereafter invented, including photocopying and recording, or in any information storage or retrieval system, without permission in writing from the publisher.

Library of Congress Cataloging-in-Publication Data

Argun, Betigül Ercan.
  Turkey in Germany : the transnational sphere of Deutschkei / Betigül Ercan Argun.
   p. cm.
  Includes bibliographical references (p.) and index.
  ISBN 978-0-415-93568-5 (alk. paper)
  1. Transnationalism. 2. Globalization. 3. Turks—Germany—Social conditions.
4. Kurds—Germany—Social conditions. I. Title.
JZ1320 .A47 2003
303.48'2561043—dc21   2002036928

ISBN 978-0-415-93568-5 (hbk)
ISBN 978-1-138-88338-3 (pbk)

To my parents Birsen Ercan and Şanver Ercan

Contents

PREFACE	xi
ACKNOWLEDGMENTS	xvii

I
INTRODUCTION TO DEUTSCHKEI

	3
Political Entrepreneurs with Transnational Linkages	4
Deutschkei	6
Political Science and Transnationalism	7
The Allegory of Field Work	8
Summary	11

II
THE DIALECTICS OF TRANSNATIONAL LINKAGES AND THE TRANSNATIONAL PUBLIC SPHERE

	17
Transnationalism and Globalization	19
Transnationalism as the Deterritorialization of Local Politics	20
Cumulative Causation: An Analysis of Migrant Networks	22
Institutional Indicators of Transnational Politics	23
Non-Institutional Indicators of Transnational Politics	27
The Transnational Public Sphere of Civil Society	28
The Teleology of the Transnational Public Sphere	31

III
MIGRANTS FROM TURKEY IN CONTEMPORARY EUROPE: A GENERAL OUTLINE — 39

Turkish Political Presence in Europe — 40
Next Generations in Transnational Politics — 42
Politicization of Groups — 43
Political Exiles — 44
The Leftists — 45
Atatürkist Thought Organized in Europe — 47

IV
TURKEY, EUROPE, AND GERMANY: A BRIEF HISTORY — 51

Young Turks in Europe — 51
German Influence on the Ottoman Empire — 53
German Influence on the Turkish Republic — 54
Turkey and the European Union — 55
Migration to Europe and Development in Turkey — 57
    Return Migration — 58
    Remittances and the Macro-Economic Effects of Migration — 59

V
BETWEEN DEUTSCHKEI AND TURKEY: THE DIALECTICS OF TRANSNATIONAL LINKAGES — 65

Diaspora as a Mélange of Groups — 66
Differentiation into Sub-National Groups — 67
Host Policies on Immigration, Citizenship, and Multiculturalism — 68
Ghettoization and Identification with Homeland — 70
Indexation to Homeland Politics — 71
Transnational Flows from Deutschkei — 73
Electoral Connections — 74
Europe and Turkish Environmentalists — 76

VI
THE DISCURSIVE TRANSFORMATION OF TURKEY PROPER — 81

The Illusion of Ethnic Homogeneity at Home — 81
The Military and the Turkish-Islamic Synthesis — 84
Coming to Terms with the Collective Shadow — 86
The Expansion of Civil Society in Turkey — 88
The Commercialization of the Media — 90
Turkey and the Internet — 93

VII
THE ALEVIS — 101

Alevism and the Politics of State Reformation — 102
Alevi Revival in Turkey: Politicization, Fragmentation, and
   Radicalization — 104
The Alevi Bridge between Germany and Turkey — 107
Alevis in Cyberspace — 114
The Alevi View of Kemalism — 114

VIII
THE KURDS — 119

Kurds and the Politics of State Formation — 120
PKK and the Internationalization of Kurdish Nationalism — 121
The Kurdish Diaspora in Europe — 123
KOMKAR: A Kurdish Civil Society in Europe? — 128
Kurds in Cyberspace — 130
KOMKAR and PKK on Kemalism — 133

IX
THE ULTRANATIONALISTS — 139

Ultranationalists (Idealists) and the Politics of State Conservation — 139
Gray Wolves in Europe — 140
The Idealist Philosophy in Flux: Islamist Nationalists — 143
The European Turkish-Islamic Union (ATIB) — 145
Turkish Idealists in Cyberspace — 147
The Ultranationalist View of Kemalism — 148

X
THE ISLAMISTS — 153

Islamists and the Politics of State Appropriation — 153
Islam a la Turca in Europe — 155
Transnational Islamist Exchanges — 156
The Official Turkish Islam in Europe — 160
Other Islamist Groups in Germany — 161
Turkish Islamists in Cyberspace — 163
The Islamist View of Kemalism — 163

XI
CONCLUSION 169

The Turkish Diaspora in the United States 171
Final Remarks 172

BIBLIOGRAPHY 175
AUTHOR INDEX 191
SUBJECT INDEX 193

Preface

WHEN PEOPLE MOVE OUT OF THEIR COUNTRIES AND SETTLE ELSEWHERE they do not stop participating in the polities of their origins. Migrants continue to be involved with their homelands not just in obvious modes that have been researched under "remittance flows" by political economists or "return migration" by anthropologists and sociologists. They also participate in homeland politics through elaborate, intricate, open or secretive connections, transfer of political expertise, and dissemination of ideas. In the contemporary world, migrants are *trans-migrants*, which renders nations in practice *trans-nations*.

Several things should be said about case selection, field work, and the methodology of this study on *transnational* connections between Turkey proper (homeland) and the Turkey in Germany (diaspora), dubbed here as *Deutschkei*.

The majority of Turkish citizens outside of Turkey proper are located in Western Europe. The fact that the Ottoman Empire, the predecessor of modern Turkey, has not been a colony (except for a brief semi-colonial experience in its last decades) has important consequences for Turkish presence in contemporary Europe. During a discussion of the subject, Ayşe Çağlar from Berlin's Free University has pointed out that the relative absence in Turkey's history of victimization by colonialism might be responsible for the dispersion of migrants from Turkey all over Western Europe, including Germany, France, Britain, the Netherlands, Belgium, Switzerland, Denmark, and Sweden, as opposed to the relative concentration, for example, of Algerians in France or South Asians in Britain. Indeed, this geographical dispersion seems to have contributed to the very existence and density of linkages between Turks and their homeland.

In a similar vein, the lack of a colonist-colonized relationship between Turkey and Europe may make it easier for the second and third generations of migrants from Turkey to maintain their native language, Turkish, at the expense of competency in the official languages of their host societies. This condition, in turn, might perpetuate interest in homeland and make integration into host cultures difficult.

Geographical proximity between Turkey and Europe plays an important role in the general strength of the ties between migrant communities from Turkey and their places of origin. Geographical proximity, facilitated by relatively inexpensive air fares, lowers the cost of the flow of ideas, goods, services, people, and capital. Today, the fact that one can reach from Istanbul almost anywhere in Europe in about three hours by air has consequences for the geographical dispersion of the Turkish diaspora, their maintenance of close ties with their culture of origin, and therefore for the density of their transnational connections.

Their dispersion in Europe notwithstanding, larger numbers of migrants from Turkey and their relatively extensive networks in Germany make this latter country a good candidate for the study of Turkish diasporic activities. The relative concentration of migrants from Turkey in Germany (around two million) may be attributed to the special historical ties between these two countries. As it will be discussed later, Turco-German relations entered their modern era when the Ottoman elites allowed German soft power to infiltrate their empire at the turn of the 20th century, because they did not feel threatened by Germany, a late entrant into the business of colonization.

Germany's relative colonial inexperience with foreign cultures may also have had consequences for the contemporary attitudes of Germans toward foreigners. Some students of immigration to Germany argue that these attitudes have permeated the German political culture, institutions, and legal system, resulting in the relatively exclusionary character of Germany's citizenship and immigration laws.

By making integration more difficult through an organic conception of national identity and exclusionary policies, German governments have promoted transnationalism, sometimes knowingly and sometimes inadvertently. This explains why groups oriented toward homeland politics are particularly active and numerous in Germany. Many Turks believe that it is unlikely for them to *become* Germans even if they were born in Germany, mastered the language perfectly, and met all the objective criteria of citizenship.

The difficulty of accepting the permanence of foreigners in Germany has also resulted in the consolidation, essentialization, and segregation of foreign cultures. Those policies made it easier for political elites to use them as an excuse

Preface xiii

to justify their active creation of self-sustaining, isolated enclaves among migrants. The pervasive feeling of "otherness" is compounded by xenophobic violence directed towards migrants, which in part explains the degree of ethnic self-segregation and introversion on the part of many Turks in Germany.

The field work for this study took place in early 1999. The main physical location was Berlin, with the largest number of Turks (about 160 thousand) in a city outside of Turkey. Other sites of research included Essen, Aachen, Cologne, and Wuppertal in the state of North Rhine Westphalia, also because of the density and large numbers of migrants from Turkey living in these areas.

The broader political temporal context was marked by the capture of Abdullah Öcalan, the leader of the PKK, by Turkish authorities in February 1999. Preparations for Öcalan's trial generated a heated debate, domestically and internationally, about the state of democracy in Turkey. The resonance of Ocalan's capture also coincided with campaign issues preceding the April 18, 1999 general elections in Turkey. The electoral chances of the Islamist, nationalist, Kurdist, and the ruling leftist parties and how the Öcalan affair would influence these probabilities were all part of the transnational debate between Turkey and Deutschkei. In a sense, the timing of these elections determined the timing of the field work. The idea was that there would be heightened political awareness and activity in the diaspora geared toward Turkish politics, making it easier to capture otherwise more elusive transnational flows, such as discursive exchanges.

The evidence presented here is not hard-core scientific data, but of a rather anecdotal and anthropological sort to illustrate certain kinds of relationships. My goal is not to make conclusive causal inferences, but to suggest the existence of correlative relations. The findings are the outcome of a kind of story telling that uses locations and events as metaphors in the advancement of the understanding of particular concepts.

The qualitative methodology employed consists mainly of elite interviews and content analysis. Interviews with political elites and opinion leaders, who are the very crafters of pervasive discourse, in conjunction with archival and document work, are used to capture what in essence are relatively informal, dispersed, and shifting networks and connections. Such interviews were conducted with representatives of civil society organizations, political asylum seekers and refugees, representatives of the second generation, academics, political representatives, consular representatives, bureaucrats, and some prominent figures of Turkish and German politics.

Deutschkei is essentially a transnational public sphere or, more precisely, a constellation of transnational public sub-spheres. These are spaces where politically significant discursive activities take place. Discourse here is understood in its broader sense, as systematic, spoken and written expression of ideas as well as practices. Therefore, discourse analysis, which takes the semantic sphere as its main unit of analysis, has presented itself as a more appropriate tool for this study.

Content analysis was conducted in media such as newspapers, journals, pamphlets, bulletins, newsletters, radio and television broadcasts, political speeches, books, and articles. These sites constituted the very locations of inquiry where opposition discourses as well as status quo preserving discourses, such as state nationalism, could be detected. In particular, the following was examined for the delineation of discursive patterns: The past issues of the newspaper *Hevi*, a publication of KOMKAR; *Özgür Politika*, a publication of the PKK; Turkish newspapers *Milliyet, Cumhuriyet, Hürriyet,* and *Türkiye*; political magazines *Nokta* (in Turkey), *8. Gün, Alevilerin Sesi* (The Alevis Voice), *Algül* (Alevi); *TBB Spiegel* (a publication of the Berlin-Brandenburg Turkish Community); *Milli Görüş Dergisi* (published by the IGMG); *IBK* (Information Bulletin Kurdistan, by KOMKAR); issues of magazines *Insiyatif* and *Kau Yaz*. Numerous pamphlets and web sites, including those of German foundations and think tanks with special interest in the affairs of Turkey and those of newspapers and Turkey-oriented German research institutions were also scanned for content and discursive structure.

Further reasons for the choice of an interpretive methodology include the following: First, there are few reliable statistical data that could respond to the questions addressed in this study—particularly to those about ethnicity. The latest national census in Turkey, which included a question with respect to the mother tongue to give a sense of the ethnic make-up in the country, was conducted in 1965. From this year onwards, all intelligent talk about ethnicity had to rely, as its quantitative basis, on projections from the 1965 data.

Second, surveys are unreliable sources of information in a context where distrust in government prevents people from disclosing their opinions freely, particularly on issues of genuine controversy. Although public opinion polling is a developing enterprise in Turkey, problems generally attributed to polling and survey techniques, ranging from question wording and sampling to self-selection, are magnified in a political setting where trust and feelings of efficacy have weak presence. Studies conducted and reports prepared by political parties have generated some of the much-needed information about the "ethnic" dimension of the Kurdish question, but reliance on such reports has its own difficulties.

The cyberspace is the quintessential transnational sphere. No study on transnationalism can ignore the cyberspace, especially at a time when some proponents of direct and high-tech democracy are so optimistic about the potential use of the Internet and the World Wide Web to generate mass participation and responsible government. Unfortunately, with the exception of the Kurds, the groups under inquiry here had elementary and minimal presence on the World Wide Web at the time of this writing. Many of the relevant web sites were under construction, incomplete, and rather anemic. Some needed substantial updating. Moreover, Germany and Turkey both have relatively underdeveloped infrastructures for Internet connectivity with expensive access. This adds to the problems many Turkish groups already experience with limited know-how and financial resources.

Although the conditions were not yet ripe for a rich field work in cyberspace, a situation which is undoubtedly changing rapidly, it was nevertheless possible to touch on some of the themes discussed in virtual political chat rooms, engage in some rudimentary homepage analysis, and to present some material from on-line publications put out by various interest groups.

Betigül E. Argun
Austin, May 2002

Acknowledgments

NO PART OF THIS STUDY WOULD HAVE BEEN POSSIBLE WITHOUT THE encouragement, guidance, and constructive criticism I have received from my mentor and supervisor Clement M. Henry from the University of Texas at Austin. I have been a fortunate beneficiary of his open-mindedness, knowledge, and insight.

I am also deeply grateful to Barbara Wolbert for sustaining so much commitment to this work. I appreciate her attention to detail and her all-time readiness to facilitate this work's progression.

I thank the members of my dissertation committee for their time and enthusiasm about this research. Walid Hamarneh, David Edwards, Benjamin Gregg, and Jeffrey Tulis have all been generous with their valuable help at the various stages of this project.

Special thanks should go to my friends and colleagues Sultan Tepe from the University of Illinois at Chicago and Konuralp Pamukcu from Istanbul University for all those thought provoking discussions that I was lucky to have with them. The very seeds of this idea were sown with their help.

My discussions with Ümit Cizre Sakallioğlu and her scholarship have also been a source of inspiration to me.

I am indebted to my family, starting with my husband Murat Argun, my son Deniz Çakabey, my parents Birsen Ercan and Şanver Ercan, my sister Elif Ercan Aslan and her husband Rüknettin Aslan, my parents-in-law Rezan Argun and Turan Argun, my aunt and my uncle Şengül Çakir and Orhan Çakir, and my pooch Pasha, who has always been the heartbeat at my feet when writing. I have to express my deepest gratitude to my mother, my mother-in-law, and my sister for helping me balance the demands of motherhood with those of work.

I thank my friends Sue Gunawardena and Bill Vaughn, who never hesitated to be there when I needed them.

How can I forget my late, dear friend Gabriele Lenden, who offered me so much help and kindness despite her debilitating medical condition. This work is a tribute to her memory. Without her, the field work could never have started. Gabi, my thoughts are with you.

Finally, I thank all my interviewees from Deutschkei for sharing their knowledge, thoughts, hopes, and plans with me. In particular, I would like to express my appreciation to Haydar Avci and Mustafa Düzgün, both Alevi historians, for making work in Deutschkei instructive and enjoyable with their expertise and assistance. Also thanks to Barbara Kellner Heinkele from the Berlin Free University, who offered much help to facilitate my field work. I also appreciate the discussions I had with Ayşe Çağlar from the same university and Jan Rath from the University of Amsterdam as valuable sources of intellectual stimulation.

The archival work for this project took place at a variety of institutions, including the Center for Turkey Studies (ZFT) and the Documentation Center of Migration from Turkey (DOMIT) in Essen; the European Center for Migration (BIVS) in Berlin; the archives and the library of the Turcology Institute at the Free University in Berlin; the archives of the youth association ADA in Berlin; Staatsbibliothek and Gedenkbibliothek in Berlin; Auslaenderbeauftragte des Senats (Commissioner for Foreigners) in Berlin; Auslaenderbeauftragte in Munich; HITIT Verlag; UFUK Kitabevi in Berlin; the Office for the Protection of the Constitution in Berlin; the Perry Castañeda Library (PCL) at the University of Texas at Austin; the Atatürk Library in Taksim, Istanbul; the Turkish Foundation of Social, Economic, and Political Problems (TUSES) in Istanbul; the library of the Turkish Grand National Assembly in Ankara; the Agency for Work and Employment in Ankara and its library; and the State Statistical Institute in Ankara.

The following is a list of some of my interviewees, with some names changed upon request for privacy purposes:

Turgut Öker, the president of the Federation of Alevi Unions in Germany (AABF); members of the Haci Bektaş Veli Cultural Association and the Cultural Association of Anatolian Alevis; members of KOMKAR in Berlin; Ziya Laçin, a writer and researcher for the newspaper *Hevi* in Wuppertal; public relations officials of IGMG in Cologne; Ömer Vehbi Hatipoğlu and Oğuzhan Asiltürk, members of the Turkish parliament from the Islamist Virtue Party (RP) at the time; an official from the Berlin Turkish Hearth, who requested anonymity;

Acknowledgments

Ismail Köse, member of the Turkish parliament from the Nationalist Action Party (MHP); Muhsin Yazicioglu, leader of the Islamist/Turkist Big Unity Party (BBP); Güray Öz, Attila Türk, Metin Ağaçgözgü, Haydar Avci, M. Cebe, and Metin Mat; Ebru Tasdemir from Sender Freies Berlin (SFB4) Multikulti; Ali Yildirim and Claudia Danschke from AYPA-TV in Berlin; producers of TRT-INT in Ankara; producer Gülnur Yesilbas from NTV; Dursun Atilgan, the head of the Organization of Atatürkist Thought in Cologne; Ali Alaybeyoğlu in Ankara from the Coordination Council for Citizens Living Abroad (YYVKK); Kenan Kolat and Bahattin Kaya from the Berlin Brandenburg Türk Topluluğu (TBB archives); Nurhan Akçayli from the University of Uludağ, founder of the Center for Research on Workers Abroad; and Rainer Münz from Humboldt University. I thank them all.

Turkey in Germany

I
Introduction to Deutschkei

O N FEBRUARY 16, 1999, THE WORLD WOKE UP TO A PIECE OF NEWS THAT caught everyone off guard except a few high-level officials and intelligence servicemen. Abdullah Öcalan, the leader of PKK, a Kurdish ethnonationalist organization, was captured by Turkish commandos in Kenya and was on his way to Turkey to face charges of treason, murder, and crimes against humanity.[1]

The news immediately gave rise to simultaneous protests by PKK members and sympathizers in more than twenty cities in Western Europe. Protests in front of Greek, Kenyan, and Israeli consulates and embassies all over Europe made the headlines globally. Angry protesters took hostages, attempted to penetrate consular buildings and to burn themselves. They organized sit-in demonstrations, expressed their frustration to the media, and engaged in clashes with the police. Berlin's police could not prevent three Kurdish protesters from getting shot and killed by the Israeli consular guards.

Frustrated European politicians and officials tried desperately to convince themselves and the public that none of these events had anything to do with Europe. Eager to present themselves as neutral outsiders, European public officials appealed to Kurds and Turks alike: "We cannot let one country's civil war play itself out on our soil" said a high-ranking member of a German opposition party.[2] People watched, with much confusion and disbelief, how minute by minute one country's domestic affairs unfolded on the international stage, from Europe to the Middle East, from the Middle East to Australia. Governments and non-governmental organizations, worried of an escalation of violent protests in Western urban centers, started appealing to the Turkish government to let

Öcalan have a fair trial, open his process to international observers, and not to convict him to death. In the meantime, angry Kurds threatened: "If Öcalan dies, Europe goes up in flames!"[3]

What complicated matters further was the fact that many of the demonstrators were refugees, legal residents, and naturalized citizens of their receiving countries.[4] Their actions not only brought issues like the constitutional status of the Kurds in Turkey, the history of Kurdish resistance in the Middle East, Turkey's relations with the West, and the composition of the Turkish state security courts to the center of international debate.[5] They also raised serious questions about laws and attitudes in Western Europe with regard to immigration, integration, and citizenship.

Immigrants were expected to integrate quietly and display signs of loyalty to their new countries only.[6] The fact that even second generation youngsters, born in Europe, were able to display such passion about what goes on in their parents' home country was upsetting to conventional wisdom and to expectations about the eventual social integration of immigrants. The unstoppable spillover of the most burning issues of Turkish politics onto the relatively stable Western European plain was upsetting to the comforting thought that what made domestic politics "domestic" was the existence of national borders.

POLITICAL ENTREPRENEURS WITH TRANSNATIONAL LINKAGES

Far from being quiet sojourners, migrants "have become major players in international affairs using their 'diasporic' status."[7] Sending as well as receiving governments and political parties are becoming more and more aware of new political networks operated by migrants.

One of the earlier works that has inspired scholars to study migrant political empowerment was Mark Miller's *Foreign Workers in Europe: An Emerging Political Force* (1981). This work anticipated the significance of transnational political linkages and discussed them in terms of migrants' *political capital*. According to Miller, contrary to the "quiescence thesis," through the lenses of which foreign workers have long been seen as powerless and voiceless, "foreign workers possess considerable resources that are of political significance not only to the migrants themselves but also in terms of national and foreign politics in both the host and sending countries."[8] Considering the fact that the communications revolution was at its elementary stages when Miller first published his work, it can be reasonably expected that in this sense much more powerful resources are at migrants' disposal today than any time in history.

New perspectives in research view contemporary migration as an ongoing and multi-level process through which people develop institutions and meanings in multiple settings.[9] Alejandro Portes points out that modern-day migrants are neither "migrants" nor "return migrants" in the traditional sense of these terms. Contemporary migrations, he writes, are distinguished from earlier forms by a cyclical back-and-forth movement through which the *transnational* entrepreneur makes use of differential economic and political opportunities spread across both countries.[10]

The systematic usage of the concept of *transnationalism* was first undertaken by Nina Glick-Schiller, Linda Basch, and Christina Blanc-Szanton.[11] These writers offered new conceptual lenses through which migrants might be seen as "transmigrants." Transmigrant communities, they write, share the significant feature of diasporas of being firmly rooted in their new country, but maintaining multiple linkages to their homeland.[12]

According to Khachig Tololyan, diasporas are "the exemplary communities of the transnational moment."[13] Diasporas develop and maintain multilateral connections with various political and social groups in their host countries, homelands, and third countries.[14] They exchange information and resources with international organizations, governments, and other relevant groups within their host country and their homelands.

Similarly, Rainer Bauböck directs attention to the so called "new status groups" in diasporas composed of people who are not foreigners anymore, but also not naturalized citizens of the receiving country. Baubock sees these multiple memberships in different societies as a decisive contribution toward "the slow emergence of interstate societies."[15]

Diasporic groups establish special organizations to promote their linguistic, cultural, religious and economic interests in both their host countries and lands of origin.[16] This enables migrants (as in the case of those from Turkey in Western Europe) to preserve and develop their identities, distinct from that of the host culture, throughout the second and third generations, regardless of their level of integration and despite the gradual dissipation of the *myth of return*.

Groups in diasporas are better organized, more vocal, and visible in the transnational space between receiving and sending countries. They create discursive fields, or transnational public spheres, that can shed much light on the politics in the land of origin, particularly when they are grounded in more permissive political environments in host countries than in the country of origin. In this sense, political activities in transnational communities, or diasporas, may be treated analytically as *accentuated* extensions of the civil society of origin and its public sphere.

DEUTSCHKEI

The web of networks established by migrants from Turkey in Germany constitutes *Deutschkei*, a syncretic union of *Deutschland* and *Türkei*, as these countries are called in German. Deutschkei is a trans-state or transnational entity, which is neither a mirror image of Turkey proper, nor does it quite display the characteristics of Germany.

This study of Deutschkei is not geared towards understanding how migrants from Turkey operate in Germany or what migration means for German or European polity or for international politics. Rather, this work is designed to be a study of Turkish domestic politics. It looks at Turkish civil society outside of Turkish national boundaries, or from the outside in, to gain a better understanding of civil society in Turkey proper. The main reason for this seemingly twisted logic lies in the very observation that identities, particularly those that do not enjoy satisfactory political representation at home, are *sharpened* in the diaspora.

The idea here is to talk primarily about Turkish politics in a novel way and to imagine how Turkish civil society might have looked like, had it been allowed to flourish more freely. Deutschkei may be envisioned as a self-contained Turkish *ecosystem* surrounded by foreign soil. This geographically imaginary, yet socio-politically very real sphere presents itself more like an extension of Turkey than as a part of Germany, even though its imaginary borders are porous, allowing it to interact with both Turkey and Germany.

The transnational community of Deutschkei consists of *Alevis, Kurds, ultranationalists*, and *Islamists*, among other groups.[17] By feeding back into the politics of origin through a variety of mechanisms, the effects of the transnational public spheres created by these diasporic groups sometimes provide a powerful critique of the system of origin (Alevis, Kurds, Islamists). Other times, the status quo in the country of origin is promoted from abroad (ultranationalists).

In order to operationalize the diasporic effects on the polity of origin, the various ways these four groups relate to the Turkish state and interpret Kemalism, the official state ideology, are examined. The politics of state *reformation* (Alevis), of state *formation* (Kurds), of state *appropriation* (Islamists), and of state *conservation* (ultranationalists) all approach Kemalism differently. As such, these discourses force Turks to reflect on their national identity and on controversial constitutional issues, including the question of ethnic minorities within national borders and the role of religion in politics.[18]

POLITICAL SCIENCE AND TRANSNATIONALISM

Political science is a late and reluctant entrant into the conceptual and empirical terrain of transnationalism.[19] There has been a tendency to view international migration as "a socioeconomic phenomenon largely devoid of political significance," in part due to the now out-dated assumption that migrants have a transitory and temporary presence.[20] As a result, there are relatively few studies that focus on the political aspects of transnational linkages between diasporas and their home governments.[21]

Where the political significance of transnationalism is acknowledged, its treatment has been confined to the "high politics" of national and international security.[22] While works, including textbooks, in the sub-field of international relations have gradually begun to incorporate discourses of globalization into their material, albeit primarily from the perspective of financial flows, they nevertheless remain silent about transnationalism.[23] In this respect, comparative politics have been even more reserved, even though comparativists have much to offer to a better understanding of transnational politics.

As a natural extension of the relative absence of political science in the area of transnationalism, there has also been a relative absence of the *state* in transnational politics.[24] In introductory government and political science courses, the common definition of government, or state, as the "legitimate use of force within *specific geographic boundaries* to control human behavior" remains to be a popular description.[25] However, we now know that on the one hand states may be capable of exerting power over their subjects outside of delineated national boundaries. On the other hand, they can be utterly incapable of exerting power even within their own national borders, precisely because of the processes of globalization and transnationalization.[26]

Important theoretical and empirical questions arise from the relative scholarly absence of the state and its institutions from the study of transnationalism: How do the nation-states handle the emergence of transnational spheres? What kinds of changes do transnational politics cause for the state, which remains the main point of reference of such politics? In short, what does transnationalism mean for the theory and practice of nation-state politics? Is it a new form of nationalism? Do transnationalism and nationalism reinforce or negate each other?

This study is in part an attempt to bring political science into transnationalism and transnational politics into political science. Accordingly, it is also an attempt to explore the relationship between migration and political "development."[27] This work raises the question "how are migration movements and the transnational communities they create connected to the possibility of enhanced political voice in sending countries?" In response, it suggests that under certain national political circumstances, such as restrictions on the freedoms of expression and self-organization, more may perhaps be learned about the local (domestic) politics by examining the interaction between its manifestation abroad and in the native setting.[28]

The existence of transnational communities with continuing interest in their countries of origin and intensifying multiple linkages to their places of origin denotes the process of the *deterritorialization* of the local/national. In a similar fashion, the fact that states increasingly are forced to share power over their nationals with transnational political formations points to the accompanying process of the so-called "denationalization of the state."[29] The conceptual fluidity that these notions offer makes it possible to *imagine* the public sphere in the diaspora as an *extension* of the public sphere in the country of origin.

Therefore, an attempt is made here to understand national politics from the *outside in*, rather than from within, by examining politics in the transnational space. Much may be understood about a country's identity and politics by looking at the activities and outputs of its citizens (or former citizens) outside of its borders. In this sense, the concept of the deterritorialization of the local may be used as a tool in a modified and regionally limited form of "second-image-reversed" analysis.[30]

Social science communities have come a long way in acknowledging the transnational dimensions of sociopolitical and economic phenomena as *constitutive*, rather than epiphenomenal elements of virtually any domestic development to be explained. Yet what transnationalism means for domestic politics is a question that continues to beg theoretical and empirical exploration. In this work the notion of the deterritorialization of the local is applied to diaspora politics vis-a-vis country of origin, with the expectation and the thesis that a clearer picture of national politics might be obtained by looking at how national politics transpire in the transnational space.

THE ALLEGORY OF FIELD WORK

Walking in the Kreuzberg district of Berlin on any given day to get a glimpse of Turkish politics may be likened to having a little ecosystem in your backyard to teach your kids the basics of life on this planet.[31] One is struck by a series of graffiti on the walls and doors of old robust buildings, each several steps away from each other. A garden variety of slogans, each belonging to a different political persuasion, make odd bed-fellows when they occupy the facades of the same street or, at times, the same building: A *Dev Sol* (revolutionary left) statement, next to an Alevi protest of the burning in Sivas, next to PKK's promise for an independent Kurdistan, next to a rallying cry about Islam being the solution, next to some fascist motto.[32]

One gets a similar feeling of awe when one watches a hundred thousand people from the glass windows of a Kreuzberg train station streaming like a political river to Marienplatz to protest the arrest of the Kurdish rebel leader. One sees banners of the German leftists, Turkish revolutionaries, and Kurdish organizations of all kind, including Islamist-Kurdist groups. Messages for brotherly cohabitation and messages that drip blood and promises of revenge all mingle as the crowd slowly passes by, giving enough time to German police cameras to get everyone in the picture for investigative purposes in the future. It is a dense microcosm of politics that would escape the eye in the land of its own reference. In that land of origin there exists, ostensibly, the same diversity, but it is spread so thinly that to encounter such juxtaposition of disparage worldviews one has to cover larger stretches of space.

Thousands of miles away from Istanbul, almost all large Istanbul mosques are represented in this German city by the very same names: *Sultanahmet, Hagia Sophia, Beyazid, Selimiye.* The Kreuzberg of Berlin is the quintessential embodiment of Turkish migrants' efforts to recreate the major symbols of the places they came from: The *Mısır Çarşisi* (the old spice bazaar in Istanbul), the *Galata Bridge*, a replica of *Pamukkale* in Görlitzer Park. The restaurants and cafes of Kreuzberg, Wedding, or Tiergarten, where one can experience the culinary diversity of almost all Turkish geographic regions, carry the names of Turkish provinces their owners come from. German street names have become turkified in everyday language: Brussaer Weg is sometimes called Bursa Weg; Imbros Weg is called Imroz Weg.[33] In an average Turkish home in Wedding, a quick look at the programming on television, or the furniture with doilies and Turkish newspapers on them, or at the tulip-shaped tea glasses with dark red Turkish tea in them, or the young girl serving tea to her guests gives no clue whatsoever that one is in *gurbet* ("place away from home" in Turkish). That realization comes only then when one looks out of the window or listens to a family conversation on life in Germany.

Just like the *Turkish Berlin*, there is an *Indian London*, an *Algerian Paris*, a *Cuban Miami*, or a *Mexican Los Angeles*, with districts of concentrated migrant populations. But these districts do not have firm boundaries. The Little Havana in Miami is *apart* from Cuba, but it is also very much *a part* of Cuba.

This researcher's personal experience on the field itself attests to the very argument that is presented here. I do not mean to suggest that one can make solid inferences pertaining to the collective from personal experiences. I mean that the personal learning experience offered by work on the field may be utilized *allegorically* to better understand and explain the thesis itself.

In this particular case, field work necessitated physical relocation and distancing to understand the political phenomenon at hand. There is nothing novel about going to another country to do field work on other cultures. Although some may argue that an outsider may fail to grasp the "inter-subjectivity" in a cultural setting and therefore simply "miss the point," geographical and paradigmatic distance can add new dimensions to the understanding of a foreign cultural phenomenon.

It is, however, a twist in logic when one goes to another country to study one's *own* culture. It is an entirely different set of circumstances when an insider of a culture looks at that particular culture from a geographical and paradigmatic distance. In my particular case this was made possible by transnational spaces created by migrant communities and the accompanying thought experiment that envisions these spaces as integral parts, natural extensions, or hinterlands of the polity of origin.

Transnational settings provide unique sets of circumstances that may enable researchers to study their subject matter, while operating within them, if their subject matter itself consists of transnational spaces. Two features of transnational spaces facilitate the discursive articulation of the transnational critique and its study:

First, *geographical and intellectual distance from the polity of origin* ensures physical security, and accordingly, freedom of expression and articulation. In the interim period between 1980 and 1983 for example, when all former political parties in Turkey were closed down by the military, these parties all could freely operate in Germany.

Second, the *higher density of networks* facilitates access and interaction between groups. The relatively smaller size of diaspora communities makes it difficult to replicate the same type and level of physical segregation that was accustomed to at the point of departure. The increased frequency of inter-group contacts has consequences for issues like societal polarization or integration.

These settings enable researchers to encounter, personally, what they otherwise would not have been exposed to in their native settings. Such encounters with the "other" are made easier in transnational spaces precisely because what may be hidden in the original environment may be *visible*, both institutionally as well as discursively, in the transnational milieu.

Put differently, the type of field work conducted here is akin to what Harry Eckstein calls "studying small countries."

> [T]he smaller the country, the more likely it is that one can get a decent grip on it in a reasonable amount of time—read the literature, interview important actors, explore its various regions and social segments—in other words, achieve

economies in inquiry. Considering the great complexity of political study that is no small advantage. (Eckstein 1996, 6)

Third, distancing proves to be highly functional for the dual purposes of approximating objectivity and of *unveiling, disclosing*, and thus *learning* about the original environment. Geographical distance creates an intellectual distance that enables one to get closer to the fringes of the paradigm, if not completely stepping out of it. While it may not be safe to maintain a fruitful intellectual existence at the margins of the paradigm in the polity of origin, it may be safer to do so in its simulacrum in the transnational sphere where one is both at home *and* abroad simultaneously. There, one gets closest to the experience of the migrant, that very actor, among others, who makes transnational connections possible. In fact, one gets a first taste of the migrants' life-world at an airport when waiting for a passport and visa check.

In more concrete terms, the following might be said about the methodological uniqueness of studying transnationalism and its various dimensions: At the end of the field work the researcher of this project has acquired a first-hand sense and account of the diversity of her own polity of origin. The point that is telling and significant in this case is the very fact that it takes such physical distancing to expose oneself to that diversity and that the costs of such exposure are much higher at home. In this way, personal experience on the field becomes a metaphor that encompasses and supports the very thesis. That is to say that Deutschkei may be a *field* where the *work* on identity politics in Turkey proper might be conducted. This field lies at once outside of the paradigm of a homogeneous Turkish nation, and is related, in intricate ways, to the very making of the myth of such homogeneity. In other words, the transnational field may be the maker *and* the destroyer of the status quo. The task is to explain how it can be both and under what conditions it might function as one or the other.

SUMMARY

What is to be explicated here is the diaspora influence on the country-of-origin politics, or more specifically, the country of origin's political development, mainly in the form of the expansion of the public sphere of civil society. Whether or not this expansion translates into political liberalization and whether or not political liberalization is in and of itself a good thing are matters that go beyond the parameters of this discussion. In fact, this presentation will show the difficulties in making conclusive normative statements about transnational effects on political development. There is much ambivalence in this respect—that is, in general terms, migration relates to development neither positively nor negatively. Only cautious claims may perhaps be made, depending upon the nature of the groups involved and their interaction with the state.

There are four components of the thesis advanced:

The first is the incorporation of politics into transnationalism. For this purpose, political institutions such as the state, political parties, civic organizations, and political associations are brought into the broader picture of transnationalism.[34]

The second component is the way the public sphere is imagined, namely, the public sphere in its transnational, *deterritorialized* manifestation. As such, migrants and their cultural, economic, and political worlds are viewed not only as building blocs of their receiving national environments, but as natural extensions and elements of their sending national milieus as well.

The third component is the concern with sub-national political groups, rather than with an entire group that originates from a nation-state. Focusing on groups as the main actors, rather than on national diasporas as homogenous blocs, contributes to the very conceptualization of transnationalism, because the transnational condition itself stimulates such differentiation among sub-national groups.

Finally and more significantly, the fourth component of the thesis lies in the recognition of the *dialectics* inherent in transnational linkages. It has generally been postulated in the literature that the arrow of influence runs from the sending country to the diaspora and not so significantly in the opposite direction. The recognition of a genuinely dialectical interaction intends to counterbalance some of the resistance that defines the way we hitherto have thought of diaspora/country-of-origin relationships.

NOTES

[1]PKK (Partiya Karkeren Kurdistan, or Kurdistan Workers Party, at the time, but now Kurdistan Freedom and Democracy Congress, or KADEK) was founded by Öcalan in 1978. Since 1984, the group has been waging a war against Turkish governments. PKK is a Marxist-Leninist organization with training camps in the Near East, Southern Europe as well as in Germany. Until recently, the political and military headquarters of PKK were located in Damascus where Öcalan had resided. When, in late 1998, Turkey exerted pressure on Syria to stop harboring Öcalan, he fled to Italy where he sought asylum and was denied. Öcalan then was captured by the Turkish intelligence officials while trying to leave the Greek Embassy in Nairobi, Kenya. PKK has a political wing, the ERNK, and an extensive political organization in Europe. It is also a member of the Kurdish Parliament in Exile (KPE) based in Brussels. The organization's main publications are *Serxwebun* and *Özgür Politika*, printed in Germany. PKK also has a television station, MED-TV, with a history of broadcasting from London to the Middle East. The group's strategic use of the Internet is also on the rise.

²The Christian Democratic Union (CDU) was the main opposition party in Germany at the time.

³Extensive coverage of the Kurdish unrest appeared throughout the February 1999 issues of *Der Spiegel* as well as in the rest of the German print and broadcast media.

⁴Germany's interior minister Otto Schilly threatened that those who participated in violent acts would be deported. This sparked a massive debate in Germany, since around seven thousand Kurds had refugee status and could not be sent back to their country of origin.

⁵State security courts were the products of the 1980 military coup and they used to consist of two civilian judges and one military judge. These courts now are all civilianized and this change took place, due to pressures from the European Human Rights Court, shortly before Öcalan's high profile trial.

⁶Informal interviews conducted by this author with some German nationals outside of the academic profession displayed a sense of impossibility for people to have multiple national loyalties. The frequent analogy was made between belonging to a nation and being a fan of a soccer team. The "either-or" proposition is formulated as "you have to pick a team. You can't be loyal to two teams simultaneously."

⁷Yossi Shain, "Transnationalism and the American Experience: On Immigration, Nationhood and Citizenship," available from http://www.oneworld.org/ips2/feb99/13_46_037.html; Internet, accessed February 1999.

The term "diaspora" has been used in the literature in its traditional sense, mainly to describe forcibly dispersed populations like the Jewish people. With respect to Turks in Germany or the Portuguese and the Maghrebi in France, William Safran for example writes that they differ from Jews and Armenians in the sense of not having been forcibly expelled, or having a lost homeland to restore, or an endangered culture to maintain. See William Safran, "Diasporas in Modern Societies: Myths of Homeland and Return," *Diaspora* (Spring 1991).

⁸Mark J. Miller, *Foreign Workers in Western Europe: An Emerging Political Force* (New York: Praeger Publishers 1981, 22).

⁹Steven Gold, "Transnationalism and Vocabularies of Motive in International Migration: The Case of Israelis in the United States," *Sociological Perspectives* 40:3 (Fall 1997), 409–428.

¹⁰Alejandro Portes "Global Villagers: The Rise of Transnational Communities." *American Prospect* 25 (March/April 1996): 74–7.

¹¹Nina Glick-Schiller, Linda Basch, and Cristina Blanc-Szanton, "Towards a Transnationalization of Migration: Race, Class, Ethnicity, and Nationalism Reconsidered," *The Annals of the New York Academy of Sciences* 645 (1992).

¹² Ibid.

¹³Khachig Tololyan, "The Nation-State and its Others: In Lieu of a Preface," *Diaspora* 1 (1991), 5.

¹⁴According to Nicholas Van Hear, the term transnational community is a more inclusive notion, "which embraces diaspora, but also populations that are contiguous rather than scattered and may straddle just one border." See Nicholas Van Hear, *New Diasporas: The Mass Exodus, Dispersal, and Regrouping of Migrant Communities* (Seattle: University of Washington Press, 1998).

[15] Rainer Bauböck, "Migration and Citizenship," *New Community* 81:1 (1991), 41.

[16] Gabriel Sheffer, ed., *Modern Diasporas in International Politics* (London and Sydney: Croom Helm, 1986), 6.

[17] The leftist groups are omitted from this study since, in comparison to the groups included, their discursive contribution to the expansion of the public sphere of civil society in Turkey has been rendered minimal due to their perceived radicalism, violent methods, and near-complete marginalization in the Turkish political system. One recent example of the exilic impact on the Turkish radical left was witnessed in late 2000 during hunger strikes by hundreds of mostly leftist political prisoners in protest of the Turkish state's efforts to re-gain control of order in twenty prisons around the country by relocating prisoners to new buildings of solitary confinement. The protests appeared to be in part orchestrated and directed by some group leaders residing abroad, communicating with inmates via cell phones and giving them tactics.

Perhaps due to their higher levels of education and socioeconomic status, which provide them with more *social capital*, migrants who consider themselves moderately leftist or social democratic in political orientation are better able to survive and thrive in their host societies without much need for migrant networks. Chapter three includes a brief discussion of leftist activists from Turkey in self-imposed or otherwise exile.

[18] A similar typology was developed by Yossi Shain in *Governments-in-Exile in Contemporary World Politics* (New York and London: Routledge, 1991). Shain focuses on exilic political opposition and divides groups into three categories: Those who aspire for statehood, those who fight for independence against a foreign invader, and those who try to overthrow the government. This model however does not include *status-quo-preserving* groups.

[19] Ishtiaq Ahmed, "Exit, Voice and Citizenship," in *International Migration, Immobility and Development: Multidisciplinary Perspectives*, ed. Tomas Hammar, Grete Brochmann, Kristof Tamas, and Thomas Faist (Oxford and New York: Berg, 1997), 159–185.

[20] Stephen Castles and Mark J. Miller, *The Age of Migration: International Population Movements in the Modern World* (Houndmills, Basingstoke, Hampshire: Macmillan, 1998), 253.

[21] The term "political" is used here both in its *ideational* and *institutional* senses.

[22] See, for example, Myron Weiner, *International Migration and Security* (Boulder, Colorado: Westview Press, 1993).

[23] Globalization and transnationalism are two different phenomena. Their differences as well as the relationship between them are subject to a brief discussion in the following chapter.

[24] Ishtiaq Ahmed, "Exit, Voice and Citizenship," in *International Migration, Immobility and Development: Multidisciplinary Perspectives*, ed. Tomas Hammar, Grete Brochmann, Kristof Tamas, and Thomas Faist (Oxford and New York: Berg, 1997), 159–185.

[25] Taken, or randomly selected, as representative of other textbooks, from Kenneth Janda, Jeffrey M. Berry, and Jerry Goldman, *The Challenge of Democracy: Government in America* (Boston and New York: Houghton Mifflin Company, 1997). Emphasis added.

[26] I use the term "transnationalism," rather than "transnationalization," throughout the study because the former term stands both for "condition" and "process."

Introduction to Deutschkei 15

²⁷Development, in the context of this work, is understood not in the necessary, linear-progressive senses of modernization and democratization perspectives. Neither does it connote becoming more like the West. Rather, the term is used in the sense of a trend towards enhanced political voice and participation, increased sociopolitical diversity, and the deconstruction of the hegemonic notions of national identity in a polity.

²⁸Inspired by the conceptual questions raised by Thomas Faist, "From Common Questions to common Concepts," in *International Migration, Immobility, and Development: A Multidisciplinary Perspective*, ed. Tomas Hammar, Grete Brochmann, Kristof Tamas, and Thomas Faist (Oxford: Berg, 1997), 247–276.

²⁹Ulrich Beck, *Perspektiven der Weltgesellschaft* (Frankfurt: Suhrkamp, 1998).

³⁰Peter Gourevitch, "The Second Image Reversed," *International Organization* 32 (Fall1978), 881–912. Gourevitch builds on Kenneth Waltz's analytical framework in *Man, the State, the War* (New York: Columbia University Press, 1959). Waltz's work offers three levels of analysis of international conflict. The second level, or the "second image,' explains the outbreak of international conflict by way of the internal structures of the states. Gourevitch reverses the second image to explain variations in the internal structures of states by looking at the international system as the explanatory variable.

³¹Around 30 thousand migrants from Turkey live in Kreuzberg, a colorful, multicultural district of Berlin. During the years of the Cold War, Kreuzberg was leaning against the Berlin Wall and was a rather unpopular division with its heavily immigrant population, counterculture bohemians, and left-revolutionary, anti-fascist youth. It is rather telling that during Ronald Reagan's visit to Berlin in the mid-1980s, the Berlin police, afraid of left-liberal protests, cordoned the entire district of Kreuzberg. With the end of the Cold War, the progressive, multicultural, and artistic environment of Kreuzberg promises to be a tourist attraction and a site where cafes, nightclubs, and ethnic restaurants coexist, just like its inhabitants have been for decades. However, as rent and prices in Kreuzberg are going up, the pressure on migrant populations to relocate may increase. Left-revolutionism and anti-fascism in Kreuzberg seem to cut across ethnic groups and nations. As a result, one sees the more conservative and religious Turks living in other districts of Berlin such as Wedding and Tiergarten.

³²The events in Sivas of July 1993 are of utmost importance to the recent development and politicization of Alevi identity. These events will be discussed in more detail in chapter seven. It should be noted here briefly that in Sivas many Alevi and Alevi-friendly intellectuals and poets were set on fire by Sunni fundamentalists.

³³Martin Greve and Tülay Çinar, *Das Türkische Berlin* (Berlin: Die Auslaenderbeauftragte des Senats, 1998).

³⁴The relative absence of economic factors as explanatory variables in this work has been a conscious choice. The choice was made to emphasize the political dimensions of the subject matter at hand in order to counterbalance the traditional stress on socioeconomic factors in the literature. The author acknowledges that economics and politics are intertwined intricately.

II
The Dialectics of Transnational Linkages and the Transnational Public Sphere

When I was elected to the Bundestag, I was celebrated by the Turkish media as the "Turkish member of the German parliament." So I had to explain to those of the Turkish migrant community who saw the issue that way that I was of Turkish *descent*. Not more and not less. Had I been a *Turkish* member of the parliament, I would have been residing in Ankara and not in Bonn or Ludwigsburg. After a while, this point got accepted. However, the next problem of origin for me was just around the corner. Because my father originated from a Circassian village in Turkey, the Turkish-Circassian community in Germany had approached me: "You are a Circassian. How come you don't emphasize that more in public?" Okay, but I don't speak a single word of Circassian. Through my father I may have some access to another interesting little part of this world, as far as one can talk about it after thirty-four years since my parents have settled down in Germany. On my mother's side, who was born in Turkey and who has lived in Istanbul until the migration, there are Greeks to be found. My mother's grandmother was Greek. In Nazi-German terms then my mother is one quarter Greek. Whoever handles ethnicity in this fashion might as well commit *harakiri*. (Özdemir 1997, 8)

THESE WORDS BELONG TO CEM ÖZDEMIR, THE FIRST GERMAN OF TURKISH descent who was elected to the German federal House of Representatives (Bundestag).[1] In *Ich bin ein Inlaender* ("I am an Insider," whereby "insider" means "native" as opposed to "foreigner" in the German language), the young member of the parliament from the Green Party talks in a humorous but frustrated manner about the *creolizing* influence of national politics and of the inescapable "straight jacket" his ethnic background has superimposed on him.[2]

As a person who was born and raised in the Federal Republic of Germany, suddenly, I was being asked on a frequent basis to take sides in the issue of Turks and Kurds. I had to prove that despite my Turkish background I was no Kurd eater. According to my opponents, from the perspective of my origins, I could not be anything but an enemy of the Kurds. At the same time, Turkish acquaintances would criticize me for attacking Turkey on issues like human rights, torture, democratic shortcomings, and of course the Kurdish question. (Özdemir 1997, 112, 113).

Özdemir, born and raised in Germany, writes that he entered German politics with a focus on issues like environmental protection and nuclear disarmament that had little to do with identity and minority politics. In the face of his ascriptive baggage and in a political milieu where large groups of minorities were desperately looking for political participation through their descriptive representatives, this deliberate single-mindedness did not and could not work.

A variety of themes run through the excerpts above, taken from Özdemir's autobiographical chronicle. These themes include the image of Turks in German society, the tendency to essentialize identity, the collective nature and force of identity, its choice-limiting power, groups' need for political representation, the discursive differentiation between Turks and Kurds, and the self-perpetuating character of transnational connections.

On numerous occasions Özdemir had been criticized vehemently by his German as well as by some of his Turkish counterparts for being too vocal about problems in Turkey, when in fact he was elected to do his job *qua German* in the German political arena.[3] He raised several eyebrows when he called, on the day of the capture of the Kurdish leader Öcalan, for amnesty for PKK fighters in the mountains, Kurdish radio and television programs, Kurdish courses in schools, and the removal of all hurdles on the way for the free participation by the Kurdish political party in the approaching Turkish national elections. However, he added, Turkey had to be given political incentives by the West to adopt such policies, and the obvious incentive would be to add her to the list of candidates for an eventual European Union (EU) membership.[4]

Özdemir, a second-generation migrant, or a German citizen with a migratory background, is both a product and a producer of transnational connections. No matter how integrated he may be the transnational political structure within which he operates does not allow him to escape the multiplicity of his own background. He works with and for the Kurds. He works with and for the Turks. He works with and for the Germans. He helps the Alevis organize themselves both in Germany and in Turkey.[5] As such, Özdemir represents the quintessential personification of transnational politics or of political transnationalism.

TRANSNATIONALISM AND GLOBALIZATION

Transnationalism is an important aspect of globalization. In fact, according to some scholars, it may be explained as a response or reaction to globalization.[6] Therefore, it should not be surprising that much of the theoretical work that went into understanding globalization can be illuminating for the understanding of the nature and the inner workings of transnationalism as well.

Nevertheless, there are some noteworthy differences between the two trends. Although transnational connections develop everywhere around the globe, they tend to be much more regional in their implications and the analytical tools to study transnationalism are better equipped with mid-range theory to explain region-wide phenomena.

The term "globalization" is generally associated with economic and financial trends. Transnationalism, on the other hand, is about political as well as economic linkages. Ulrich Beck, who dwells on the question of what globalization means, writes that massive dislocation of people has not only rendered the idea of closed spaces entirely fictitious, but has also challenged the institutional separation between politics and economics. In a sense, according to Beck, globalization entails the politicization of society.[7] World society without a world-state means a society not politically organized at the macro-level. That in turn means that new transnational spaces of the moral and the sub-political are opened, as exemplified in consumer boycotts or in questions of transcultural communication and critique.[8]

Globalization is generally understood as a unifying process, whereas *divergence* and messy ideological matter like nationalisms are inherent in transnationalism. The distinction between globalization and transnationalism, or "the distinction between the universal and impersonal character of the former versus the political and ideological dimensions of the latter is indicated in ... the use of the suffixes –*ization* versus –*ism*, respectively."[9] Indeed, the term "*trans*national ... ironically, draws attention to what it negates: the national."[10] In other words, although transnationalism and the emergence of transnational spaces constitute an aspect of globalization, transnationalism resonates "with nationalism as a cultural and political project, whereas globalization implies more abstract, less institutionalized, and less intentional processes occurring without reference to nations."[11]

Despite this nexus with nationalism, transnationalism, like globalization, has dented the unity of the nation-state and the national society by deterritorializing the local. The fact that almost everything that happens on the face of the planet is no longer locally bounded means that new actors, new identities, new social spaces and processes emerge.[12] There is a movement from the national to the so-called transnational state as a result of distance and territory becoming irrelevant (*Aufhebung der Entfernung*). According to Anthony Giddens, we live in a "phenomenological" world in which space shrinks and in which space and time are "liberated from their local markers."[13]

Thus, what happens in transnational spaces is, to a significant extent, outside of nation-states' control. In fact, more often than not, transnational spaces emerge as an unintended consequence of state action. Rather than initiating it, the state reacts to activities in the transnational space. By the same token, the more states try to control their transnational extensions, the less control they are able to exert on them. In this sense, transnational politics may be seen as the grand facilitator of exogenous influences on the state and the transnational critique may function like a surrogate system of political checks and balances.

TRANSNATIONALISM AS THE DETERRITORIALIZATION OF LOCAL POLITICS

Anthropologists were among the first social scientists who came to the realization that culture and identity could no longer be analyzed as local and territorially bounded. There are now calls for a new ethnography and anthropology to understand the "delocalized" or the *re-localized*.[14] In fact, the rupture between locality and territory has reached such proportions that some scholars like Roland Robertson talk, instead of globalization, of *glocalization*, or global localization, whereby global trends adapt to local realities and the local and the global coexist in various forms and places.[15]

In other words, in contrast to the claims made by theorists of "global convergence," what is happening today may not be described as the "McDonaldization" of the world.[16] Rather, the local is resisting homogenization in two ways: First, local cultures connect to the global without losing their *localness*, but by adapting to it. In a sense, the local and the global are not mutually exclusive, but the local needs to be understood as an aspect of the global and the global culture can only be understood as a contingent, dialectical process with conflicting, paradoxical, ambivalent, and contrasting elements.[17]

Second, local cultures reproduce themselves in borderless, transnational realms that cut across nation-states.[18] Put differently, local specifics are being situated transnationally, and sometimes even globally. Instead of integrating into host societies, relocated people tend to create simulacra of countries of origins in transnational spaces.

There is something inherently and intensely political about transnational spaces within which cultures of origin are recreated. Even those who are re-localized for non-political reasons experience the politicizing effects of the kinds of self-perception, communal solidarity, and exposure to other groups that are unique to the very experiences of relocation and dislocation.[19]

According to Arjun Appadurai, deterritorialization sometimes produces *exaggerated and intensified* senses of criticism or attachment to politics in the home state.[20] This happens because what characterize the new era of globalization are the "new role for imagination in social life" and the "transnational construction of imaginary landscapes."[21] In this sense, the homeland is partly invented, existing in part in the imagination of deterritorialized groups and sometimes it can be so fantastic and one-sided that it fuels new conflicts.[22] Appadurai gives the example of the creation of *Khalistan*, an invented homeland of the deterritorialized Sikh population of England, Canada, and the United States, to illustrate the potential for conflict in such "ethnoscapes."[23]

Deterritorialization also creates the mechanisms that perpetuate such imagination of the homeland. Apart from the known effects of the global media on the imagination, such as satellite television and new forms of electronic communication, deterritorialization creates new markets for networks such as film companies and travel agencies, which thrive on migrants' need for contact with their homeland.[24] Appadurai's depiction of the making of *virtual neighborhoods* and *imaginary landscapes* in the transnational space is reminiscent of Benedict Anderson's "imagined communities."[25] The new ingredient in Appadurai, however, is the deterritorialization of nationalism.

Along the same lines, Martin Van Bruinessen discusses the emergence of a non-military and a politically sophisticated Kurdish nationalism in Europe. He offers the example of a "high Kurdish" in the process of development, namely *Kirmanci*, transcending other Kurdish dialects, becoming the language of writing, and thus facilitating the dissemination of nationalist ideas to unify the Kurdish diaspora at a discursive level.[26] Here, indeed, Benedict Anderson's and Jürgen Habermas's analyses of the effects of "print capitalism" on the emergence of European nationalisms and on the emergence of a critical public sphere respectively find one of their applications in the twentieth century, in the midst of Europe and by a non-European nationalism.[27]

The policies of sending and receiving country governments contribute to the politicization of transnational spaces. Sending countries may utilize outreach strategies toward migrant communities in order to have their national loyalties preserved for purposes such as having pressure groups abroad or maintaining continuous sources of financial flow. Political parties of the sending country may have their own outreach programs. On the other hand, receiving countries may adopt policies geared towards *disaggregating* migrants' official national identities into group-specific identities and thereby foster, actively and sometimes unintentionally, the divisions between ethnic and religious groups coming from the same land of origin.

Transnational political spaces inherently are realms where issues of political significance are discussed and acted upon. They are public spheres consisting of discursive communities that can produce new political ideas and put a new spin on old ones. In the transnational public sphere, where there are fewer impediments on the expression of thought, what cannot be said at home might sometimes be articulated at a diminished cost.

The World Wide Web with its numerous sites and Usenet groups with their various chat rooms are near-perfect examples of transnational public spheres. In these cyber-salons, composed of quasi-Rawlsian subjects, subversive political thoughts find their expression without fear of prosecution.[28] Depending upon the character of the political regime in the country of origin, citizens' activities abroad and *netizens'* discursive sorties from the cyberspace may produce, in varying degrees, amplified versions of emancipating, identity-unveiling, status-quo disrupting or preserving discourses that may have politically significant consequences in receiving as well as sending societies.[29]

CUMULATIVE CAUSATION: AN ANALYSIS OF MIGRANT NETWORKS

Most previous research on migration has focused on the question "why do people migrate?" The question "what would happen when people continue to migrate" is a relatively new one. Rather than asking the cause-effect oriented question why and how migration occurs, the *processual,* as opposed to *causal,* approach is interested in what happens once migration starts.[30] Migration, from this perspective, is seen as a *continuous* process with economic, political, and social implications. The type of causation, if it at all can be established, can best be captured under the rubric of *cumulative causation* or the so-called *determining* effects of early migration on later migration. In other words, once migration starts and continues as a process, it prepares the framework within which later processes and results of migration take place.

Migrant networks are the incubators of the cumulative effects of earlier migration on later migration. As a result they deserve special attention. Ludger Pries writes that "[t]he first step in the expansion of scientific reflection over migration processes is not only, in an isolated fashion, to explore the social, cultural economic, and political circumstances in the receiving and sending regions, but the social networks and the migration chains inside the migration systems, which practically function as communications channels between the two worlds in two geographical spaces."[31] Indeed, consecutive migrants follow the footsteps of pioneer migrants and depend on networks formed by them to survive the trauma of deterritorialization.

Networks are also the main vehicles of the deterritorialization of the local. "In its most general form spatial movement can be understood as a transfer not only from one place to another, but also from one social unit or neighbourhood to another. This transfer may strain, rupture, change or reinforce previous social ties."[32] The transfer of entire localities from places of origin to new settings in receiving societies takes place through migrant networks and through the process of *chain migration*. As such, networks are the primary facilitators of chain migration.

Networks perpetuate themselves as part of the very process of migration and, in doing so they are responsible for making migration a continuous phenomenon. Continuity is one of the features of contemporary migratory movements that distinguishes them from previous ones and gives them their transnational character. It takes *social capital* to build networks. Social capital consists of resources such as information on jobs in a potential destination country, knowledge of the means of transport, or loans to finance a journey to the country of destination. These resources reduce the costs of further migration and therefore facilitate chain migration, which itself is, along the logic of cumulative causation, a self-feeding and a self-reproducing process.[33]

Migration from Turkey to Europe in general and to Germany in particular has primarily been labor migration with a predominantly rural sociological genesis. This may in part explain the high levels of networking among migrants from Turkey in Europe, their reliance on networks for the accumulation of new social capital and the linkages that they preserve, and in some instances enhance, with the country of origin.[34] Indeed, one comparative study on Colombian and Dominican migrants in New York City during the 1980s found that those with already high levels of social and financial capital needed networks less than those who had lower levels of such capital. By the same token, immigrants who relied on social networks tended to integrate less socially and culturally. They had weaker language skills and had lower paying jobs.[35]

INSTITUTIONAL INDICATORS OF TRANSNATIONAL POLITICS

Some forms of diaspora influence on the country of origin are based on strong institutional ties and therefore are easier to detect. Institutional influences include forms of participation in the home country polities that may be classified as *financial* (remittances, investment, consumption, donations, and fund raising), *consular* (diplomatic activities, outreach programs, and lobbying), *elec-*

toral (voting), and *associational* (networks, civic organizations, and political parties).

In the particular case of Turkey, previous attempts to operationalize the reverse effects of migration tended to focus primarily on *one-time* migration and on financial variables producing social and economic change. These include changes in the socioeconomic relationships in the country of origin caused by return migration, particularly, changes in the socioeconomic status of women; changes in the macroeconomic indicators of the economy of origin, such as the employment rate and the balance of payments affected by return migration, the flow of remittances, and tourism revenues obtained from annual vacations in the country of origin; workers cooperatives, real estate investments, and development projects financed by remittances; problems with re-integration; and the education of returnees' children.[36]

There is now noteworthy research on migrant networks around the world, which attempts to capture not only the back-and-forth-ness of contemporary migration, but also its effects on the political, social, as well as economic institutions of the origin. Daniel Elazar, for instance, shows how Israeli institutions are fashioned after those of the diaspora.[37] Patricia Landolt discusses the Salvadoran transnational institutions that link El Salvador to Salvadoran settlements in the U.S.[38]

In their works that discuss the transnational space between the state of Puebla in Mexico and New York City, Robert Smith and Ludger Pries show that there is a continuous coming and going, a circulation of transmigrants, who, for a certain period, look for jobs in the United States, go back, and later migrate again, as well as a constant flow of information and goods between the two areas.[39]

Pries writes that migrants transform the country of arrival qualitatively. But simultaneously the localities of origin remain the central reference points in their life projects.

> In New York they organize support committees that install drinking water pipelines or restore churches in the communities of origin. They collect money, through telephone conferencing they ask questions to the native authorities and participate in the decision making. They take video and audio recordings to send home to keep in touch. In the U.S. they consume Mexican TV programming. Their organizations (e.g. *Frente Indigena Oaxaquena Binacional*) and journals (e.g., *La Mixteca Ano 2000*) deal with issues ranging from the economic interests of the migrants to their human rights, remittances, direct investment, home construction, land improvement, water facilities, vacations, village celebrations. (Pries 1998, 69)

Smith and Pries both describe a lively scene of economic activities in New York, particularly of the *Puebla Food Incorporation*, distributing *tortillas* all around the city. The remarkable parallel is the *pide* (Anatolian flat bread) distribution to *döner kebap* (gyro) restaurants in Berlin among Turkish migrants. Further parallels may be found between neighborhoods in Queens and part of the Amsterdam Street where the Mexican cultural and economic infrastructure lies on the one hand and Kreuzberg and Oranienstrasse in Berlin where the Turkish economic infrastructure has developed on the other.

Migrants' increasing economic strength add to their developing political potential. The emergence of migrants as potential and actual political forces gives rise to all sorts of government outreach programs to incorporate them into national political systems. In Haiti, a country politically divided into nine administrative departments, overseas Haitians are recognized as the tenth department complete with their own ministry.[40] The Chinese government has, in recent years, stepped up contacts with overseas Chinese around the world and created the Overseas Chinese Affairs Commission (OCAC) not only to serve Chinese interests abroad, but also to have this institution serve as a bridge between the Chinese government and Chinese residing abroad.[41] The government of El Salvador, for example, has provided free legal assistance to political refugees, fleeing their own regime, so that they may obtain asylum and remain in the United States, remitting some one billion dollars annually.[42]

Some governments give incentives to their expatriate nationals to function as their "arms" abroad. The *Direzione dell'Emigrazione* in the Italian foreign ministry coordinates and gives financial support to migrants' associations and organizations. Consular officers sometimes initiate organizational activities where they have not emerged spontaneously.[43] The *Instituto Espanol de la Emigracion*, attached to the office of the secretary of labor in Spain, encourages the creation of associations that strengthen Spanish identity and permit emigrants to maintain strong ties with their home country.[44]

Steven Vertovec writes that

> [g]overnments of the same nations have started to perceive their expatriate communities as a source of investment, entrepreneurial initiatives, markets for home country companies and even political representation abroad ... The mobilization of third world governments in pursuit of economic and political benefits of transnationalism has taken several forms that range from the creation of a specialized industry or government department in Haiti and Mexico, the granting of dual citizenship and the right to vote in national elections in Colombia, and new legislation allowing the election of representatives of the diaspora in the national legislature in Colombia and the Dominican Republic. From these policies, it is clear that sending governments do not want their

immigrants to return, but rather to achieve a secure status in wealthy nations to which they have moved and from which they can make sustained economic and political contributions in the name of patriotism and hometown loyalties. (Vertovec 1999, 467)

Luis Guarnizo has shown in his research on Mexico and the Dominican Republic (1994, 1996) that the state reaches beyond national borders to capture remittances and migrant support through incentives like health and welfare benefits, property rights, voting rights, rights to dual citizenship and so on.[45]

The Mexican state, for example, has over the recent years recognized not only the enormous economic but also the political potential of migrants for exercising pressure on the United States government in favor of Mexican national interests.[46] The Program for Mexican Communities Abroad (PCME) aims at encouraging Mexicans and people of Mexican origin to maintain ties with Mexico.[47] It was created to gain migrants' support for the government and the ruling party and to prevent embarrassing mobilizations abroad in favor of the opposition. In the context of the new U.S.-Mexico partnership under the North American Free Trade Agreement (NAFTA), the Mexican government sought, in particular, to stop damaging demonstrations abroad against human-rights violations and fraudulent electoral processes at home.

In the end, the program and accompanying legislation to extend U.S. citizenship to Mexican immigrants ended up extending the migrants' capacity to mobilize and to be heard, both in the United States and in Mexico. Thus, the president of the Zacatecan Confederation in Los Angeles reported in 1997: "Though the Consulate created the Federation to control us ... it did not anticipate the result."[48] *Radio Bilingue* in Fresno, California, headed by an Oaxacan Mixtec Indian, was used by Oaxacan organizations in both countries to put pressure on the Mexican government for the release of kidnapped Indian leaders: "If something happens in Oaxaca we can put protesters in front of the consulates in Fresno, Los Angeles, and Madera" declared a local organizer. His view was supported by consular officials who lamented that Oaxacan Indian demands had to be given greater attention when made in California than in Oaxaca.[49]

Similarly, Ludger Pries discusses the direct political connections in the U.S.-Mexican case:

> Since the presidential elections in 1988, the critical electoral potential of the transmigrants who disproportionately vote against the PRI became more obvious. Now the Mexican government is making an active and targeted effort to establish and maintain economic and politico-cultural connections with the transmigrant communities. The mayors of small Mexican communities visit New York in order to propose investment projects to the migrant associations

to benefit village development back at home. The Mexican government actively supports the development of *Guadelupana-Groups* in New York. Thus labor migration is no longer seen as a passive security valve for the economy but as an active potential of capital and human resources for one's own economic and social development. (Pries 1998, 66)

NON-INSTITUTIONAL INDICATORS OF TRANSNATIONAL POLITICS

The consequences of migration and the transnational traffic resulting from the reverse effects of migration flowing from the diaspora to the country of origin go beyond economic results and extend not only to political institutions but also to political culture. Some works on migration to and from the United States at the turn of the century show how returnees carried religious and political ideas, skills, and know-how to their lands of origin. [50]

Non-institutional forms of such influence may be harder to pin down. Such forms may be categorized as *unconventional* (terrorism, violent protest), *ideational* (such as discursive structures and the transnational dissemination of political ideas), and *contextual* (such as impact exerted through regional organizations). As Alejandro Portes points out, "the less institutionalized initiatives of ordinary immigrants and their home country counterparts represent the more novel and distinct development ... and, hence, the one that deserves the greatest attention."[51] The case of migrants from Turkey in Western Europe offers a good field where transnational activities of a rather low level of institutionalization (what Portes calls *grassroots transnationalism*) can be studied.

Sending states, which have a long history of emigration, tend to have more developed and articulate migration policies, commensurate institutional structures, and a pervasive network of consular offices to channel and control the migration process in all stages. Turkey, on the other hand, is a relative newcomer to emigration. Prior to 1960, Turkey did not systematically export labor. The first major goal of Turkish migration policies was to export as many workers as possible, without considering possible consequences.[52] Therefore, despite massive emigration, compared to other countries, Turkey has the least developed official network of organizations in receiving lands. While consular activities have been extended in recent years, the Turkish government has not been able to rally significant Turkish organizations around such activities. The reasons are primarily political, but they also reflect Turkey's inexperience in dealing with issues that arise from migration.

Much of diaspora activity vis-à-vis Turkey is of non-electoral nature because Turkish nationals abroad can only cast their votes at border stations of mainland Turkey. Non-electoral forms of participation in homeland politics include protests, boycotts, publications, recruitment, and lobbying of host governments in favor of or against homeland policies. Some national leaders at home acquire training and expertise while they spend time as political activists abroad. Civic associations in the diaspora support political formations back home by offering their organizational expertise, finances and/or ideology.

Unlike those of any other sending country, Turkish organizations in host societies consist of numerous extremist groups, reflecting ideologies from the extreme right and religious groups to those of the extreme left. Unlike in Italian and Spanish cases, where the state has been successful in tying emerging and existing groups into a comprehensive network, Turkish organizations formed their own ideologically divided peak associations abroad. The apparent inability of the Turkish state to exert greater influence over the process of emigration has meant that a number of interest groups outlawed in Turkey have seized the opportunity to seek converts among increasingly alienated migrant populations.[53]

Turkish networks abroad take informal as well as formal forms and Turkish grassroots media have existed in a highly irregular fashion, depending, for systematic output, on regular availability of funding. The exchange that takes place with Turkey, although frequent and dense, is not always systematic and patterned.

A rather indirect, informal, and discursive mode of influence or political participation comes in the form of *transnational critique*. Transnational politics may offer alternative ways of thinking about national issues and may at times culminate in the emergence of new political movements, parties, and civil society organizations in the country of origin through the transfer of ideas, discourses, and political expertise from abroad.

THE TRANSNATIONAL PUBLIC SPHERE OF CIVIL SOCIETY

At its worst, the cultivation of subversive ideas abroad may have profound destabilizing effects on a regime which is already suffering from legitimacy problems. At their best, such ideas can provide the checks and balances or the auto-critique mechanisms that a political system may be lacking endogenously. Physical and juristic distance from the power structures of the origin helps the transnational space to offer a viable alternative milieu where critical discourse can flourish and thereby enhance the political voice of citizens abroad.

The plural and diverse configuration of transnational communitie facilitates an environment of contestation and a clash of opposites.[54] In fact, some analysts see the presence of a multiplicity of discourses and opinions and the lack of centralized command structures as the main characteristics that distinguish diasporas from ethnic groups.[55]

Migrants' heightened political awareness and the facilitating environment provided by the transnational space together make up the vital ingredients for lively political exchange that is expected to take place in *the public sphere of civil society*. There are important reasons why this Habermasian notion is attractive for the study of transnationalism and is a useful conceptual container to capture what is meant by diasporic feedback in the form of transnational critique.

First, Jürgen Habermas's conceptualization of the "public sphere" distinguishes this realm from the more institutional infrastructural bases of civil society. From a strictly analytical standpoint, the Habermasian public sphere is an arena distinct *both from the state and the market*. The public sphere is "an operationalization of civil society's capacity for self-organization, one that emphasizes plurality and reason."[56] In other words, the public sphere develops independently from the specific direction of state power. The fact that this arena is separate from the realm of state authority makes unhindered rational conversation about issues of political significance within it possible.

Second, the public sphere is *political*. The genesis of the public sphere may be traced back to nonpolitical settings such as cafes and salons, the world of letters, and the flow of commercial goods. But when a critique of privileged institutions such as the church and the state came out of those settings in the eighteenth century, the sphere itself became politicized.[57]

The *public-ness* of the public sphere itself has a politicizing effect on issues that enter its realm. But the simple move from the private to the public is not sufficient for politicization.[58] As Jose Casanova's analysis of the deprivatization of religion as a contemporary phenomenon shows, the political-ness in the move from the private to the public lies rather in the "relocation from a pre-modern form of public-ness to the public sphere of civil society" or a "change in the type of publicity."[59] In particular, when previously private issues that are articulated in the public sphere place demands on the state, they acquire a political character.

Third, the public sphere of civil society possesses an *emancipating* potential or a "potential as a foundation for a critique of society based on democratic principles."[60] Critical reasoning vis-a-vis the state constitutes the central function of the civil public sphere. It is a medium of criticism that targets entrenched structures of political power.[61] In this sense, transnational public spheres "have the potential to liberate nationals within them who are able to escape in part the totalizing hegemony that a strong state may have within its national borders."[62] Discourses that emerge in such spheres articulate forms of community consciousness and solidarity that maintain identifications outside the national time/space.[63]

Fourth, participation in the public sphere is *discursive*. This is why it resonates so well with Habermas's conception of social integration. According to the Habermasian model, social integration emerges in and through the discursive participation of individuals, groups, social movements, and institutions in a public sphere of civil society where the collective construction, reconstruction, contestation, and affirmation of the common good takes place. [64]

Robert Wuthnow's study of the Protestant Reformation, Enlightenment, and Marxism as discourses that challenged the status quo demonstrates the significant moments in history when the discursive and emancipating potential of the theory of the public sphere manifested itself. These were periods in which the horizons of thought expanded through discourses that challenged the status quo. Ideas were produced, disseminated, and proliferated through sermons, pamphlets, letters, books, newspapers, party platforms, political tracts, philosophical treatises, propaganda, instructions in the ways of worshipping, theological writings, literature, plays, and other formalized modes of cultural production in institutionalized contexts such as churches, salons, and so on. Ideas dealing with the lasting questions of freedom, faith, civic order, and the like managed to disengage from their social situations by which they were shaped and have a broader cast.[65]

The specific dimension of country-of-origin polity on which this work focuses is the expansion of the public sphere of civil society. The findings presented in this study do not go as far as suggesting that political activities of migrants and the discourses that emerge abroad have *direct* effects on political events in the country of origin or in any way set the parameters of public discourse in that country. In fact, one of the biggest challenges a study of this kind has to face is to establish clearly the *link* between political identification among members of the diaspora with the land of origin on the one hand and the actual effects on politics of origin on the other.

Rather, a more modest claim is made here that there seems to be a reciprocal exchange between national and transnational realms which needs more exploration and that this exchange has a potential to gain importance in the future. What goes on in the transnational community matters for the trajectory of ideas about national identity, citizenship, social integration, and democracy in the native setting.

In a sense, one might suggest that had there been less restriction on freedom of thought, expression, and organization in Turkey the Turkish society might have, politically, looked more like its simulacra in Europe today. This counterfactual proposition may be utilized as a conceptual tool—that is, as a kind of hypothetical thought experiment to study opposition movements more easily and perhaps more reliably. This argument assumes that Turkish politics may be developing more "naturally" in Europe than at home.

In another sense, however, it might be claimed that had Turkey been a genuinely liberal polity, the so-called "Turkey in Europe" might have been less political and less radical. This argument is based on the premise that there is in fact something out-of-the-ordinary about diaspora politics and that diasporas may be particularly radicalized.

Finally, the claim may be made that had it not been for Turkey in Europe, Turkish polity today would have been, perhaps, more restrictive. This counterfactual best conforms to the thesis presented here. Starting with Young Turks at the turn of the century, the Turkish public sphere in Europe has contributed and continues to contribute to political development in Turkey proper. Therefore, the more recent mechanisms of this political influence should also be explicated by situating them in the wider net of relations between contemporary Turkey and contemporary Europe.

THE TELEOLOGY OF THE TRANSNATIONAL PUBLIC SPHERE

Is there a positive normative relationship between transnationalism and political development? Is the emergence of destabilizing anti status quo discourses in and of itself a good thing? How does civil society relate to democratization? Whether or not migration and the transnational linkages resulting from it affect political development in sending societies positively is a question with no conclusive answer.

Some observers see an affirmative relationship between transnationalism and political development at home. Alejandro Portes writes that

> [i]n general, the overall bearing of transnational activities on sending countries is positive, in both economic and political sense, even though they do not necessarily bolster the existing social and political order. Migrant remittances and business investments promote economic growth and, in this sense, contribute to stability in their nations. But migrant transnational political activism is more likely to line up with the forces of change, promoting democracy, lesser corruption and lesser violation of human rights at home. (Portes 1999, 474, 475)

On the other side of the debate, Sheri Berman's historical study of civil society in Weimar Germany, which deals directly with this normative issue, gives a more qualified answer. In contrast to optimistic neo-Tocquevillian theories of civil society and democracy, Berman's study of associational life in the Weimar Germany shows that "associationism should be considered a politically neutral multiplier—neither inherently good nor inherently bad, but rather dependent for its effects on the wider political context."[66]

Berman argues that studying civil society without paying attention to the nature of the ties that bind it to the larger political context of development, which includes political institutions and parties, little could be understood of what makes democracy work. She shows that in the case of the Weimar polity, weak political institutionalization, the absence of strong and responsive political parties, and a segmented civil society with groups catering to the elite rather than establishing connections with grassroots constituencies might have enhanced political instability.

> If a country's political institutions and structures are capable of channeling and redressing grievances and the existing political regime enjoys public support and legitimacy, then associationism will probably buttress political stability by placing its resources and beneficial effects in the service of the status quo. This is the pattern Tocqueville described. If, on the contrary, political institutions and structures are weak and/or the existing political regime is perceived to be ineffectual and illegitimate, then civil society activity may become an alternative to politics, increasingly absorbing citizens' energies and satisfying their basic needs. In such situations, associationism will probably undermine political stability, by deepening cleavages, furthering dissatisfaction, and providing rich soil for opposition movements. (Berman 1997, 427)

Within the wider political context, the reaction of nation-states to their diasporas, to the individual groups in their diasporas, as well as to extra-national influences may vary significantly. As a response to the dual processes of globalization and transnationalism, nation-states may become introverted. But they just as well may orient themselves actively toward the outside, may change and improve their politics, and redefine their identity.[67]

Although the thesis advanced here in great part conforms to the notion that the expansion of the public sphere of civil society is overall a positive development and that transnationalism is a contributing factor in this process, it should be restated that transnational spaces may breed progressive as well as conservative forces and that transnational activities may have both positive and negative destabilizing effects back at home.

The case of Deutschkei and its relationship to Turkey shows that the transnational public sphere of civil society contains both pro-change and status-quo preserving groups, giving force to the claim that the nature of the transnational feedback is normatively complicated, uncertain, and relatively unexplored. How political groups relate to the state and how the state responds to these groups may ultimately determine the overall outcome.

NOTES

[1] In July 2002, due to a financial mismanagement crisis, Özdemir announced that he would resign from his position as the Green Party spokesman and that he would not be a candidate in the parliamentary elections held on September 22, 2002.

[2] For the notions of "creolization" and the "straight jacket of culture" see Ayşe Çağlar, *The Prison House of Culture in the Studies of Turks in Germany* (Berlin: FUB, 1990).

[3] At the time of this writing Özdemir was being bombarded with criticism by the daily liberal *Hürriyet*, a Turkish newspaper widely published in both Turkey and Germany, for what was interpreted as anti-Turkey remarks in his speeches and the way he conducted himself toward Turkey as a parliamentarian in Germany.

[4] This interview took place on *Inforadio*, a Berlin broadcast station, on February 16, 1999. The eventual EU candidacy of Turkey did realize in Helsinki later that year.

[5] Özdemir mentions this connection in his political autobiography *Ich bin Ein Inlaender: Ein Anatolischer Schwabe im Bundestag* (Munich: DTV Premium, 1997).

[6] Alejandro Portes, "Transnational Communities: Their Emergence and Significance in the Contemporary World System," Working Paper Series 16 (April 1995).

[7] Ulrich Beck, *Was ist Globalisierung?* (Frankfurt: Suhrkamp: 1998), 46.

[8] Ibid., 54.

[9] M. Kearney, "The Local and the Global: The Anthropology of Globalization and Transnationalism," *Annual Review of Anthropology* 24 (1995), 549.

[10] Hannerz, Ulf, *Transnational Connection: Culture, People, Places* (London and New York: Routledge, 1996), 6.

[11] M. Kearney, "The Local and the Global: The Anthropology of Globalization and Transnationalism," *Annual Review of Anthropology* 24 (1995), 548.

[12] Ulrich Beck, *Was ist Globalisierung?* (Frankfurt: Suhrkamp: 1998, 47.

[13] Anthony Giddens, *The Consequences of Modernity* (Stanford, CA: Stanford University Press, 1990), 21.

[14] Ibid. (for the term "delocalized")

[15] Roland Robertson, "Glokalisierung: Homogenitaet und Heterogenitaet in Raum und Zeit," in *Perspektiven der Weltgesellschaft*, ed. Ulrich Beck (Frankfurt: Suhrkamp, 1998), 192–221.

[16] Ulrich Beck, *Perspektiven der Weltgesellschaft* (Frankfurt: Suhrkamp, 1998); Benjamin R. Barber, *Jihad vs. McWorld* (New York: Times Books, 1995).

[17] Roland Robertson, "Glokalisierung: Homogenitaet und Heterogenitaet in Raum und Zeit," in *Perspektiven der Weltgesellschaft*, ed. Ulrich Beck (Frankfurt: Suhrkamp, 1998), 192–221.

[18] Ibid.

[19] Samuel Huntington, in his well-known thesis on the "clash of civilizations" raises the claim that close encounters between cultures very different from each other would have radicalizing politicizing effects and would lead to conflict rather than increased mutual understanding. According to Huntington, whose arguments should be read with much caution, dislocation incurred by speedy and massive migratory movements have inherent destabilizing

political consequences, precisely because people become more aware of their differences when they interact with each other.

[20] Arjun Appadurai, *Modernity at Large: Cultural Dimensions of Globalization* (Minneapolis and London: University of Minnesota Press, 1996), 37, 38.

[21] Ibid., 31.

[22] Ibid., 49.

[23] Ibid., 38.

[24] Ibid., 83.

[25] Benedict Anderson, *Imagined Communities* (London and New York: Verso, 1983).

[26] Martin Van Bruinessen, "Shifting National and Ethnic Identities: The Kurds in Turkey and the European Diaspora," *Journal of Muslim Minority Affairs* 18 (1998): 39–52.

[27] Here, I use the term, "non-European" in a geographical sense. The reference is to Kurdish nationalism. This movement is non-European in the geographical sense, but not, for example, in the structural linguistic sense. Kurdish is an Indo-European language with close affinity to Persian.

[28] Here I refer to the concept of "the veil of ignorance" in John Rawls, *A Theory of Justice* (Cambridge, Massachusetts: Harvard University Press, 1971). Similar to the "ideal speech situation" envisioned by Jurgen Habermas in the perfect functioning of a critical rational public sphere, the subject in Rawls is also imagined as a neutral player in collective negotiations, with all her/his "identity politics" shoved behind a veil.

[29] Social sciences are on their way to developing a web jargon, with notions like *netizens, cyber-separatism, nodalities*, and so on. This author believes that at the time of this writing it is premature to talk about virtual communities in this fashion, as if they were liberated entirely from the non-virtual trenches of the nation-state paradigm. Nations and states still *share* power with deterritorialized, virtual, non-national, and non-statal actors, rather than having been replaced by them.

[30] Thomas Faist, "From Common Questions to Common Concepts," in *International Migration, Immobility, and Development: A Multidisciplinary Perspective*, ed. Tomas Hammar, Grete Brochmann, Kristof Tamas, and Thomas Faist (Oxford: Berg, 1997), 247–276.

[31] Ludger Pries, "Transnationale Soziale Raume," in *Perspektiven der Weltgesellschaft*, ed. Ulrich Beck. (Frankfurt: Suhrkamp: 1998), 72. Also see Robert C. Smith, "Los Ausentes Siempre Presentes: The Imagining, Making and Politics of a Transnational Community Between New York City and Ticuana, Puebla," Manuscript, Institute for Latin American and Iberian Studies, Columbia University, (October1992). For the argument in favor of focus on networks and linkages, see Monica Boyd, "Family and Personal Networks in International Migration: Recent Developments and New Agendas," *International Migration Review* 23:3 (1989); James T. Fawcett, "Networks, Linkages and Migration Systems," *International Migration Review* 23 (1989), 671–680; Alejandro Portes, "Transnational Communities: Their Emergence and Significance in the Contemporary World Systems," Working Paper Series 16 (April 1995), available from http://www.jhu.edu/~soc/.ladark/.working_papers/.16; Internet; Thomas Faist "A Preliminary Analysis of Political-Institutional Aspects of International Migration: Internationalization Transnationalization, and Internal Globalization," ZeS-Arbeitspapier 10 (1995), Center for Social Policy Research, Bremen..

[32] Thomas Faist, "The Crucial Meso-Level," in *International Migration, Immobility, and Development: A Multidisciplinary Perspective*, ed., Tomas Hammar et al. (Oxford: Berg, 1997), 187–217.

[33] Ibid.

[34] The Center for Turkey Studies in Essen, Germany, is particularly oriented in collecting evidence of Turks' integration into the German economy. The Center's projects are based primarily on the premise that Turks are settled in Europe and have become an integral part of Europe's economy and politics.

[35] G. Gilbertson and D. T. Gurak, "Household Transitions in the Migrations of Dominicans and Colombians to New York," *International Migration Review* 26 (1992), 22–45.

[36] Some examples are L. Van Velzen, *Peripheral Production in Kayseri, Turkey: A Study of Prospects for Industrialization Arising from Small and Middle Scale Enterprises in a Peripheral Growth Pole* (The Hague: NUFFIC, 1977); Michael J. Piore, *Birds of Passage: Migrant Labor and Industrial Societies* (Cambridge: Cambridge University Press, 1979); Rhinus Penninx, "A Critical Review of Theory and Practice: The Case of Turkey," *International Migration Review* 16:4 (1982), 781–818; Barbara Wolbert, "Pass und Passagen: Zur Dynamik und Symbolik von Migrationsprozessen am Beispiel der Rückkehr Türkischer Arbeitsmigranten," *Kea* 10 (1997), 49–69.

[37] Daniel Elazar, "The Jewish People as the Classic Diaspora: A Political Analysis," in *Modern Diasporas in International Politics*, ed. Gabriel Sheffer (London and Sydney: Croom Helm, 1986), 212–258.

[38] Patricia Landolt, "Salvadoran Transnationalism: Towards the Redefinition of National Community," Working Paper Series 18, (2000), Johns Hopkins University, Program in Comparative and International Development. For transnational connections between Algeria and France, see Gilles Kepel, *Allah in the West: Islamic Movements in America and Europe*, trans. Susan Milner (Stanford, CA: Stanford University Press 1997); Catherine de Wenden, "France's Policy on Migration from May 1981 till March 1986: Its Symbolic Dimension its Restrictive Aspects, and its Unintended Effects," *International Migration* 25 (1987), 211–220; between Pakistan and Britain, Pnina Werbner, *The Migration Process: Capital, Gifts, and Offerings Among British Pakistanis* (Oxford: Berg, 1990); between Germany and Turkey, Barbara Wolbert, *Der Getoetete Pass: Ruckkehr in die Türkei: Eine Ethnologische Migrationsstudie* (Berlin: Akademie Verlag, 1995); between London and Hong Kong, James L. Watson, *Emigration and the Chinese Lineage: The Mans in Hong Kong and London* (Berkeley: University of California Press, 1975); and between Boston and the Dominican Republic, Peggy Levitt, *Transnationalizing Civil and Political Change: The Case of Organizational Ties Between the United States and the Dominican Republic*, (Ph.D. dissertation, MIT, 1995).

[39] Ludger Pries, "Transnationale Soziale Räume," in *Perspektiven der Weltgesellschaft*, ed. Ulrich Beck (Frankfurt: Suhrkamp: 1998), 60. Also see Robert C. Smith, *Los Ausentes Siempre Presentes: The Imagining, Making, and Politics of a Transnational Community between New York City and Ticuana, Pueblena*. Institute for Latin American and Iberian Studies, Columbia University, October 1992.

[40] Linda G. Basch, Nina Glick-Schiller, and Christina Szanton-Blanc, *Nations Unbound: Transnational Projects, Post-Colonial Predicaments, and De-Territorialized Nation-States* (Langhorne, Pa: Gordin and Breach, 1994).

Turks jokingly used to refer to Munich as the 68th province of Turkey when Turkey used to have 67 administrative provinces. Berlin is still referred to, both by Germans and Turks, as the largest Turkish city, outside of Turkey, in the world.

[41] Information available from http://www.cultural-division.org/info/yb97/htm/ch9_4.htm; Internet.

[42] Stephen Vertovec, "Conceiving and Researching Transnationalism," *Ethnic and Racial Studies* 22 (March 1999), 445–462.

[43] Stephen Adler, "Emigration and Development in Algeria: Doubts and Dilemmas," in *Guests Come to Stay: The Effects of European Labor Migration on Sending and Receiving Countries*, ed. Rosemarie Rogers (Boulder and London: Westview Press, 1985), 478.

[44] Philip Martin L., *Administering Foreign-Worker Programs: Lessons from Europe* (Lexington, Mass.: Lexington Books, 1982).

[45] Luis E. Guarnizo, "The Rise of Transnational Social Formations: Mexico and Dominican Republic." Unpublished paper.

[46] Bryan R. Roberts, Reanne Frank, and Fernando Lozano-Ascencio, "Transnational Migrant Communities and Mexican Migration to the U.S," *Ethnic and Racial Studies* 22 (March 1999), 251.

[47] Ibid.

[48] Robert Smith, "Mexican Immigrants, the Mexican State and the Practice of Mexican Politics and Membership," *LASA Forum* 24 (Summer 1998), 21.

[49] Ibid., 20. Also see Steven Vertovec, "Conceiving and Researching Transnationalism," *Ethnic and Racial Studies* 22 (March 1999), 475.

[50] See Daniel Cinel, *The National Integration of Italian Return Migration: 1870–1929* (Cambridge and New York: Cambridge University Press, 1991); R. Bourne, "Transnational America," *Atlantic Monthly* 118 (1916), 86–97; William I. Thomas and F. Znaniecki, *The Polish Peasant in Europe and America: Monograph of Immigrant Groups: 1918–1920* (New York: Dover, 1958); Mark Wyman, *Round-trip to America: The Immigrants Return to Europe, 1880–1930* (Ithaca: Cornell University Press 1993).

[51] Alejandro Portes, Luis E. Guarnizo, and Patricia Landolt, "Introduction: Pitfalls and Promises of an Emergent Research Field," *Ethnic and Racial Studies* 22 (March 1999), 223.

[52] Suzanne Paine, *Exporting Workers: The Turkish Case* (London: Cambridge University Press 1974); Stephen Adler, *The Turkish Conundrum: Emigration, Politics and Development, 1961–1980* (Geneva: ILO, 1981).

[53] Stephen Adler, "Emigration and Development in Algeria: Doubts and Dilemmas," in *Guests Come to Stay: The Effects of European Labor Migration on Sending and Receiving Countries*, ed. Rosemarie Rogers (Boulder and London: Westview Press, 1985), 479.

[54] For a philosophical argument on behalf of the necessity of the clash of opposites for political liberalism see J. S. Mill, *On Liberty* (Indianapolis: Hackett Publishing Co., 1978).

[55] Pnina Werbner, *Embodying Charisma: Modernity, Locality, and Performance of Emotions in Sufi Cults* (London and New York: Routledge, 1998).

[56] Craig Calhoun, "Civil Society and the Public Sphere," *Public Culture* 5 (1993), 273.

[57] Daniel Bell, "The 'Public Sphere,' the State and the World of Law in Eighteenth Century France," *French Historical Studies* 17 (Fall 1992), 915.

[58] The bourgeois public sphere existed in opposition to the royal representative public sphere, which derived its values from private domestic experience.

[59] Jose Casanova, *Public Religions in the Modern World* (Chicago and London: The University of Chicago Press, 1994), 221, 222.

[60] Robert C. Holub, *Jurgen Habermas: Critic in the Public Sphere* (London and New York: Routledge, 1991), 3.

[61] Benjamin Nathans, "Habermas's 'Public Sphere' in the Era of French Revolution," *French Historical Studies* 16 (Spring 1990), 622.

[62] M. Kearney, "The Local and the Global: The Anthropology of Globalization and Transnationalism," *Annual Review of Anthropology* 24 (1995), 553.

[63] Paul Gilroy, *There Ain't No Black in the Union Jack* (London: Hutchinson, 1987); Clifford, James, "Diasporas," *Cultural Anthropology* 9:3 (1994), 308.

[64] Jose Casanova, *Public Religions in the Modern World* (Chicago and London: The University of Chicago Press, 1994).

[65] Robert Wuthnow, *Communities of Discourse: Ideology and Social Structure in the Reformation, the Enlightenment, and European Socialism* (Cambridge Mass.: Harvard University Press, 1989), 4, 5.

[66] Sheri Berman, "Civil Society and the Collapse of the Weimar Republic," *World Politics* 49 (April 1997): 401–429.

[67] Ulrich Beck, *Was ist Globalisierung?* (Frankfurt: Suhrkamp, 1998), 93.

III
Migrants from Turkey in Contemporary Europe: A General Outline

It was another cold, rainy Berlin day in March, but there was much action inside the buildings and shops of Kreuzberg—the "Turkish Berlin," or the "little Istanbul" as the inhabitants would like to think of it. Members of ADA on Reichenbergerstrasse, a left-leaning group of Turkish youngsters, were particularly busy, getting ready for an important meeting. A representative of the Freedom and Democracy Party (ÖDP) was going to discuss the political situation in Turkey and ÖDP's prospects in the upcoming general elections. The representative had arrived the day before on invitation by ÖDP sympathizers—ADA being one of them.

ÖDP had been an outspoken critic of the structural problems in Turkish politics. Those gathered at ADA's small Kreuzberg apartment that night expected their party to receive about three percent of the votes in the elections. Considering that Turkey was a "military democracy," according to the ÖDP representative, that would have been a satisfactory result for the time being. The actual sharing of political power was a long shot for a new party like ÖDP, but until then there was valuable work to be done in opposition.

Kamil came to Berlin several years ago for his undergraduate study. Things did not work out the way he had planned though. He dropped out of college, married a German woman, and was now unemployed. Fortunately he had found himself a place at ADA, "an association of anti-fascist Turks," as he put it. The small apartment was the first story of a building owned by some German anti-fascists. They had been letting their Turkish "comrades" convene on the first floor and use the space for meetings and archival work. But finances were getting tighter for them too, so lately they had been asking for a couple of hundred Deutschmarks for monthly rent from their Turkish friends.

Kamil was living upstairs with his wife, taking care of the place, making tea, and hanging out with the anti-fascist crowd. He also was helping with the library and the archive. "It's the most comprehensive among all Turkish organizations in Berlin," he said proudly pointing with his head to the archive. An entire wall of the apartment was covered with dossiers of newspaper clippings and writings about "fascists'", Kurds', leftists', and Islamists' activities in Turkey as well as in Germany. Older issues of ADA's own irregular journal *Insiyatif* were stored in a separate section. Turkish newspapers were scattered all over the place.

A group of young people entered the room several hours before the meeting. After getting their tea and lighting their cigarettes, they turned on the television. On TRT-INT, the international broadcast of the Turkish state-owned network, news and commentaries about the preparations for the Kurdish rebel leader's upcoming trial captured everyone's attention. As they were having dinner, shuffling through newspapers, or playing backgammon, Turkish politics was just as present in the air as cigarette smoke. Comments about the connection between the trial and the elections followed, as Kamil and a couple of others started moving chairs around and making more tea to get ready for the evening. Soon the room was going to be filled with more anxious people, more cigarette smoke, and heavy questions about homeland politics.

The speaker would first be interviewed for the *Spreekanal* (public access television). Then he would start his speech by repeating what he said to the camera. He would talk in intelligent, abstract terms about ÖDP's platform. He would talk about the party cadres and about things that make them different than the establishment parties. At the end of a traditionally long speech, the audience would ask informed questions that would demand answers in "more concrete terms please!" Who would be the probable coalition partners? What would happen if the Islamists gain more than 20 percent? How would ÖDP's relations with the military be? What about the economy, foreign affairs, corruption? There would be complaints about the lack of an outreach plan to migrants in Europe in ÖDP's program. The meeting would end with a reluctant solicitation for financial contribution to the party, no matter how small it may be. And no matter how unemployed or dissatisfied they may be, pledges would come from the members of this small but concerned group of Turkish public abroad.

TURKISH POLITICAL PRESENCE IN EUROPE

Although it is estimated that about 80 percent of more than two thousand Turkish associations in Germany have a distinct political orientation, this was not the case at the beginning of labor migration.¹ Initially, the purpose behind most migrant gatherings was primarily social. Over time, structural changes have occurred, both in the organization and in the objectives of migrant associations. In the late 1960s and throughout the 1970s labor unions and student organizations were highly politicized. In the 1980s, while the political activities of workers and students subsided, mosque associations and religious "roof" organizations (*Dachverbände*) flourished.

The nature of the initial stages of migration in the early 1960s dictated transitory arrangements. Not only was there a rotation system in place that was designed to keep migration temporary and the turnover high but most laborers had also come alone, leaving families behind until an eventual reunification with them in Turkey. Workers lived together in dormitories and had little reason to mingle with the rest of the society. This pattern changed when the rotation system did not agree with good business sense. The suspension of the rotation system, accompanied by chain migration, the need of the German economy for women workers, and German government's plan to stop the recruitment of new workers in 1973 (*Anwerbestopp*) precipitated a wave of family reunions and expanded the volume of migration to Germany from Turkey.

In the 1980s and the 1990s, the exchange between the two countries became an everyday matter. Student exchanges, bridal transfers from Turkey, businesspeople going back and forth, vacationing, military service and so on acquired regularity. Turkish presence in Germany had become permanent, yet the *myth of return* and the continuing sense of temporary-ness still rendered integration undesirable and dictated that migrants create their own economic and cultural infrastructure, rather than utilizing what was available (or not available) in the host society. As a result, a Turkish micro-society with distinct networks and, at times, conflicting ideological orientations and minority identities started developing in Germany.²

The chain migration of at times entire villages and towns resulted in the congregation of first generation migrants around the notion of *hemşehrilik* (regional loyalties) in European cities. The best known of these representations of entire localities are the town of *Emirdağ* in Belgium and *Kulu* in Sweden.³ In his comparative study of Portuguese and Turkish communities in the Netherlands with respect to their children's education, Flip Lindo found stronger mechanisms of social control and sanctions among Turkish communities due to chain migration. Chain migration meant that families "did not build their communities from scratch, but rather developed them on the basis of already established relationships. ... The result was a large number of tightly knit communities of co-villagers or of former inhabitants of clusters of neighboring villages. These communities encourage not only strong local cohesion, but have used relations with kin and co-villagers to build up close ties with communities elsewhere in Europe."[4]

With the slowing pace of chain migration over the years, mostly due to more rigid immigration policies of the host, regional loyalties were replaced by ethnicity and religion. General feelings of being a Turk in Germany, a Turk from Berlin, a Turk from Kreuzberg, or a Muslim in a Christian world became prevalent among second and third generation youngsters, even though they have little emotional and geographical knowledge of their land of origin in comparison to their parents.[5]

NEXT GENERATIONS IN TRANSNATIONAL POLITICS

Şükran Ketenci, a columnist for the daily *Cumhuriyet*, once wrote: "Even those who say that they decided to live in Germany and not to go back to Turkey continue to be oriented, with their life styles and their interests, towards Turkey. ... When are the early elections scheduled? How much does a kilogram of meat in Turkey cost now? ... Just recently have we [migrants] begun to ask questions like 'why don't we have voting rights?' We are just now trying to accept the fact that we cannot save Turkey all the way from Germany by simply debating amongst each other."[6]

The main reference point for the second generation Turks continues to be Turkey and the Turkish culture. Migrant networks and dense social checks and balances resulting from them make sure that ghettoizing dynamics apply to the second, third, and even fourth generations. Keeping the old identity and acquiring mainly the practical and not necessarily the substantive aspects of the new one has become the trend in Deutschkei. The overwhelming support from Turkish migrants for dual citizenship demonstrates this trend.[7]

The fear that their children would lose their identity to the Christian-German culture has led Turkish parents to create "counter-cultural havens," fully equipped with their own facilities.[8] The advent of Turkish satellite broadcasting and the growing density of migrant networks, including cultural clubs and sports associations, have contributed to parental success in this area.

Aytac Eryilmaz, the director of the Center for the Documentation of Migration from Turkey (DOMIT), attributes the low level of competency in German, from which later generations of Turkish children suffer, in part to the continuous flow of so-called "national brides" from Turkey, who can speak only Turkish. This, he argues, is one of the important factors that slow down Turks' integration into Germany.

Similarly, Faruk Şen, the director of the Center for Turkey Studies in Essen, who is more inclined to highlight the successes of Turks' integration into European structures, writes that since 1985 migration from Turkey to Western

Europe has been dominated by "family formation" rather than by family reunification. What is meant by family formation is a new marriage to a partner in the country of origin, leading to the migration of the latter to the country of settlement of the former.[9] Thus, intermarriages with Germans are not widespread phenomena.

German policies themselves contribute to such introversion. For example, Turkish children, because of language difficulties, are sent to *Sonderschule* or *Hauptschule* that are special schools for handicapped children or children with a variety of learning difficulties rather than to *Realschule* that offers the necessary preparation to attend college or *Gymnasium*. Some observers argue that in this way Turkish children are systematically deprived of the opportunity to penetrate the service sector in Germany and thus marginalized, although, since 1983, some relative improvements in this area have been recorded.[10]

POLITICIZATION OF GROUPS

When they first relocated from Turkey to Germany, the pioneer migrants brought the "coffeehouse culture" of their Anatolian provinces to German cities. Somewhat similarly to the coffeehouses and salons of the nineteenth century France that Habermas investigates, coffeehouses in Near and Middle Eastern cities, towns, and villages have been the elementary settings for formal and informal, discursive and associational activity among men. As of today, these social institutions continue their role as facilitating environments of public debate, where men exchange ideas about social events and politics at all levels.[11] So it is not surprising that the seemingly leisurely activities of playing cards and drinking tea, coffee, and alcoholic beverages have become the foundations of solidarity and associationism among migrants beginning with the 1970s. In a short period of time, migrants found out about ways to avoid paying taxes by turning their coffeehouse associations (*kahve dernekleri*) into organizations working for public benefit.

In the 1970s, in a parallel development, some Turkish political parties, particularly the Nationalist Action Party (MHP), started operating foreign offices in Germany. Some existing associations would also tailor themselves according to political parties and movements in Turkey. There were also former activists whose frustration could find its expression and an outlet in this "Hyde Park," which they saw as an extension of the Turkish political landscape for their particularistic projects toward their land of origin.

The 1980s were marked by substantial structural changes in political life in Turkey in the aftermath of the military coup of September 12, 1980, which also resonated among migrants and exiles in Europe and in Deutschkei. By putting down the political left, this conservative coup paved the way for the political right to fragment, diversify, and dominate the political system. The *Turkish-Islamic Synthesis*, endorsed by the military as the cultural infrastructure to legitimate the new system, worked to the advantage of the Islamists, the ultranationalists, and the economic neo-liberals more than any other group. The 1990s witnessed serious divisions among the Turkish ultranationalists and were also marked by the rise of Alevi organizations in Western Europe, in reaction to the Sunni dominated Islamization in Turkey.

Xenophobic outbursts in Germany by the far right also had their decisive impact on migrant groups' politicization. The burning of a five-member Turkish family in Solingen in May 1993 by setting their home on fire was the turning point that accelerated the dual processes of *ghettoization* on the one hand and the radicalization of the political landscape of Deutschkei on the other, with serious negative implications for Turks' social integration.[12] The most visible effect of the attacks was the strengthening Turkish ultranationalism in Europe.

POLITICAL EXILES

"I absolutely do not accept any amnesty whatsoever. Some of us should stay right here just so it be a lesson to the world."[13] This was how Şanar Yurdatapan, a famous Turkish composer in exile and a political activist, responded to the question whether he would accept an amnesty from the Turkish government, receive his citizenship back, and return home.

Political exiles from Turkey, who fled in large numbers to Europe in the late 1970s and early 1980s, particularly after the military coup of 1980, were mostly leftists, although almost the entire Turkish political continuum was represented abroad.[14]

Only a few of the political exiles, like Yurdatapan, had the energy, time, and the finances to sustain a vocal critique of their polity of origin. Most have lost the leisure to sustain engagement in politics. Many have become more worried about pocket book issues as they grew older and took responsibilities in family life.

Today, some of the exiles have gained their citizenship back. Others continue to live under official refugee status and receive financial support from their host governments or organizations like the United Nations. A few had acquired new citizenship. Some continue their intellectual endeavors by writing for newspaper columns or for journals and by organizing panels, protests, conferences, and forums. Others express themselves through poetry, music, and literature. Some of them, over the years, have engaged in extensive associational activity, hoping to mobilize public opinion and a critical mass of dissidents to stimulate political change in Turkey. All have hoped and some continue to hope to go back to Turkey. Very few, however, would acknowledge today that the mode of associational activity that they conducted had produced any solid results, other than enabling them to establish networks in Europe, which they later utilized for non-political, business-related endeavors.

The exiles claim that the mode of new associational activity should shift more towards umbrella organizations and federations with large grassroots bases and that their focus should be repositioned on issues relevant to life in Europe rather than life in Turkey.

THE LEFTISTS

Mr. Cebe was a veteran of political associationism. From 1975, since he arrived in Germany, until 1987, he co-founded and worked for numerous organizations whose main purpose was to change Turkey politically. He reflects, with some regret, on the strategies and tactics of the Turkish youth in the 1970s and the 1980s to protest the flaws of the regime in Turkey. He has not visited Turkey for 22 years, yet he still dreams in Turkish, still reads Turkish newspapers regularly, and he still is in the habit of scanning the German press for news exclusively from Turkey.

"This was the case with all Turkish political activists in the 1970s," he remembers. "There was a tremendous tension between the awareness of the need to focus on the problems of Turkish migrants in Germany and the desire to see things change politically in Turkey. In particular, immediately before and immediately after the 1980 military coup, the number and intensity of political activity vis-à-vis Turkey rose. Peace committees were established against torture, persecution, and capital punishment. An increased numbers of political exiles coming from Turkey, in addition to labor migration and family reunions, have contributed to this situation as well."[15]

What were they talking about? Why was their focus consistently on Turkey? "We were constantly debating that the two realms of activities, the one with respect to Turkey and the one where problems resulting from migration, should be separated and handled with equal urgency. But in practice, we couldn't do that. People who were supposed to be active in both areas were the same people and we were more equipped to deal with problems in Turkey than with problems here. For one thing, we did not have a good command of German. There was also an emotional dimension to the whole thing. When people are tortured and die in Turkey, it is inevitable that your heart and attention shifts to that direction."[16]

They organized hunger strikes, printed and distributed regular information bulletins. They organized protest marches, most notably the ones in 1981 and 1984 to the European Parliament in Strasbourg. When the "civil junta" (as the leftists would call the center-right civilian government that followed the 1980 military coup) in 1985 prosecuted 56 intellectuals out of 1256 who signed a declaration for reform, two thousand activists supported the petition from Europe and the United States. *Türkei Information*, a publication of the leftist Federation of Workers Association in Federal Germany (FIDEF), for example, criticized the military "junta," worked as a watchdog of ultra-right activities in Germany, and commemorated the Kurdish New Year *newroz*, which was a significant, subversive symbol at the time in Turkey. In 1982, the publication focused on the legal process by the regime against the Peace Committee, which consisted of leftist intellectuals.[17]

"Because of language difficulties and because of the prevailing mindset, we could not use the German media and political institutions effectively. Moreover, we were very fragmented. All political groups that existed in Turkey were represented here and they were all working independently from each other. It was very difficult to achieve the critical mass of numbers when a march was organized."[18]

To what extent did all of this affect Turkish politics? "I cannot say that all was in vain. If only fifty people were executed back then and not more, I think the activities of this or that organization abroad had something to do with it. We were able to mobilize the German public opinion against the regime in Turkey. Many prominent theologians, scientists, parliamentarians supported us. But in retrospect, I can see that we could have accomplished a lot more, had we been equipped to take advantage of the media and the institutions in this country. Had our minds been less preoccupied with Turkey, we could have done more for our people here. We were like Don Quixote back then. We were like cavalries on old and sick horses, out there, trying to change the world. We are in a way a lost generation. Any movement that cannot use the media effectively will have little chance in this day and age. The new generation is equipped with the language and know-how to do what we could not."[19]

While leftist groups, especially the radical leftists, constitute marginal fringe groups on the political landscape of Turkey, they are better organized in Deutschkei and have a larger appeal there. These groups were highly active in the 1970s and particularly effective from 1975 to 1981, as counterbalancing forces against the right-of-center establishment in Deutschkei. As such they helped the extra-national political environment to fully reflect the political polarization between the right and the left in Turkey.[20]

ATATÜRKIST THOUGHT ORGANIZED IN EUROPE

The clean-shaven, middle-aged man in suit and tie was asked the question why 3.5 million Turks in Europe still have not received the right to vote in national elections of their country of origin through mail or at ballot boxes in consular facilities. Since 1995 they could participate in this mode only at the Turkish border. As the head of the Association of Atatürkist Thought in Europe (AADD), my interviewee was a representative of the Turkish state. So it could be safely assumed that his answer would be indicative of how the Turkish presence in Western Europe, particularly in Germany, was seen by the Turkish state. Indeed, why was it that this proposal—to let Turks abroad vote in their residential areas—was always on the parliament's agenda but could never be realized? Why was it that voting abroad was not encouraged and made easier? Why did Turkish citizens have to travel all the way to the border to cast their votes? "Can you imagine," he asked, "the commotion at the doors of the consulates? Who is going to organize all of that? You think it's easy? ... If we let them vote by mail, how are we going to verify the identity of the voters?"

The main reason, however, appears to be political damage control rather than practical considerations. In the face of the Islamists' extensive organization and propaganda activities in Europe, Turkish governments seem to be concerned with the potential electoral effects of political extremism, which is perceived as dominating the political views of Turks abroad.[21] As a result, there has been little political will to facilitate voting rights for Turkish citizens abroad. Although the general tendency among migrants has been to vote for social democrats in Germany and opt for conservatives in Turkey, migrants' electoral preferences in 1999 reflected more or less the aggregate choice and the general outcome in Turkey proper.[22]

The radical Islamist movement of the *Kaplancilar* in Germany, with their self-declared "*caliphate* state in exile" and *jihad* against the Turkish state has played an important role in stimulating Turkey to have a counterbalancing official presence abroad.[23] It is no coincidence that the AADD, with three thousand members, is also based in Cologne where most radical Islamist Turkish organizations have their headquarters.

For the first time in Turkey's history, the 1982 constitution contained stipulations about Turks abroad and consular outreach programs directed towards them. Article 62 proclaims that the state is responsible to take the necessary measures to protect family unity and social security, facilitate the education of migrants' children, provide for their cultural needs, the *maintenance of their ties with their homeland*, and help them return home.[24]

Turkish consular outreach in Deutschkei includes Turkish Coordination Councils that encompass small associations. These coordination councils are organized around the Turkish-Islamic Union of Religious Affairs (DITIB) and around consular circles. It is argued that they are informally connected to the National Security Council (MGK) in Turkey and that their main function is to organize reactions to anti-Turkey initiatives.[25] The Bavarian Turkish Coordination Council has been particularly active in this regard.

NOTES

[1] Aytaç Eryilmaz, the director of DOMIT, the Documentation Center of Migration from Turkey, interview by author, Essen, March 1999.

[2] Ali Gitmez and Czarina Wilpert, "A Micro-Society or an Ethnic Community? Social Organization and Ethnicity amongst Turkish Migrants in Berlin," in *Immigrant Associations in Europe*, ed. John Rex et al. (Gower, 1987), 86-124.

According to the figures published by the Ministry of Labor and Social Security in their 1998 Annual Report, Turks in Germany run about 47 thousand work places. Among them those who work for themselves generate an annual volume of 69 billion DM and employ 80 percent Turks and 20 percent non-Turks. The number of civic associations, established by migrants from Turkey, is around 1722 in Germany.

[3] These communities contain extended families and distant relatives. Young people are pressured to marry "one of their own" rather than mingle with the host culture.

[4] Flip Lindo, "Ethnic Myth or Ethnic Might? On the Divergence in Educational Attainment Between Portuguese and Turkish Youth in the Netherlands," in *Post-Migration Ethnicity: De-Essentializing Cohesion, Commitments, and Comparison*, Gerd Baumann and Thijl Sunier, ed. (Amsterdam: Het Spinhuis, 1995), 154.

[5] Ibid.

[6] *Cumhuriyet*, May 14-20, 1989.

[7] A survey on citizenship, conducted by the Center for Turkey Studies in Essen showed that 48.7 percent of the respondents said they would become German citizens only under the condition that they would not lose their Turkish citizenship—*Milliyet*, March 1999.

[8] The biggest concern for conservative Turkish parents is to provide an educational environment for their kids free of Christian influences, drugs, and sex. The fact that most preschools in Germany are run by churches has been an impetus to the establishment of Turkish and Islamic preschools and schools. German local governments have given legal and financial support to these projects.

[9] Faruk Şen et al., *Migration Movements from Turkey to the European Community*. (Brussels: Center for Turkish Studies, 1993), 17.

[10] Ibid.

[11] Not unlike the bourgeois public sphere of the 18th century Europe, the traditional Turkish coffeehouses continue to exclude women.

[12] During an interview on Turkish television (NTV) in February 1999, Faruk Sen, the director of the Center for Turkey Studies in Essen discussed how the neo-fascist burnings of

Turks in *Solingen* and *Mölln* had made migrants from Turkey in Germany more introverted and more resentful toward the host society.

¹³*Nokta*, 19 July 1987, 13.

¹⁴ By 1987, there were over 200 political exiles of Turkish descent in Europe, stripped of their citizenship. From 1979 to 1994, around 13 percent of the Turkish nationals in Germany were comprised of political asylum seekers. Approximately one-third of these were ethnically non-Turkish.

¹⁵Interview by author, tape-recorded, Cologne, March 1999.

¹⁶Ibid.

¹⁷This organization was founded in 1977 as a non-governmental organization (NGO). It was a member of the World Peace Council demanding the ban of all weapons of mass destruction, the abolition of all military bases, transition to a general and controlled arms reduction process, abolishment of all types of colonialism and racism, self-determination, and the like. The main charge against the committee was that it cooperated with communist fronts in and out of the country and engaged in common activities with leftist parties in order to get rid of the military bases in Turkey and to end Turkey's NATO membership.

¹⁸Interview by author, tape-recorded, Cologne, March 1999.

¹⁹Ibid.

²⁰Among the most noteworthy Turkish leftist organizations in the diaspora are the Federation of Turkish Migrant Associations (GDF), the Federation of Democratic Workers Associations in Germany (DIDF), the Federation of Workers Association in Federal Germany (FIDEF), the Revolutionary Left (DEV-SOL), the Turkish Communist Party (TKP), the Turkey Populist Revolutionist Federation (HDF), and the Turkish Workers Party (TIP). In addition, the German *Verfassungsschutzbericht,* issued by the Office for the Protection of the German Constitution, includes the following Turkish leftist organizations as extremist formations on German soil: Revolutionary Peoples' Liberation Party-Front (DHKP-C)—a spinoff of Revolutionary Left (Devrimci-Sol) and the Turkish Peoples' Liberation Party-Front/Revolutionary Left (THKP-C/Devrimci Sol). According to German *Verfassungsschutzbericht*, 1997, over 40 thousand (without Kurds) out of 1.5 million Turks in Germany are presumed to be members of these "extremist" organizations. In addition, there are Kurdish formations like the PKK and Islamic formations like the IGMG and the ICCB that are considered to be extremists by the German state.

²¹Kamil Atilgan, the head of AADD, interview by author, tape-recorded, Cologne, March 1999.

²²Migrants' aggregate preferences in the last general elections in 1999: DSP 29 %, FP 22,9%, MHP 18.7 %, ANAP 12.6 %, CHP 6.2 %, HADEP 1,65 %, ÖDP 1,17 %, BBP 1.07 %, BP 0.18 %. Source: Kurthan Fişek "Birkaç Günlüğüne Almanya'daydim, Gozum Dikiz Aynasindaydi" *Hürriyet*, 1 June 1999.

²³ See for more on *Kaplancilar* in chapter ten.

²⁴The 1982 Constitution of Turkey (1996). Emphasis added.

²⁵Aytaç Eryilmaz, the director of DOMIT, interview by author, Essen, March 1999.

IV
Turkey, Europe, and Germany: A Brief History

To traditional Muslims they were nothing but infidels and atheists, "the victims of an overexposure to the decadent values of a degenerate Europe"[1] In reality they were highly resentful of European interference in the empire's domestic affairs. Most were socialists and freemasons, but some would embrace a variety of Islamic values and try to reconcile them with science, materialism, and nationalism.

It is during their era that the seeds of the Ottoman/Turkish patriotism, anti-imperialism, and nationalism were sown. Thus, the Turkish war of independence (1919–1923) against the great powers of the time was first waged *outside* rather than inside the country by these young Ottoman dissidents called the Young Turks.[2]

YOUNG TURKS IN EUROPE

> A thorough examination of the *Weltanschauung* of the Young Turks between 1889 and 1902 leaves no doubt that, except for the shift in focus on nationalism, the official ideology of the early modern Turkish state was shaped during this period. The Young Turks who lived long enough to witness the coming into being of the Turkish Republic saw many of their dreams fulfilled—it was a regime based on a popular materialist-positivist ideology and nationalism. The new regime worked to be included in Western culture while exerting an anti-imperialist rhetoric and convened a parliament composed not of elected politicians but of virtually selected intellectuals working on behalf of the people without cooperating in any capacity with the 'ignorant' masses. The impact of the Young Turks on shaping the official ideology of early modern Turkey went far beyond the political changes they affected. (Hanioğlu 1995, 216)

The Young Turks' presence and activities abroad constitute one of the earliest examples of modern transnationalism. Europe was an important arena where the Young Turks gained organizational expertise, developed new strategies for governance, and cultivated their ideas about Ottoman and Turkish nationalism. Their purpose was to dethrone sultan Abdulhamid II and replace his despotic rule with a more liberal and more secular parliamentary system by revising the Constitution of 1876.

In the Ottoman capital the Young Turks constituted a secret society. But in Europe, in Paris, Geneva, Salonika, and in other cities they were visibly active. They published their ideas in Ottoman as well as in European languages and maintained open contacts with governments, organizations, and groups sympathetic to their cause. Political discussions in the Beşiktaş Scientific Society frequented by the Young Turks in the early nineteenth century Istanbul resembled those of the eighteenth-century salons subject to Habermas's analysis.[3]

The Young Turks' gains on the European stage, particularly at a time when the proper ways of modernization and Westernization were being debated as strategies for the Ottoman survival and change, have contributed significantly to the revolution of 1908, a significant historical step in Turkish constitutionalism. Following the revolution, the Young Turks and their organization, the Committee of Union and Progress (CUP), ruled the empire until the end of the First World War, which the Ottomans entered on the side of the Germans.

The founders of modern Turkey, including Mustafa Kemal (Atatürk) and the two presidents that followed him, were former CUP members.[4] More significantly "the official ideology of modern Turkey, as shaped during this period by the early Young Turks, has continued to exert its influence even today on Turkey's intellectual and political life."[5] Considering the fact that Atatürk himself was socialized into the Young Turk mode of thinking about what was good for the empire and later for Turkey, the Young Turks' far-reaching influence, facilitated by their presence in Western Europe, is noteworthy.

Europe has always been an important source of political, administrative, and economic change in the Ottoman/Turkish history. Accordingly, Europe through the European Union (EU) plays a significant role in inducing change in contemporary Turkey as well as in other candidate countries expecting to become full members.[6] Political Islam and Kurdish ethnonationalism, the two main issues that have been exerting the strongest pressures on Turkish official discourse, "came to the foreground in the late 1980s concomitantly with the consolidation of the European Community. Their advent on the political agenda as a major bone of contention in Turkey's eligibility for European-ness has opened a Pandora's box of previously accepted truths for the Turkish elite."[7]

One Turkish parliamentarian comments on the European extension of Turkish politics as follows:

> A hundred years ago there was a Young Turk movement developing in European capitals. This movement was being supported and financed by many European organizations. A hundred years later today in many European cities there are now a so-called 'Young Kurd' movement and a 'Young Islamist' movement. If the Young Turks had an influence on the Ottomans, and they did, it is only natural to expect the Young Kurds, the Young Islamists, or neo-Islamists, however you may call them, to affect political thinking and structures in Turkey. This will be more so in the future. It is necessary to understand this well. ... What we need to do is to democratize endogenously without waiting for it to happen due to foreign pressures.[8]

GERMAN INFLUENCE ON THE OTTOMAN EMPIRE

In 1877, Carl Detroit from Berlin became the chief commander of the Turkish army in Europe and was given the responsibility by the Ottoman Sultan to defend Istanbul against the Russians. By this time Detroit had already converted to Islam and become Mehmet Ali Pasha. The following year he was sent as the Ottoman delegate to the Congress in Berlin, which was held under the leadership of Otto Von Bismarck of the new German Reich, and where the fate of the militarily weakened Ottoman Empire was to be discussed. It was from this time onwards, when the Ottomans started incurring heavy territorial losses in Europe, that the pace of the military and economic exchange between German and Turkish empires started increasing.[9]

At the turn of the 20th century young Ottomans were being admitted, for training purposes, to the German army and prospective Turkish doctors and engineers were studying at German schools. The first Turkish *Gastarbeiter* came to Germany during this period and many Turkish political dissidents enjoyed asylum in Germany. It was no coincidence that the first communist party of Turkey was established in Germany.[10] The Turkish "Hyde Park" was located in the heart of Europe in the first three decades of the 1900s.

The era of the Young Turks (1908–1918) also witnessed a heightened infatuation with the fledgling German economy, military, and technology. Some of the Young Turk publications (for example, *Osmanli* in 1900) would appear in German and promise good relations with Germany under a Young Turk government.[11] The Young Turks were dreaming about an empire in Asia. German orientalists like Ernst Jaeck fueled such *pan-Turkist* ideas by embracing them enthusiastically. Germans also supported not only sultan Abdulhamid's pragmatic Islamism, but also the Young Turks' idealist Islamism. Enver Pasha, who was a member of the CUP and who was responsible for the Ottoman Empire's entrance into the First World War on the side of the Germans, was trained in Germany. In the years preceding the First World War, Turkey was on her way to becoming a German satellite.[12]

According to Ilber Oltayli, German imperialism in Turkey is the earliest example and the forerunner of 20th century imperialisms that operate with soft rather than hard power. Oltayli writes that the Ottomans were more accepting of German influence, because, unlike other powers, Germans under Bismarck appeared to be interested in the territorial integrity of the Ottoman Empire. The Germans did not have a colonial past and the fact that they had no colonies in Muslim lands was important for the pragmatic pan-Islamist policies pursued by Abdulhamid II. Unlike the British or the French, Germans, with their own autocratic politics, were not in a position to pressure the despotic regime of Abdulhamid II to democratize. Since they entered the international political arena relatively late, there were no unaffected minorities left for the Germans in the Ottoman lands to influence politically. Therefore, Germans seemed to be a natural ally for the Ottomans.

Germany's main concern was to gain access to the Persian Gulf through the Ottoman lands. Germans were also interested in the vast Ottoman holdings as a precious source of raw material as well as a market for the products of their late but remarkable economic advancement. Soon German industrial products would invade the Ottoman markets and trade between Germany and the Ottoman Empire would flourish.[13]

German influence on the Ottoman Empire exerted itself through German reformers in the Ottoman military and bureaucracy, in such areas as customs, finance and banking, law enforcement, administrative and justice systems, and through the construction of the Baghdad railway.[14]

The Baghdad railway, which had positive effects on Turkish agriculture and the quality of life in the regions surrounding it, is the ultimate embodiment of German presence in the Ottoman Turkey. Deutsche Bank acquired the privilege to construct and manage the railway in 1890. German capital also engaged in port constructions and local public utility initiatives.[15] Beginning with 1934, loans from German companies have played a significant role in jumpstarting the Turkish economy by expanding trade relations between the two countries at a time when there was virtually no native capital to get the job done.

GERMAN INFLUENCE ON THE TURKISH REPUBLIC

Although the Ottomans remained largely oblivious to German intellectualism, this was not the case in the young Turkish Republic. In the late 1930s and early

1940s modern Turkey hosted many Jewish scholars who fled Nazi Germany. These Jewish Germans have contributed profoundly to the initial stages of the development of a modern system of higher education in Turkey.

Gerhard Kessler, a professor of sociology and economics, from the University of Leipzig, became a co-founder of the first Turkish trade union. Ernst Reuter, the later mayor of Berlin during the 1948 blockade, taught political science in Ankara and many of his students later became governors, ministers, and high-level bureaucrats. Celal Bayar, the minister of economics at the time, would frequently consult Max von der Portens, who was the industry consultant for the Heinrich Brunning government (1930–32) in Germany, before taking major decisions. Fritz Bade was responsible for organizing the Turkish dry fruit export as a source of foreign exchange. Philosopher Hans Reichenbach, the "German Bertrand Russell, also taught in Ankara. These scholars, until 1971, reinvigorated the various departments of the University of Ankara, including medicine, music, economics, and law.[16]

TURKEY AND THE EUROPEAN UNION

On December 26, 1999, CNN International was reporting that Turkey's candidacy for full membership in the European Union (EU) was accepted in Helsinki, Finland. Highly unusual, however, was the map that was accompanying the report in the background, behind the reporter. It was a map of Turkey where the areas that are considered heavily populated by Kurds were carved out. It looked as if the cookie monster had taken a big bite off the southeastern part of Turkey. To the Turkish eye, it was a bizarre, out-of-the-ordinary shape. Drawing a map of the sorts inside of Turkey (as a young boy of a returnee from Germany had done once and been prosecuted in the juvenile court for it) could be sufficient reason to spend some precious time in jail. Perhaps the CNN map was a bad joke, or an honest mistake, or the product of anti-Turkish lobbying (as most Turks would believe). Whatever it was, it was strangely becoming of the report itself. The cut-off chunk was perhaps the harbinger of the pressures yet to be put on Turkey with regard to the once-and-for-all settlement of the Kurdish question, among other things, before becoming an EU member.

Turkey's aspiration to become a part of the West and of a supranational political structure like the EU has become an integral aspect of Turkish national identity and domestic politics. Through such transnational aspirations Turkey exposes herself to the deconstructing effects of the transnational critique on a daily basis. Political activities in the diaspora have also been putting significant pressure on the legal/political system in Turkey since the days of the Young Turks in Europe. In the contemporary context, within which the EU's carrot-and-stick stimuli on Turkey operate, those effects are even more pervasive, more continuous, and more frequent.

Meltem Müftüler-Bac, in her study of the relations between the EU and Turkey writes that the prospect of Turkey's integration into the European core was an important factor in influencing the country's internal dynamics.[17] "The pressures exerted by the EU provided the external stimuli for structural change in Turkey as well as for specific policy change."[18]

Turkey signed an Association Agreement with the European Economic Community (EEC), the predecessor of the EU, in 1963. Following this development, Turkey began to send its workers to Europe. "Turkish migrants, who came mostly from rural areas, were exposed to the culture of Western Europe. When they returned on holidays to visit their villages, they opened up these rural areas to the outside world. Therefore, the attitudes and the expectations of Turkish people gradually began to change as a result of integration with Europe."[19]

In 1981, following the military takeover the year before, the Joint Parliamentary Committee of the European Union froze all relations with Turkey because of the military's dissolution of the Turkish parliament. When former party leaders were arrested, the European Union decided to suspend all aid to Turkey and Turkish membership of the Parliamentary Assembly of the Council of Europe was also suspended.[20]

Europe insisted on rapid normalization and democratization of political life following the 1982 coup. After every resolution and declaration by the EU, a high-ranking Turkish official visited Brussels to explain the situation.[21] In January 1987, Turkey recognized the right of its citizens to make individual applications to the European Commission on Human Rights and ratified the United Nations and European Conventions for the Prevention of Torture. In 1990, Turkey signed the Paris Charter along with other members of the Conference on Security and Cooperation in Europe (CSCE) on minority rights and the protection of minority cultures, languages, and religions. In April 1991, the Turkish government permitted the use of the Kurdish language, thereby repealing the restrictive 1983 law on minority languages. In the same period, Articles 141, 142, and 163 were removed from the Turkish Penal Code, in response to European claims that these articles restricted political participation and a ministry of human rights within the Turkish cabinet was established to adapt to EU standards in this area.[22]

Turkey has utilized her European diaspora to obtain German support for her bid for EU membership. "Germany was instrumental in promoting the consideration of Turkish membership in the early 1960s. Not surprisingly, this was during the period when German recruitment of Turkish workers was just beginning. ... In 1973, German help was important in obtaining a twenty-two-year transition period. The economic downturn surrounding the 1973 oil shock and Germany's subsequent desire to decrease the size of its immigrant population reduced German support for Turkish membership. The fear of most European states was that Turkish membership would result in a new flood of Turkish workers."[23]

Faruk Şen, the director of the Center for Turkey Studies in Essen, argues that the Turkish community in Europe now reflects the diverse ethnic make-up of Turkey proper and that this would add color to Europe. "Currently there are 15 countries, 29 different people, and 34 languages within the borders of the European Union. The Ottomans had 72 ethnic groups living within their borders. European multiculturalism will be enhanced with Turkey's membership."[24]

The presence of a significant migrant population from Turkey in Europe and Turkey's rocky relationship with the EU are intricately linked with Turkey's historical desire to become part of the West. Turkey's relations with Europe provide the larger context within which Deutschkei's transnational condition acquires more importance for Turkish as well as European politics. This is not to say that transnational connections are in absolute need of such contexts. It is, however, to say that Turkey's persistent, pro-West foreign policy orientation makes her more susceptible to influences from abroad. The contemporary manifestation of the desire to be a part of the West, namely, the bid for full EU membership constitutes the broader institutional link that makes Turkey-related activities outside of national borders and the government's outreach to counter, foster, or control them all the more meaningful.

Although her candidacy has been declared in Helsinki in 1999, Turkey has yet to meet the various criteria set on June 22, 1993 in Copenhagen for all potential EU members. These include democracy, the rule of law, human and minority rights, a functioning market economy, the capacity to withstand the market forces and competition within the union, and the ability to fulfill other obligations arising from full membership.

MIGRATION TO EUROPE AND DEVELOPMENT IN TURKEY

Empirical and case-specific studies do not contain conclusive findings about the aggregate effects of migration on development. As mentioned before, according to the perspective adopted in this work "the migration-development relationship is complicated, unresolved, unsettled, uncertain, critical, and even unexplored, or both positive and negative for emigrant as well as immigrant countries."[25]

The most observable effects of migration on development have been captured in the literature under the headings of *return migration* and *remittances*.[26]

Return Migration

Return migration from Europe to Turkey is now being replaced with de facto or de jure permanent settlement and transmigration. The back and forth movement between sending and receiving countries takes place on a more or less continuous basis.[27]

Return migration has been analyzed, particularly by sociologists, in terms of the changes it causes in the class structures of the lands of origin, with the premise that emigration can be a stimulus for social change and that returnees may contribute to the expansion of the middle class in their hometowns and villages.[28] Others have studied the effects of return on macro variables like national savings rates, productivity, qualification levels, unemployment, or in terms of its sociological effects on women and family.

There are general studies, as well as specific ones on Turkey, that show that return migration has not necessarily been an overall beneficial factor for the economy. At the village level, there are some success stories. At the aggregate level, returned Turkish migrants do not seem to have constituted a strategic factor in Turkey's economic development. In fact, according to one analyst, around 70 percent of the migrants did not return and those who remained abroad were the most skilled and ambitious.[29]

To some degree, returnees have contributed to upward mobility in Turkish society. Between 1983 and 1984 a relatively large number of migrants returned from Germany to Turkey.[30] The majority, around 76 percent, preferred to settle in cities near their hometowns or villages, a sign perhaps of potentially urbanizing effects of return migration.[31] Returnees also tended to be among the wealthiest in their villages of origin. Around 80.5 percent of the returnees accrued a certain amount of savings during their stay in Germany. Around 18 percent had established their own businesses.[32] However, their saved capital has rarely gone to productive sectors and when it did, often it was eaten up by big capital. A large portion of the money has gone to the purchase of homes and real estate.[33] The unfortunate fate of experiments and self-help projects subsidized by the government, such as the so-called "village development cooperatives" and "worker companies," attests to this picture.[34]

Michael Piore points out that migration in some countries may function as a political and economic *safety valve*, that is, as an outlet for a surplus population whose aspirations and expectations cannot be met at home and that would otherwise be pressed more vigorously through the political process at home. Nermin Abadan-Unat, for example, argues that when Turkey's first Five-Year Development Plan (1962–67) was formulated, the export of excess unskilled labor to Western Europe was thought of one of the possibilities for alleviating unemployment.[35]

In the long run, however, migration may, by exposing the population to foreign standards of living and patterns of work, actually reproduce the very aspirations that policy makers aim to satisfy. The assimilation of industrial values may lead to the very kind of consumption patterns that foster expenditures on foreign imports.[36] Indeed, Turkish return migrants and their families have not been eager to spend their foreign earnings on locally produced goods and services. Instead, these earnings have often been used to finance imports of consumer products.[37]

Abadan-Unat paints a more positive picture in terms of the relationship between migration to Europe and development in Turkey. "Their preference to live off rental income or small business produces a type one might call the 'proletarian bourgeois.' Nonetheless, the *Almancilar* [a colloquial term for returnees from Germany] represent a new generation of those who dared to look for a future outside the national borders. As such they have made a permanent impact on Turkey's economic life, social structure and politics."[38]

Abadan-Unat argues that *Almancilar* have "caused in rural Turkey a chain reaction of social change; changes in the economy, in technological innovation, in telecommunication and transport, and finally, to some extent in social stratification and political participation."[39] They changed, she writes, the attitudes in rural areas toward "the ownership of land, the value of landowning, and the intentions of villagers for land usage."[40] They imported tractors and invested heavily in livestock. They brought TV sets, VCRs, refrigerators, and fax machines with them into a country that was relying primarily on import substitution strategies to develop and therefore was a closed market to foreign goods. *Almancilar* have invested in home building and improvement, purchased new-style furniture. Beyond changing the consumption patterns of villagers, they caused positive changes, albeit marginal, in social values regarding fatalism, pre-arranged marriages, and the status of women.[41]

REMITTANCES AND THE MACRO-ECONOMIC EFFECTS OF MIGRATION

The more positive effects of international migration on sending developing countries lie in the remittances and the business investment potential of migrants.[42] Indeed, the migration of Turkish workers, skilled as well as unskilled, has exercised its influence most strongly through workers' remittances.

Remittances, in addition to exports, are a source of foreign exchange for the sending country. They may even be a partial substitute for direct foreign aid in the long-term.[43] The foreign exchange obtained from both remittances and export income may enable the country to obtain imports. These imports may contribute to domestic production as inputs. Remittances may also raise aggregate demand. The owners of businesses who sell consumer goods to those who receive and spend remittances may invest the funds in "productive" ways such as expanding their business. Some analysts claim that labor migration helped greatly to postpone the crisis of the Turkish economy in the late 1960s and early 1970s by preventing foreign exchange starvation, which was the inevitable outcome of the strategy of import substitution (ISI) in inefficient and noncompetitive consumer goods industries.[44]

Even though only a negligible part of the massive flow of remittances was channeled into direct productive investment in the industrial sector, remittances seem to have helped to keep the levels of income and employment in Turkey higher than they could have otherwise been by increasing demand and imports.[45] However, other analysts argue that remittances might, in this way, have fueled inflation and have permitted Turkey to follow an import-substitution strategy (ISI).[46]

According to Şen, the function and impact of external labor migration on Turkey can be better assessed within the scope defined and determined by ISI, which was adopted following the military intervention of 1960. Since external competition was non-existent due to protectionism, production was directed exclusively to the internal market. Although the volume of production increased, this did not correspond to simultaneous increase in export potential. Moreover, increases in industrial production required increases in the import appeal and therefore the foreign exchange account of the manufacturing sector always showed a deficit.[47] Remittances contributed to foreign exchange availability and to the widening of the internal market. Market expansion could also be attained both by the remittances themselves and by the demonstration effect of consumer goods brought back from abroad by workers.[48]

Whatever its aggregate effects were, according to A. Y. Gökdere, the main impact of labor migration has been on the service sector. Migrants have expanded demand for transport, banking and communications services. Turkish workers abroad stimulated business and tourist travel between EU countries and Turkey, which further enlarged the Turkish service economy.[49]

NOTES

[1] A.L. Macfie, *Profiles in Power: Atatürk* (London and New York: Longman, 1994), 4. Mehmet Talat, Kazim Karabekir, Enver Pasha, Abdullah Cevdet, Ahmed Cemal, and Mehmet Cemal were the most notable Young Turks known to Europeans.

[2] There are other examples akin to the Turkish experience. The cradle of Algerian nationalism during the 1930s was in France among the migrant population rather than in Algeria

proper. Algeria's first nationalist newspaper, the *Etolie d'Afrique du Nord*, was published in Paris in the 1920s. This migrant population was an important financial resource for the National Liberation Front (FLN). See William B. Quandt, *Revolution and Political Leadership: Algeria*, 1954–1968 (Cambridge: MIT Press, 1969).

During Algeria's war of independence, the Algerian diaspora in France also served as a base of operations for the war in Algeria proper. *The Amicale des Algeriens en Europe*, essentially a branch of the National Liberation Front (FLN, is a contemporary illustration of the political role of a public sphere abroad. This group's significant impact on Algerian politics occurred in 1976 during a major national debate on the "Charte Nationale," the war constitution. The *Amicale* organized meetings and discussion groups in France to discuss a draft version of the document and generally played an important role as a transmitter of ideas between national authorities and the emigrants. See Stephen Adler, "Emigration and Development in Algeria: Doubts and Dilemmas," in *Guests Come to Stay: The Effects of European Labor Migration on Sending and Receiving Countries*, ed. Rosemarie Rogers (Boulder and London: Westview Press, 1985), 263–284.

[3]Şerif Mardin, *The Genesis of Young Ottoman Thought* (Princeton: Princeton University Press, 1962), 17.

[4]M. Şükrü Hanioğlu, *The Young Turks in Opposition* (New York and Oxford: Oxford University Press, 1995), 3.

[5]Ibid., 3.

[6]In 1993, the European Council meeting in Copenhagen outlined certain political and economic conditions to be satisfied by candidate countries before accession, known as the "Copenhagen criteria," which included stable democratic institutions, observance of the rule of law, human rights and minority rights, and a capacity for competitive market economy.

[7]Ayşe Öncü, "Small Worlds and Grand Projects," in Metin Heper et al., eds., *Turkey and the West: Changing Politics and Cultural Identities* (London: I.B. Tauris, 1993), 260.

[8]Ömer Vehbi Hatipoğlu, a parliamentarian of Kurdish descent from the Islamist Welfare Party, interview by author, tape-recorded Ankara, August 1998.

[9]Klaus Schwarz, "Ein Rückblick," in *Das Türkische Berlin*, ed. Martin Greve and Tülay Çinar, (Berlin: Die Ausländerbeauftragte des Senats, 1998), 7–10.

[10]Ibid.

[11]Ibid.

[12]Ilber Oltayli, *Osmanli Imparatorluğu'nda Alman Nüfuzu* (Istanbul: Iletisim Yayinlari, 1998).

[13]Ibid., 59.

[14]Ibid.

[15]Hebert Feis, *Europe: The World's Banker (1870–1894): An Account of European Foreign Investment and the Connection of World Finance with Diplomacy before the War* (Yale University Press, 1930).

[16]Alfred Joachim Fischer, "Deutsche Emigranten in der Turkei," in *Das Türkische Berlin*, ed. Martin Greve and Tülay Çinar (Berlin: Die Ausländerbeauftragte des Senats, 1998), 10–12.

17 In August 2002 the Turkish parliament passed a series of legislation, including the repeal of the death penalty and the right to education in minority languages, to bring the country's legal infrastructure more in line with the criteria set by the European Union for full membership.

18 Meltem Müftüler-Bac, *Turkey's Relations with a Changing Europe* (Manchester and New York: Manchester University Press, 1997), 108.

19 Ibid.

20 Ibid., 79.

21 Ibid., 80.

22 Ibid., 83, 84.

23 Wesley D. Chapin, "The Turkish Diaspora in Germany," *Diaspora* 5:2 (1996).

24 Yalcin Bayer, "Avrupa'da Türk Mozaiği," *Hürriyet*, 10 February 1999.

25 Kenneth Hermele, "The Discourse on Migration and Development," in *International Migration, Immobility, and Development: A Multidisciplinary Perspective*, ed., Thomas Hammar, Grete Brochmann, Kristof Tamas and Thomas Faist (Oxford: Berg, 1997), 134.

26 There are exceptions, particularly works dwelling on the Mexican immigrant communities in the United States and their relations with their places of origin. Also see Matthew Frye Jacobson, *Special Sorrows: The Diasporic Imagination of Irish Polish, and Jewish Immigrants in the United States* (Cambridge: Harvard University Press, 1995).

27 For a good empirical discussion of transmigration, see Patricia Landolt, *Salvadoran Transnationalism: Towards the Redefinition of National Community*, 2000, Working Paper # 18, The Johns Hopkins University, Program in Comparative and International Development.

28 There are also studies on immigrants to the United States at the turn of the century, such as R. Bourne, "Transnational America" *Atlantic Monthly* 118 (1916), 86–97; on the return of the dissatisfied and the disenchanted see Wilbur Shepperson, *Emigration and Disenchantment: Portraits of Englishmen Repatriated from the United States* (Norman: University of Oklahoma Press, 1965); on those who came back with savings accumulated in the United States to buy land, such as Michaela di Leonardi, *The Varieties of Ethnic Experience: Kinship, Class, and Gender among California Italian Americans* (Ithaca, New York: Cornell University Press 1984); or to buy businesses such as Mark Wyman, *Round-trip to America: The Immigrants Return to Europe, 1880–1930* (Ithaca: Cornell University Press 1993).

29 Rhinus Penninx, "A Critical Review of Theory and Practice: The Case of Turkey," *International Migration Review*, 16/4 (1982): 795, 796.

30 Specifically, between October 31, 1983 and June 30, 1984, 221 thousand migrants returned to Turkey. This was mainly due to German policies that distributed 10500 DM to those who would return permanently.

31 Faruk Şen et al., *Migration Movements from Turkey to the European Community* (Brussels: Center for Turkey Studies, 1993), 48.

32 Ibid.

33 Oya Baydar-Engin, "Die Kehrseite der Auswanderung—die Rückkehr: Fakten, Probleme, Forschung, Theorien," in *Türkische Migranten in der Bundesrepublik Deutschland*, ed. Sami Özkara (Köln: Önel Verlag, 1990), 292.

³⁴The Ministry of Industry and Commerce offers returnees loans for workshops and cooperatives in designated industrial zones to stimulate industrial development. Worker companies (*işçi şirketleri*) are regional, cooperative undertakings to benefit the migrants and their families abroad, as well as the returnees, by investing their money in productive enterprises that would guarantee them employment upon return and would contribute to the development of communities in rural areas from where migrants have originated. Of the 322 workers companies, many of them have closed down or have gone bankrupt due to bad management and general economic downturns in Turkey. For more on this, see Nermin Abadan-Unat, "Turkey: Late Entrant into Europe's Work Force," in *The Politics of Migration Policies: Settlement and Integration: The First World into the 1990s*, ed. Daniel Kubat (New York: Center for Migration Studies, 1993), 307–336.

³⁵Nermin Abadan-Unat, "Turkey: Late Entrant into Europe's Work Force," in *The Politics of Migration Policies: Settlement and Integration: The First World into the 1990s*, ed. Daniel Kubat (New York: Center for Migration Studies, 1993), 307.

³⁶Michael Piore, *Birds of Passage: Migrant Labor and Industrial Societies* (Cambridge, Massachusetts: Cambridge University Press, 1979), 116, 117, 128, 129.

³⁷Ibid.

³⁸Nermin Abadan-Unat, "Turkey: Late Entrant into Europe's Work Force," in *The Politics of Migration Policies: Settlement and Integration: The First World into the 1990s*, ed. Daniel Kubat (New York: Center for Migration Studies, 1993), 320.

³⁹Nermin Abadan-Unat, "Impact of External Migration on Rural Turkey," in Paul Stirling ed., *Culture and Economy: Changes in Turkish Villages* (Cambridgeshire: The Eothen Press, 1993), 201–215.

⁴⁰Ibid., 204.

⁴¹Ibid.

⁴²Indeed, workers' remittances have played, and continue to play, an important role in the economic development of countries like Turkey, Morocco, Portugal, the Philippines and so on. In smaller countries, such as El Salvador, Guatemala, and the Dominican Republic, remittances now rival or surpass traditional exports as the main source of foreign exchange and entire sectors of the economy are increasingly dependent on migrant investments. Ludger Pries writes that there are entire villages in Mixteca Poblana, which practically lead a *rentier* existence, depending on the money sent home from abroad.

The ratio of remittances to merchandise exports in 1993: Turkey: 19, Egypt 221, El Salvador 142, Yemen 53, Morocco 48, Pakistan 23. Emigrants make up 4 percent of the total population in Turkey. This percentage is 17 for Egypt, 44 for Jordan, 3 for Mexico, 4 for Pakistan, and 2 for Philippines. Kenneth Hermele, "The Discourse on Migration and Development," in *International Migration, Immobility, and Development: A Multidisciplinary Perspective*, ed., Tomas Hammar, Grete Brochmann, Kristof Tamas and Thomas Faist (Oxford: Berg, 1997), 137.

⁴³Kutlay Ebiri, "The Impact of Labor Migration on the Turkish Economy," in *Guests Come to Stay: The Effects of European Labor Migration Rogers on Sending and Receiving Countries*, ed. Rosemarie Rogers (Boulder and London: Westview Press, 1985), 210.

[44] Workers' remittances were not sufficient, however, to compensate for the effects of the rise in oil prices and the subsequent inflation in the world economy. Remittances do not count for more than 2–3 percent of the GNP in Turkey. In 1993, remittances, as a percentage of foreign exchange earnings, were 9.6 percent. This number was 26.3 percent for Jordan, 25 percent for Bangladesh, 13.4 for the Philippines, and 11.3 percent for Syria. Source: *International Migration Policies*, The United Nations, Department for Economic and Social Information and Policy Analysis, Population Division: (1995).

[45] Rhinus Penninx, "A Critical Review of Theory and Practice: The Case of Turkey," *International Migration Review* 16:4 (1982), 798, 222.

[46] Philip Martin L., *The Unfinished Story: Turkish Labor Migration to Western Europe* (Geneva: ILO, 1991), 44. In 1965, 45 million dollars entered Turkey as remittances. In 1992, 3 billion dollars entered the country this way. From 1964 to 1981, workers sent foreign exchange remittances through official channels equivalent to 60 percent of total export earnings, which compensated for half of the trade gap.

It is estimated that migrant workers have about 6 billion DM in German banks which successive Turkish governments have not been able to attract.

[47] Faruk Şen et al., *Migration Movements from Turkey to the European Community* (Brussels: Center for Turkish Studies, 1993), 7, 8.

[48] Ibid., 8, 9, 10.

[49] A. Y. Gökdere, *Yabanci Ülkelere Işgücü Akimi ve Türkiye Ekonomisi Üzerine Etkileri* (Ankara: Türkiye Iş Bankasi, 1978).

V
Between Deutschkei and Turkey: The Dialectics of Transnational Linkages

THE ESSEN BRANCH OF THE FEDERATION OF TURKISH ASSOCIATIONS OF Northern-Rhine Westphalia announces that they are donating 55 thousand DM to the Foundation for the Strengthening of the Turkish Army.[1] In Cologne, a Turkish migrant declares himself *caliph* and the head of an Islamic state in exile, denouncing the existence of the Turkish state and declaring both Germany and Turkey *Dar-ül Harb* (un-Islamized foreign soil subject to *jihad*).[2] Again in Cologne, Alevi activists raise money for the victims of Sunni attacks in Turkey and call on the Turkish government to liberalize their constitution. In Frankfurt, the ultranationalists work hard to raise money for their party in Turkey to win elections and devise strategies to counteract Kurdish attacks in Europe against the Turkish state.

"Particularly after Solingen we became a little introverted," explains Faruk Sen, referring to the neo-Nazi's burning of a Turkish family in 1993. "We separated our mosque associations, sports clubs, discos. We watch Turkish television. In the midst of Europe we live Turkey a little too much. ... Of the two million Turks living in Germany half spend their vacations every year in Turkey. This goes for the third and the fourth generations as well. It's not easy to find another nation like this. ... We are highly organized, but fragmented. You know how the saying goes: when seven Germans get together they establish an association. When seven Turks get together they establish an association and three factions emerge out of it."[3]

DIASPORA AS A MÉLANGE OF GROUPS

Studies on diasporas have tended to take the national origins of an entire people as their main units of analysis. However, with the advent of the post-national and transnational era and with the "discursive construction of diaspora at a time when there has been a relative weakening of the meaning of the nation-state," it makes more sense to view diasporas as a melange of diverse factions.[4]

Sub-national groups in diaspora may have different experiences of discrimination and identification in sending as well as receiving countries. As Steven Vertovec notes, diaspora, as a type of consciousness, is constituted both negatively by the experiences of discrimination and positively by identification with an historical heritage.[5] Along the same lines, Ishtihaq Ahmed writes that "[t]he social groups which share a common identity with the ruling elite depend on the survival of the state. ... The states treat protests and other forms of moderate employment of voice among such groups differently from that taking place among ethnic minorities."[6] Some groups try to reconstitute a lost homeland or to maintain an endangered culture. Others try to enhance their position in the existing power structures. That is to say that diasporas contain groups that may advocate the status quo as well as groups that challenge it. Diasporic groups may be forces of conservation as well as of change.

Groups in diasporas also tend to display higher levels of differentiation than their equivalents in the country of origin. Deutschkei consists, among others (such as leftists and secularists), of Kurds, Alevis, ultranationalists, and Islamists. These four groups have been chosen for this study because they have a substantial political presence in Europe. Each of these groups has developed its own subsidiary public sphere, particularly organized and effective in Germany. More importantly, these groups have always been and continue to be oriented, sometimes at the expense of integration in host polities, towards affecting Turkish politics in Turkey proper. These groups not only have better organizational experience than their counterparts back home, but leadership skills, as the cases of Alevis and Kurds show, and substantial financial resources as the cases of Kurds and Islamists demonstrate. Moreover, they share the resources at their disposal with their functional equivalents back home.

All four of these groups position themselves differently vis-à-vis the state of origin. Each group's interpretation of Kemalism, the official ideology of the Turkish state, is used here to capture, in more concrete terms, variation in such positioning. As a direct result of their particular ways of relating to the Turkish state, these groups also differ in their ways of linking themselves to the idea of "home," in devising strategies for recreating their homes abroad, and in influencing homeland politics from abroad. Therefore, we cannot talk about a single, discernable effect on the expansion of the public sphere of civil society. There are qualitative differences between groups that are dispossessed of a land or striving for statehood (Kurds) and those who have a physically existing nation-state to identify with (Islamists, ultranationalists, and Alevis).

The overall predominance of some types of political activities and forms of political participation over others may also vary from one group to another. For instance, since stateless groups may be excluded from conventional participation at home, their methods may take more unconventional forms that are based on physical force rather than on negotiation, persuasion, and consensus building.[7] On the other hand, those who want to reform and preserve the state employ conventional political methods. The Alevi public sphere, much more than other groups examined here, approximates a realm of rational-critical debate that provides equal access to all and where conflict is resolved through consensus.[8]

With the exception of ultranationalists, who have the state's endorsement back home more than other groups examined and who therefore act as conservative forces that reinforce the existing order, all of these groups organize themselves along relatively subversive political ideas. As such, they are, to varying degrees, upsetting to the political status quo back in Turkey.

DIFFERENTIATION INTO SUB-NATIONAL GROUPS

Group differentiation among Turkish migrants in Germany has started much earlier than popular political awareness of ethnic and religious heterogeneity in Turkey.

The first signs of such differentiation abroad along ethnic lines might be traced back to the early 1980s when the Kurdish Culture and Information Center was founded in Berlin. This organization would express demands for separate Kurdish language classes for the Kurdish children who had to share preparatory classes for foreigners (*Ausländerregelklassen*) with Turkish children, but who could speak neither Turkish nor German. Kurdish representatives at the center would claim that many Kurdish families and particularly women tended to associate exclusively with fellow Kurds. As a result, they were not well informed about German public policies and services concerning foreigners because they did not understand Turkish in which much of such information was circulated.

Mathilde Jamin, who has chronicled the early stages of migration from Turkey to Germany, reminds the readers of a relatively recent compilation of migration data that show that neither Islamism nor Kurdish ethnicity was an issue in Germany of the 1960s and the 1970s. Jamin writes that in those days the image of a Turkish woman corresponded to the relatively emancipated female worker who, at times, came alone, without her spouse to work in Europe. This image was quite different from the "headscarf" issue that surrounds debates on Muslim women from Turkey today. Similarly, from a European perspective, the dominant image Germans have about Kurds and Kurdish "oppression" in contemporary Turkey had not started developing until the middle of the 1980s. In the 1960s and the 1970s, migrants of Kurdish descent, who came from Turkey, shared the same living conditions in Germany with their Turkish compatriots. In fact, according to Jamin and Aytaç Eryilmaz, Turkish workers associations, in those years, had more Kurdish members than they do today.[9]

Indeed, until the late 1970s relatively few migrant workers emphasized their Kurdish identity. Most of them, especially those of rural origins, were reluctant to become involved in politics. Europeans as well as their countrymen in Turkey labeled these guest workers as "Turks" and this remained, in most contexts, the relevant identity for them. Except for a few population samples, the workers have never been systematically asked for their own ethnic self-definitions.

The 1980 military coup in Turkey led to a great influx of politicized, mostly young Kurds as asylum seekers into Europe. Their presence, accompanied by news from home about the guerrilla war in southeast Turkey, worked as catalysts for the emergence of a Kurdish ethnic self-awareness.[10] Some analysts argue that, had regular surveys been conducted, a significant increase in the percentage of persons describing themselves as Kurds over the past two decades would have been seen.[11]

HOST POLICIES ON IMMIGRATION, CITIZENSHIP, AND MULTICULTURALISM

German politics in general and German immigration policies in particular have a significant impact on the form and content of migrants' activities in Germany and the way they relate to Turkey. As Andreas Ackermann notes, "[a] lot of times it is the state institutions of the receiving country that instrumentally create a split in ethnic and national identity and perpetuate cultural stereotypes in order to keep the migrants out."[12] Indeed, the entire ethnic and religious-cultural diversity of the Turkish society, while deliberately understated in Turkey, has been flourishing freely in German cities in the last two decades.

Along these lines Martin Greve and Tülay Çinar write that

> [i]n an attempt to grasp the complexity of the migrant groups, which were for decades treated as more or less a single uniform entity, their splintering was presented strongly in the German public and as such this splintering was inadvertently and actively stimulated. Today buzzwords like Kurd, Alevi, or funda-

mentalist define the German discursive scene much more than they do the Turkish scene. (Greve and Çinar 1998, 19).

One outstanding reason for this splintering with important policy effects is the preoccupation of German intellectuals and media with "multiculturalism" as an instrument to resolve problems emanating from the burning issues of integration, citizenship, xenophobia, and the like. Multiculturalism in Germany has resulted in policies that favored and encouraged ethnic and religious differentiation among migrants. For example, city governments, Berlin in particular, would finance cultural activities by civic organizations founded by foreigners that would bring forward the cultural diversity in their lands of origin.

The absence of overarching supervisory organizations in Germany, like the Directorate for Religious Affairs (DIB) in Turkey, has also played an important role in the heterogenization and deprivatization of religion and ethnicity. Both the German government (and for a long time until the early 1990s the Turkish government as well) regarded the development of Islam in Germany as an issue outside of their jurisdiction and authority. With the lack of the legal imposition of uniformity and with the encouragement of self-expression, identity politics proliferated and became an effective instrument in interest articulation and claims making.[13]

Germany also kept interest in Turkey among migrants alive by making interest and stake in the German polity difficult. A new immigration and naturalization law went into effect on January 1, 2000 that introduced the *jus soli* principle for citizenship, in addition to the existing and still dominant *jus sanguinis* rule, by granting automatic citizenship to those born on German soil after December 31, 1999 and whose parents has been residing in Germany for eight years.[14] However, the new law rejects "dual citizenship" by requiring that those born in Germany to foreign parents choose, by the age of 23, between their parents' citizenship and German citizenship.

Moreover, procedural difficulties in attaining citizenship have not been eliminated with the new law. Migrants willing and eligible to naturalize must pass a language test, which excludes many older migrants. As in the past, the law continues to allow for considerable local discretion in making the decision whether or not to grant citizenship, even when all requirements are fulfilled.[15]

Turkish policies with respect to the migrants also do not make things easy. Turkey charges about 4700 dollars from persons who want to give up their Turkish citizenship without doing their military service.[16] Turkish newspapers in Germany have been systematically urging Turks not to apply for German citizenship because they would have to give up their Turkish citizenship without which it might be difficult to inherit land, own a business, or be buried in Turkey.

The fact that the new German law, and particularly the provision about dual citizenship, has received a rather cold welcome from migrants from Turkey shows that Turkish nationals are not keen on losing their institutional and psychological ties to Turkey. "Of course I want the same rights as the Germans" said a Turkish national in an interview, "but I don't want to break my ties with Turkey."[17] In fact, after the law went into effect, applications in Berlin for citizenship went down by 25 percent in comparison to the previous year. "We were not prepared for this reaction," said Cem Özdemir, the German Bundestag member of Turkish descent and a key backer of the bill at the time. "Even those who applied under the old law have asked for their applications back."[18]

According to one perspective, Germany's immigration law continues to exacerbate the negative effects of anti-immigrant actions by neo-Nazi activists. The solidarity and security provided by ghettoization against these negative sentiments in the receiving society, like a boomerang, comes back and haunts immigrants by impeding efforts to have migrants associate with the natives.

GHETTOIZATION AND IDENTIFICATION WITH HOMELAND

The voluntary or involuntary adoption of "ghetto mentality," as dubbed by one analyst, forces migrants to live "abroad among themselves."[19] This mentality is pervasive in Deutschkei.

Migrants' cultural demands create the structures necessary to reproduce and sustain their cultures. The need for kosher meat, proper burials, contacts with their points of departures (to oversee their investment and property there for example) all create ethnic and religious businesses and networks with people benefiting from these new industries. These businesses and other migrant networks are important factors in the dual processes of identification with the homeland and politicization of the diaspora.

Nermin Abadan-Unat, Yasemin Karakaşoğlu, and Gerd Nonneman show how ethnic businesses contribute to the formation and the politicization of migrant communities, to the cultivation of their interest in homeland politics, and to the preservation of their ties with homeland institutions through *ethno-industries*.[20] In fact, Abadan-Unat suggests that it would be a mistake to interpret the emergence of ethnic businesses in receiving societies as a sign of migrants' integration into the national economies of their countries of arrival.[21]

The effects of chain migration and family formation by importing so-called "national brides" from the origin on non-integration have been discussed before. The restrictive policies of the host polity with regard to immigration and naturalization, multicultural policies of the host governments that provide funding for ethnic and religious practices, migrants' fear of losing their identity on foreign soil, their fear of xenophobia, the provision of a variety of cultural products by migrant networks, and, last but not least, the indulgence in satellite broadcasting from the origin contribute to self-segregation or ghettoization.

The Turkish broadcast media play a significant role in exacerbating ghettoization. In Berlin, 95 percent of the Turkish households have access to cable TV and satellite broadcasting from Turkey. It is said that Kreuzberg has become a "forest of satellite dishes," a statement that can easily be verified by a simple glance at the buildings' roofs and balconies.[22] In fact satellite dishes in Deutschkei, like national flags, distinguish the apartments where Turks live from those of non-Turkish dwellers.[23]

Finally, there are powerful groups in the diaspora that work against the integration of migrants into receiving societies. Even where there is observable integration, identification with the new home at different levels does not preclude political identification with the country of origin.[24] Non-integration provides an environment that facilitates political identification with and indexation to homeland. Therefore, non-integration abroad seems to be the *raison d'être* of groups that have a stake in the system back home.

INDEXATION TO HOMELAND POLITICS

Some researchers point out that immigrant communities in Europe do not resemble those traditionally found in the United States.[25] Barbara Schmitter-Heisler writes that unlike the ethnic enclave communities common in the United States, immigrant communities in Europe exhibit a different configuration. In terms of their strong organizational political ties with the countries of origin, they may be better characterized as "states within states" or "political exclaves." In other words, these communities are not traditional, relatively self-contained communities, but differ because of their ties to the sending state.[26]

One may argue that Turks seem to be particularly interested in homeland politics and particularly politicized in this respect than other groups in Germany. According to Kevin Robins, a "distinguishing feature of the Turkish communities in Europe, particularly since the 1980s, is their high degree of politicization—politicization that relates directly to ideological divisions and struggles within Turkey."[27]

Indeed, the reasons for higher levels of politicization may lie primarily in the nature of the homeland regime and in Germany's overall approach to politics in Turkey. The Kurdish issue, for instance, has been the locomotive force of most political migration to Germany from Turkey (or, according to some observers, of economic migration in political disguise). The existence of an intense minority of Kurdish activists in Germany (second to Sweden, which hosts an intense minority of Kurdish nationalists and intellectuals) is in part explicable by the opposing ways the Kurdish question is viewed by Turkey and Germany. While the German public sees a struggle for independence in Kurdish resistance, Turks see it as a self-serving separatist movement, sponsored by European and Middle Eastern countries to destabilize Turkey. These opposing interpretations prepare an environment within which the Kurdish issue is thoroughly politicized.

Feelings of exclusion from the political system in Turkey contribute to politicization, radicalization, and at times to the channeling of much political energy into non-conventional means of influence. Turks abroad cannot vote at Turkish elections within the countries they live. They also do not, yet, form an effective lobbying force inside Germany. Nevertheless, by presenting an "incalculable" opposition force, the Turkish and Kurdish movements in Deutschkei do possess some political capital and have an impact on both countries.[28]

From the perspective of Albert Hirschmann's model of *exit, voice,* and *loyalty*, some scholars have argued that it is when the option of exit in the country of destination and the option of voice in the county of origin are blocked that the transnational field becomes an attractive area of study.[29] This may be particularly true of Turkish transnationalism.[30] The fact that political voice is limited in Turkey with regard to certain constitutionally significant issues makes political activities of people from Turkey in the transnational space all the more meaningful for the overall evolution of Turkish politics.

In their studies of politics of migration, Mark Miller and Myron Weiner emphasize the political system in the country of origin and the networks developed by migrants as explanatory variables for the cultivation and maintenance of interest in homeland politics. Weiner writes the following:

> The more repressive the home country, the more likely that political organizations become active among foreign workers within the host country, so long as the host country has an open policy. Thus, Turkish and Arab foreign workers have brought the politics of their home countries into that of their hosts. For these groups the goal is not necessarily to influence the foreign policy of their hosts toward their home governments, but to have a direct involvement in the internal politics of their homeland. A kind of mini-Turkish and mini-Arab polity thus develops within the countries of Western Europe. For this reason, the governments of the host countries—and especially their intelligence and police services—take a keen interest in the internal politics of the countries from which their foreign workers come. (Weiner 1986, 66)

Miller cautions, however, that "the maintenance of political identification with the homeland is only a necessary and not a sufficient condition of influence by foreign workers upon their homeland."[31] In other words, the linkages between identification and actual impact need to be fleshed out.

TRANSNATIONAL FLOWS FROM DEUTSCHKEI

As discussed earlier, while ethnic differentiation of migrants from Turkey into sub-national groups with accompanying interest articulation and institutional demands was on its way in Europe, in Turkey the word "Kurd" could not be uttered in public media until the early 1990s. Prior to that there was a deliberate effort on the part of successive administrations and the media to keep the Kurdish unrest in the conceptual containers of "separatism" and "regional underdevelopment." Put differently, the Kurdish question presented itself much more clearly and early as a matter of identity politics in Germany than in Turkey where the issue has been seen primarily as militant separatism fed by foreign conspiracy or a by-product of feudal power structures.

Similar to the growing Kurdish awareness, Alevi revival in Europe not only preceded a similar revival in Turkey, but Alevism as an ethnic, religious, and cultural identity has been and still is experienced more fully and intensively in the diaspora. While the numerous and differentiated Alevi organizations in Europe can freely and officially use the term "Alevi" in their names, proceedings, and self-identification, those in Turkey, including political parties that articulate specifically Alevi interests, had to adopt names of prominent Alevi poet-philosophers, acronyms, or conceptual terms to by-pass broadly interpreted legal provisions that prevent ethnic designations from being used for associational and political purposes.[32]

The Alevis' large-scale organization in Deutschkei also predated their associational activities in Turkey proper. Alevis constituted large numbers of the first generation immigrants to Europe. The first politically active Alevi umbrella organization, namely, the predecessor of the Federation of Alevi Unions in Europe (AABF), was established in 1991 in Ginsheim-Gustavsburg, Germany. In Turkey, such an initiative did not find its full realization until 1993. The same year, the Alevi-Bektashi Counsel of Representatives (ABTM) was formed in Nevsehir, Turkey. In the coming into being of this organization as well as its effectiveness Alevi migrants' organizational experience in Europe played an important role. In fact, the president of the AABF also served as the chairperson of the ABTM from its inception until 1996.[33]

The Islamization of Turkish ultranationalists in Europe, on the other hand, took place in tandem with similar such developments in Turkey. Here again, the coup of 1980 was the significant turning point. The coup that ended the civil war between the leftists and the idealists (rightists) had particularly harsh consequences for the political left but it did not spare the radical right either. Many politically active ultranationalists managed to escape to Europe immediately before the time of the takeover. Significant numbers of those who remained were jailed.

The continuous exchange between the right wing exiles in Europe and their counterparts in Turkey has contributed to the synchronization of the post-coup developments in Turkish ultranationalism. Frustration and disappointment with their harsh treatment by the state, for which they thought they were fighting and sacrificing their lives, created an anti-state sentiment among grassroots fascists for a while. The necessity to justify this resentment ideologically and to develop a discourse critical of the state, Turkish idealists (as most ultranationalists call themselves), particularly those who were imprisoned, started, more and more, to resort to Islam. Islam, with its conservative populist critique of the secular modernist state system, provided an indispensable cognitive map for the politically charged but seriously disoriented Turkish idealism (ultranationalism).[34]

Similar events were taking place in Europe, albeit in a more radicalized fashion. Like other subversive ideas, the Islamist discourse could find its fuller articulation in Europe. This process of the Islamization of Turkish ultranationalism was quite divisive. Those who put emphasis on the religious dimension of Turkish identity gradually separated themselves from the adherents of the original doctrine, both in Europe and in Turkey.[35] Not only have new institutions, in the form of political parties and pressure groups emerged, but new political discourses have surfaced from this ideological separation as well. Musa Serdar Çelebi and Muhsin Yazicioğlu are the two leaders of the Islamist/Turkist movement in Europe and Turkey respectively. The connections between these formations, namely, the European Turkish Islamic Unions (ATIB) in Germany on the one hand and the Big Unity Party (BBP) in Turkey on the other are mostly informal and ideational, rather than organic and institutional.

The task of the sections ahead is to identify and analyze these elusive connections. The analysis will also include a closer look at the exchange between the relatively more secular and pre-Islam-based nationalism of the Federation of European Turkish Idealist Associations (ADÜTDF) in Germany and its partisan counterpart, namely, the Nationalist Action Party (MHP) in Turkey.

ELECTORAL CONNECTIONS

The lack of a system of *absentee voting* has long been a thorny issue in Turkey's relations with its diaspora. Turks abroad have continuously demanded the provision of procedures that would enable them to vote at consulates or via mail. They also have asked for representation in the Turkish parliament in Ankara *qua* diaspora.

In 1986, Turkish citizens settled abroad were granted the right to vote at national border entrances 70 days prior to the general elections in Turkey.[36] During the April 18, 1999 elections, voter turnout at the border station Kapikule was 100 percent.[37]

As it was the case with previous elections, voters were offered transportation to the border. Discounted charter planes, specifically organized for the elections, carried voters to Kapikule. Each time the Islamists and the ultranationalists were particularly active in mobilizing voters and facilitating the process of voting for them.

Indeed, the inhabitants of Deutschkei have long been engaging in vibrant political activity prior to Turkish elections.

> During the 1995 local elections in Berlin, there was a visible activity among immigrants from Turkey, even though a large percentage of them lacked voting rights. Their mobilization followed an agenda beyond the immediate act of voting and electing their own representatives. Turkish immigrant groups not only made demands for the right to vote in German and European Union elections but also used Berlin elections as leverage for elections in Turkey. Their election platforms particularly focused on the recognition of dual citizenship, eradication of racism and discrimination, extension of Europe-wide voting rights and free movement rights, along with other local issues relating to youth, education, and the elderly. One consequence of this heightened activity around elections was to re-ignite debates about rights of immigrants and replace them on Berlin's public agenda. Another was the initiative taken by the Turkish government to facilitate the participation of Turkish citizens abroad in national elections. Thus, through their politicized mobilization, immigrant groups brought together and affected multilevel agendas, as they positioned themselves in local public spheres. (Soysal 1996, 14, 15)

Right before the latest elections in 1999, the Turkish Supreme Election Board rejected the proposal of instituting a system of postal voting and required that ballots be cast in person. The large number of potential voters in Germany, it was argued, makes it difficult to organize a ballot on a single-day and that there are too few Turkish consulates to handle the numbers.[38]

In 1995, when a proposal in the parliament to liberalize this policy seemed particularly promising, Turkish political parties, anticipating potential voters abroad, increased their efforts to mobilize migrants. Parties like the center-right Motherland Party (ANAP) had their own associations campaigning in Europe and ANAP leader Mesut Yilmaz actively pursued the votes from 1.3 million potential voters abroad for his party. Although he did not quite reach his goal, in 1991 and 1995 ANAP and the Islamist Welfare Party (RP) obtained the majority of the diaspora votes.

In recent years, Turkish governments have also become increasingly aware of the political capital in the hands of the "naturalized" Turks with voting rights in Germany. The center-left Republican People Party (CHP) has been maintaining contacts with the Social Democratic Federation of Peoples' Associations (HDF) in Germany, which supports SPD in German politics.[39] The HDF members say that they are in a "critical" solidarity with the social democratic movement in Turkey. By the term "critical" they mean that they want to offer the expertise that they have achieved to the social democratic movement in Turkey through a critique that would reform and make the movement stronger.

The Libertarian Turkish-German Friendship Council (HÜR-TÜRK) is a supporter of the center-right AP/ANAP/DYP political trajectory in Turkish politics. HÜR-TÜRK was established with the help of the German Christian Democrats (CDU) and has 54 member organizations in Germany.

Five weeks before German general elections in 1994 ANAP leader Yilmaz addressed German-Turks in Germany and reminded them of the European Union's decision to exclude Turkey from the next round of talks about membership. Yilmaz blamed the CDU-led coalition for this exclusion and openly called for Turkish-German electoral support on behalf of the opposing SPD. He also met with representatives of Turkish associations from Germany in Ankara, campaigning in the same direction. In a similar fashion, during the latest elections in Germany in 1998, the head of the center-left CHP in Turkey, Deniz Baykal, campaigned among Turks in Germany against the Kohl government. Not surprisingly, 70 percent of the German Turks eligible to vote voted for the center-left SPD.[40]

EUROPE AND TURKISH ENVIRONMENTALISTS

Not unlike environmentalist movements elsewhere in the world, the Green movement in Turkey has also been influenced strongly by the German Greens.[41] The Green Party in Turkey, which emerged in the early 1990s and became official in 1994, was given impetus by German environmentalists, who first brought the issue of *Caretta Caretta* sea turtles to the public agenda. Among the natural habitat of these sea turtles, that are categorized as endangered species, are the Aegean and Mediterranean coastlines of Turkey, particularly, *Dalyan* in the Mugla province. German environmentalists mobilized their Turkish counterparts and the media with demonstrations, sit-ins, and speeches. They were phenomenally successful in energizing a massive public opinion against development projects in Dalyan to protect the sea turtles. With this event the German Greens played a significant role in raising environmental awareness in Turkey the effects of which have later spilled over to other issues.

In this respect, it is worth noting that the first German-Turkish Bundestag member, Cem Özdemir, was a member of the German Green Party known as Bündnis 90/Grünen. This party, while in coalition government with the social democrats, has created an association called Immi-Grün e.V., which focuses on migrants' problems and immigration policies.

NOTES

[1] July 28, 1998.

[2] Cemalettin Kaplan had organized and led the radical Islamic group Kaplancilar in Germany, whose self-declared goal is to replace the secular republic in Turkey with an Islamic state. Kaplan's son now leads the group.

[3] Faruk Şen, the director of the Center for Turkey Studies in Essen, interview by NTV, (Summer 1999).

[4] John Stratton, "Displacing the Jews: Historicizing the Idea of Diaspora," *Diaspora* 6 (1997).

[5] Steven Vertovec, "Three Meanings of 'Diaspora,' Exemplified Among South Asian Religions," *Diaspora* 6 (1997), 281.

[6] Ishtiaq Ahmed, "Exit, Voice, and Citizenship," in *International Migration, Immobility, and Development: A Multidisciplinary Perspective*, eds., Tomas Hammar, Grete Brochmann, and Kristof Tomas (Oxford: Berg, 1997), 159–185.

[7] Similarly, radical leftist groups, who are marginalized back home, tend to use unconventional methods that include frequent resort to violence. Some radical Islamists and ultranationalists also engage in occasional terrorist acts. Although most Islamists seem to prefer conventional methods of participation such as electioneering, the Federal Office for the Protection of the Constitution includes the IGMG, the largest Islamist organization in Germany, as an extremist threat to the constitutional order both in Germany and Turkey.

[8] There are problems with some of the premises that underlie the Habermasian conception of the public sphere, which was a bourgeois public sphere in its inception. Free and equal access, rational debate under the conditions of "ideal speech," and the emergence of consensus are assumptions that cannot support contemporary applications of the concept, just as they did not fully support the bourgeois public sphere in the seventeenth, eighteenth, and nineteenth centuries. As Nancy Fraser rightfully argues, "revisionist historiography neither undermines, nor vindicates *the* concept of the public sphere *simpliciter*, but it calls into question assumptions that are central to the *bourgeois, masculinist* conception of the public sphere, at least as Habermas describes it." (117) For a discussion of these assumptions, see Nancy Fraser, "Rethinking the Public Sphere: A Contribution to the Critique of Actually Existing Democracy," in *Habermas and the Public Sphere*, ed. Craig Calhoun (Cambridge, Massachusetts: The MIT Press, 1996), 109–143.

⁹Mathilde Jamin and Aytaç Eryilmaz, *Fremde Heimat: Eine Geschichte der Einwanderung* (Essen: DOMIT, 1998), 24.

¹⁰ German authorities estimate the number of Kurds in their country as around 400 thousand, based on the assumption that they make up roughly 20 percent of the population in Turkey.

¹¹Martin Van Bruinessen, "Shifting National and Ethnic Identities: The Kurds in Turkey and the European Diaspora," *Journal of Muslim Minority Affairs* 18 (1998): 39–52, 44, 45.

¹²Andreas Ackermann, "Ethnologische Migrationsforschung: Ein Uberblick," *Kea* 10 (1997), 17.

¹³Martin Greve and Tülay Çinar, eds., *Das Türkische Berlin* (Berlin: Die Auslaenderbeauftragte des Senats, 1998), 28.

¹⁴Wesley D. Chapin, "The Turkish Diaspora in Germany," *Diaspora* 5:2 (1996), 275–300.

¹⁵This information is acquired from the German Embassy in Ottawa, Canada. Considering the power of socialization in the family and the community, to what extent this forced choice is going to help migrants from Turkey to integrate into the German society is uncertain. To its credit though, the law reduces the duration of residency necessary for naturalization from fifteen to eight years. Currently, there are 220 thousand Turks, who so far have been naturalized into German citizens. One million and 450 thousand Turks fulfill the requirements for citizenship. The new law also enables foreigners to vote in local elections.

¹⁶ *Migration News*, 7/1, January 2000.

¹⁷Ayla Jean Yackley, "Turks, Fearing Loss of Heritage, Reject German Citizenship," *The Turkish Times*, 1 March 2000.

¹⁸Ibid.

¹⁹Nermin Abadan-Unat, "Turkey: Late Entrant into Europe's Work Force," in *The Politics of Migration Policies: Settlement and Integration: The First World into the 1990s*, ed. Daniel Kubat (New York: Center for Migration Studies, 1993), 307–336.

²⁰Nermin Abadan Unat, "Ethnic Business, Ethnic Communities, and Ethno-Politics among Turks in Europe," in *Immigration into Western Societies: Problems and Policies*, ed. Emek M. Ucarer and Donald J. Puchala (London and Washington: Pinter, 1997). Also see Yasemin Karakasoglu and Gerd Nonnemann, "Muslims in Germany with Special Reference to the Turkish-Islamic Community," in *Muslim Communities in the New Europe*, ed. Gerd Nonneman, Tim Niblock, and Bogdan Szajkowski (New York: Ithaca Press, 1996).

²¹Nermin Abadan Unat, "Ethnic Business, Ethnic Communities, and Ethno-Politics among Turks in Europe," in *Immigration into Western Societies: Problems and Policies*, ed. Emek M. Ucarer and Donald J. Puchala (London and Washington: Pinter, 1997).

²²From a documentary on Turks in Germany on the private Turkish television station NTV, 1998.

²³ In 1996, for 58 consecutive hours, TRT-INT conducted a donation drive for the Mehmetcik Foundation in Turkey, in support of the Turkish G.I. Joes and their families who died or were injured in the war against the Kurdish guerillas.

²⁴The term "integration" is rather problematic. Different groups give different meanings to this term. While for most Germans it means something closer to full assimilation, for Islamist and ultranationalist groups from Turkey it means receiving citizenship rights which

would then guarantee free and full practice of the culture of origin with minimum influence from the culture of destination. German multiculturalists, particularly social democrats and the Greens, advocate dual citizenship and the state's endorsement of both cultures, which underlie that duality.

[25] Barbara Schmitter-Heisler, "Sending Countries and the Politics of Emigration and Destination," *International Migration Review* 19 (1983), 469–484.

[26] Ibid., 481.

[27] Kevin Robins, *Negotiating Spaces: Media and Cultural Practices in the Turkish Diaspora in Britain, France, and Germany*, (Economic and Social Research Council: 1999), 3. Turkish newspapers are read in Europe more than they are read in Turkey in proportion to the respective populations. Turks abroad can only vote at border stations and that only those who have a stake or feel intensely about political issues bear the costs of traveling or are transported by certain far-right political parties.

[28] Ludger Pries, "Transnationale Soziale Räume," in *Perspektiven der Weltgesellschaft*, ed. Ulrich Beck (Frankfurt: Suhrkamp1998), 76.

[29] Bryan R. Roberts, Reanne Frank, and Fernando Lozano-Ascencio, "Transnational Migrant Communities and Mexican Migration to the United States," *Ethnic and Racial Studies* 22 (March 1999), 253.

[30] Turkish migration to Europe has both political and economic components. Although Germany, since 1973, no longer allows economic migration from Turkey, it continues to be liberal in its admission policies with respect to "political migrants." Despite the neatness of the official ruling in this regard however, neither the German government nor academics studying migratory movements into Germany from Turkey can easily discern economic from political, or voluntary from involuntary factors. It remains, however, to be true that while political voice is limited for certain groups in Turkey, once in Germany, economics makes exit from Germany to Turkey a non-option for most groups.

[31] Mark J. Miller, *Foreign Workers in Western Europe: An Emerging Political Force* (New York: Praeger Publishers 1981, 22).

[32] The general principles of the 1982 Constitution and Part II, Article 5 of the Law of Associations stipulate that organizations based on linguistic, racial, class, religious, and sectarian differences may not be established.

[33] Zentrum für Türkeistudien, *Jahrbuch* (1998), 107.

[34] Tanil Bora and Kemal Can, *Devlet, Ocak, Dergah: 12 Eylül'den 1990'lara Ülkücü Hareket* (Istanbul: Iletişim Yayinlari, 1994).

[35] Ibid.

[36] Nermin Abadan-Unat, "Turkey: Late Entrant into Europe's Work Force," in *The Politics of Migration Policies: Settlement and Integration: The First World into the 1990s*, ed. Daniel Kubat (New York: Center for Migration Studies, 1993), 307–336.

[37] All of the 66097 registered voters cast their votes. Turkish citizens who live within the borders of the European Union comprise 4 percent of Turkey's general population. 160 thousand, half of those eligible to vote, live in Germany.

[38] *The Turkish Daily News*, 1 October 1999.

³⁹The organization founded in Duisburg in 1977 has around 7 thousand members. Martin Greve and Tülay Çinar, eds., *Das Türkische Berlin* (Berlin: Auslaenderbeauftragte des Senats, 1998).

⁴⁰ In the same elections, five candidates of Turkish origin ran for federal office and three of them were elected to the Bundestag.

⁴¹Aytaç Eryilmaz, the director of DOMIT, interview by author, tape-recorded, Essen, March 1998.

VI
The Discursive Transformation of Turkey Proper

I N FEBRUARY 1999, DURING AN INTERACTIVE DISCUSSION ABOUT THE CAPTURE OF the Kurdish leader Öcalan on CNN, one of the Turkish guests, a New York based reporter for the Turkish daily *Radikal*, was asked a question, which compared the plight of the Kosovar Albanians with the problems of the Kurds in Turkey. The reporter could not hide her astonishment at the analogy explicit in the question. It was clear that she did not have a prepared response to such a comparison, even though, at the time, Serbia's Kosovo question and Turkey's Kurdish question happened to occupy the top of the international agenda simultaneously and analogies of the kind were highly likely to cross people's minds. She gave the answer that came most natural to her: "Well, from the perspective of the Turkish government, there is no distinction between Kurds and Turks."

This of course is a simple and spontaneous formulation of the "neutral state" thesis, according to which the state is, in theory, ethnically blind in its policies.[1] But the reporter's response is more interesting in the sense that it gives an idea about Turkish collective thinking with respect to the concept of "ethnicity" and the majority's resistance to coming to terms with a differentiation that "outsiders" take for granted.

THE ILLUSION OF ETHNIC HOMOGENEITY AT HOME

In an article that compares ethnic conflicts in Serbia and Turkey, Florian Bieber captures the essence of Turkish collective mentality regarding ethnicity:

> Both Turkey's Kurds and Kosovo Albanians live in nation states of other nations. The Turkish republic of Atatürk was not only a secular state, but also

claimed to establish a civic nationhood based on the inhabitants of the country. Thus every Kurd was suddenly a "Turk." This concept made the recognition of minorities redundant. The civic concept of nationhood was never truly implemented, as the language was Turkish and the acceptance in the new state could only be achieved by assimilation to Turkish-ness. Serbia and inter-war Yugoslavia never even offered a concept of nationhood, which could accommodate Albanians. The very concept of Yugoslavia excludes all non-Slavs from being a constituent component of such a state. (Bieber 1998, 2, 3)

Until the 1990s, in the popular imagination and the official idiom of the Turks and the Europeans alike, Turkish nationals in Europe were all categorized as "Turkish workers." In the early 1990s, however, Kurdish, Islamist, and Alevi activities abroad made it more and more obvious at home that some extraterritorial Turkish nationals were experiencing their ethnic and religious differences more freely outside of Turkey. In the late 1980s, and particularly in the 1990s, both Turkey and Europe came to the realization that Turkish *Gastarbeiter* could no longer be seen and treated categorically as *Turkish* simply because they migrated from Turkey.

Article 88 of the first constitution of the Turkish Republic drafted in 1924 spelled out citizenship as follows: "Everyone who belongs to the Turkish society, regardless of religion or race, is considered a Turk. ... The adjective 'Turk' is a legal definition." Thus, a "neutral state" with respect to religion and ethnicity was the intention of the Kemalist project of modernity in its early stages. The Turkish understanding of the concept of "minority" was only inclusive of non-Muslim "peoples of the book," such as Greek Orthodox, Christians, Jews, and Armenians. Over time it has become a comforting belief that reality on the ground corresponded to the theory of the neutral state and that ethnicity was a non-issue in Turkey.

A relatively recent interview with the Turkish minister of foreign affairs of the time, conducted by a French newspaper, illustrates not only Turkey's official position on ethnicity and minority rights, but also the hegemonic paradigm that encompasses public discourse in Turkey ranging from campaign slogans to school textbooks:

Question: How would you define the "Kurdish issue"?
Answer: One should not use any ethnic or racial perspective when analyzing the fabric of Turkish society. Such an approach can only serve the toleration or even justification of violence. Ethnicity has some meaning in the Western European tradition. It led to the darkest pages of its recent history. It still disturbs the moral and political scene, where racism and racist political parties are on the rise.
In Turkey, it is fortunate that nobody is interested in the ethnic origins of their fellow citizens. ... If we were to ask our parliamentarians what their ethnic origins are, we would end up with many different answers. They would include

Caucasian, the Balkans, or Kurdish and so on. I reject the attitude of most Western European countries when they suggest that one should stress the ethnic origins of our people. ... In Turkey, the Ottoman interpretation and practice of Islam was the main feature of cultural identity and a multitude of ethnic groups were allowed to exist. Ethnicity or 'race' was not an element of political or social differentiation. The most distinctive element was religion and the concept of minority stemmed from that factor. ... Turkey, like France is a unitary state. Our constitutional system stipulates that all citizens are equal before law. This is why there is no room for concepts such as autonomy or minorities based on ethnicity.[2]

At a level of lesser diplomatic tact, a prominent Turkish columnist's reaction to Britain's licensing of the Kurdish MED-TV and Germany's permission of PKK publications like *Özgür Politika* is also indicative of Turkish sensitivity to European multiculturalism and ethnopolitics:

If a television station constantly calls for terrorism and violence from the heart of Europe, curses Turkey and glorifies terrorism, naturally it is not doing this by itself and with its own resources. ... I claim boldly that had Europe not supported it, Turkey would not have gone through the PKK terror. The PKK is the instrument of imperialism and imperialists do not like Turkey. ... The left-right conflict we witnessed in the past was their product. The Alevi-Sunni conflict that they cooked up, but did not occur, was their product. The fight between Kurds and Turks is an imperialist game. ... The imperialists had to find a new instrument after the Armenian terror organization ASALA was put down by the Turkish state. *That instrument was discovered in Europe and was called PKK.*[3]

In the early 1920s, at the time of its founding, modern Turkey had little choice but to situate itself on a shaky alliance between the rich anthropological diversity of Asia Minor and the sociopolitical unity imposed by the process of nation building.[4] However, the transition from a multi-ethnic empire to a nation-state required that the new political formation reconcile this inherited diversity with a new, *unifying* formula for coexistence.

In the early stages of nation building, particularly when an anti-imperialist war against Western powers was being waged, the new formula for coexistence appeared to be relatively contractual and consensus-based.[5] The "Turkish nation" was a construct yet to be realized.[6] Having inherited strong state institutions, the Turks did not have to face the problem of state building. But nation building did present a challenge. Ayşe Kadioğlu uses the phrase "the state looking for its nation" to describe the Turkish experience in the 1920s.[7] This meant that the state of the new Turkish Republic had been trying to formulate a solid understanding of a Turkish nation from which it could derive legitimacy.

In the state's quest for its nation, distortions have occurred in the initially civic definition of citizenship.[8] Following independence, the three demands of nation building, namely, *bureaucratic centralization, secularization*, and the attempts to find a *unifying supra-identity*, created considerable tension between the objective criteria of ethnicity and the subjective sense of belonging and loyalty to a new nation.

Centralization immediately deprived some groups, particularly the Kurds, of their previous status of administrative and cultural autonomy. Secularization hurt the privileged status of Sunni religious figures and threatened the social order of the Kurdish tribes, while working to the advantage of non-Sunni minorities, including the Alevis. Finally, the adoption of Turkish-ness as the all-encompassing national identity frustrated the hopes for neo-Islamism or neo-Ottomanism that would have preserved a relative continuity with the status quo ante. Resistance to nation building by de-privileged groups made nation building less contractual and more ideological. With the gradual de-contractualization of this process the official interpretation of the founding philosophy of the state became less flexible.

In the early stages of modern Turkey, the periodic oscillation between the civic and ethnic variants of national identity has manifested itself in the form of uprisings that aimed at breaking with the main tenets of the founding philosophy, including republicanism, secularism, and the doctrine that sanctifies the new borders (*Misak-i Milli*).[9] From the perspective of the state, such ruptures have generally been seen as subversive anti-system outbursts that needed to be put down. From the large body of literature covering instances of popular opposition to Kemalism and modernity in Turkey, the endogenous causes of disruptions in the Turkish self-image are well accounted for. Here attention is given to possible influences and facilitating circumstances that appear to be *exogenous* to the national borders of Turkish politics, but nevertheless are a part of the same set of dynamics.

THE MILITARY AND THE TURKISH-ISLAMIC SYNTHESIS

By reducing the left to insignificance and impotence, the military intervention on September 12, 1980 not only fragmented the Turkish party system but also caused its general shift to the right. The *Turkish-Islamic synthesis* is the cause as well as the effect of that shift. This formula, which blends Islamic themes with Turkish-ness (unlike the old formula of Turkish-ness which reached out to the pre-Islamic period), was seen by the military as panacea against leftist radicalism. The Hearth of Intellectuals (*Aydınlar Ocağı*), set up by leading politicians, scientists and journalists in 1970, was embraced by the new military and civilian political elite who wanted to *officialize* the role of religion in public life, while at the same time and in a paradoxical fashion to glorify a new form of Kemalism.

In his discourse analysis of the ideational presence and the trajectory of the Turkish-Islamic synthesis in history textbooks from the 1940s until 1993, Etienne Copeaux traces the genesis of this political thinking and describes the elusive yet powerful nature of this ideational construct as follows:

> Because it does not belong to any specific political group or party, it is not easy to study this strand of thought. Its discourse is produced and reproduced by the two senses of belonging that take either Kemalism or Islam as their point of reference. The Turkish-Islamic synthesis finds its overt expression in many books, newspapers, and cultural journals. But, in educational and academic historical discourse its ideas manifest themselves only covertly. Its relations with political power are also not very clear. Although it is not possible to say that it has become a state ideology, it has nevertheless penetrated into discourses produced by and for certain state institutions. (Copeaux 1998, 5)

With the adoption of the Turkish-Islamic synthesis Kemalism changed its character and the Turkish democracy re-militarized, re-islamized, and re-nationalized itself. The National Security Council (MGK), State Security Courts (DGMs), and the Constitutional Court became the building blocs of the institutional infrastructure of the post-1980 regime. While the military exerts a direct influence on the first two of these institutions, its effects on the latter are rather indirect, through the parameters set by the military-made constitution of 1982.[10]

The configuration and the status of the MGK and the DGMs have been problematic for the prospective full membership of Turkey in the European Union, because the MGK does not have a functional equivalent in other European polities.[11] According to the constitution, the cabinet gives "priority" to the "decisions" taken by the MGK with respect to precautions necessary to protect the existence and the independence of the state, the indivisibility and the unity of the nation, and the peace and security in society.[12] With this institution, the military preserves the space it has carved for itself in Turkish politics since the early 1980s.

The role played and nurtured by the Turkish military in domestic politics and the changes that have taken place in that role over the years are intricately connected to the ways ethnicity and religion are perceived and handled in Turkey. Throughout the 1980s the military was acting as the protector of secularism and trying to counterbalance the revival of religious politicking that it has initiated by mandatory religion courses in public schools, among other policies. Similarly, the military has also been trying to preserve its monopoly over public political discourse on the Kurdish question and the role of religion in politics. Although the military certainly has had and continues to have significant success in setting the standards for civilian discourse on such existential issues within Turkey, there is a public sphere that develops beyond its reach and exerts constant pressure on its objectives.

One important aspect of this new sphere is made up by the unintended and unexpected consequences of Turkish migration to Europe. In combination with the privatization of the media, those outcomes contribute, in subtle ways, to the civilianization of Turkish politics and the expansion of the Turkish public sphere.

COMING TO TERMS WITH THE COLLECTIVE SHADOW

According to some analysts, the reaffirmation of cultural traditions and primordial loyalties in Turkish migrants represents a radical departure from official state policies in Turkey concerning religion and ethnicity, and as such, they can be seen as the unintended and unforeseen consequences of Turkish migration to Europe.[13]

> The large-scale migration of Turkish workers to Western Europe has posed an important challenge to the secularist principles of the Turkish state. Once settled in Europe, many Turks adopt a discernibly more Islamic orientation. ... By virtue of living in Europe the migrants can freely carry their commitment to its most conservative extremes. As a result, in an interesting and unexpected way, Western Europe, particularly West Germany, has become the center of intense activism by religious sects and movements, some of which are proscribed in Turkey. The revival of Kurdish ethnic consciousness among the migrant workers has followed a similar pattern. Turkey's Kurdish ethnic minority has participated heavily in the outflow of labor. In addition to providing them with economic benefits, migration has enabled many Kurds to reinforce their ethnic allegiances. Again, this has resulted from a mix of personal psychological needs and the absence of legal constraints in the host societies on free expression of Kurdish ethnic interests ... As in the case of religious revivalism, the growing saliency of this ethic resurgence stands in sharp contrast to official state policies in Turkey concerning ethnicity. (Sayari 1986, 96)

A very important function of the expansion of the civil public sphere in the Turkish case was to uncover the illusion of homogeneity that was pervasive in the national collective psyche.

One interesting political psychoanalysis of the Turkish national consciousness has been undertaken by Vamik Volkan and Norman Itzkowitz in *Turks and Greeks: Neighbors in Conflict* (1997). These authors concur that, at the time of the founding of the Turkish Republic in the early 1920s, internal homogeneity was of utmost importance to the Turks, because the new Turkish nation (which was a radical reaction to the Ottoman Empire) was not to be a continuation of Ottomanism, namely, of a multi-ethnic empire. "Large groups in the process of developing a new mass consciousness usually adopt a 'purification policy.' This may include a wholesale projection of the groups' unwanted parts."[14] Projection involves attributing to others an unacknowledged, unconscious part of ourselves—something that lies outside of our conscious awareness."[15] "Unless we do conscious work on it," the negative side of the psyche is "almost always projected; that is, it is neatly laid on someone or something else so we don't have to take responsibility for it."[16]

In the Turkish experience, projections onto internal diversity took place in the name of distinguishing oneself from the Ottoman past and becoming a sovereign nation-state. Territorial integrity and national unity became *existential* issues. The problem of *beka* (defined in terms of the psychology of territorial loss; the shrinking from a massive empire to a relatively small nation-state) and what the Turks call the *Sevres syndrome* continues to prevent the Turks from tackling the issue of ethnic diversity rationally.[17]

In C. G. Jung's "theory of the shadow" psychological opposites provide a way for our psyches to correct one-sidedness.[18] Jung believed that the unconscious included dormant or latent potentials that are yet to be realized and that, because the shadow is a natural part of our psyche, we can benefit from the insights that can be gained from encounters with it.[19] Put differently, the *shadow* is the negative side of the personality. We *suppress* (knowingly delete) some characteristics from our personality and/or we *repress* them, that is, convince ourselves that the unwanted characteristic does not exist in us.[20] Becoming conscious of the shadow requires considerable effort and this effort meets with considerable resistance. Healing starts with seeing through the shadow with a little self-criticism.[21]

There has been little systematic attempt made to directly apply Jung's theory of the shadow to collectivities such as nations or ethnic groups. Rather, the literature in psychology with respect to this area contains allusions to certain historical periods such as the Nazi era or to generalized categories such as the "Western culture."[22] Nevertheless, there is a general understanding in this literature that "different cultures affix different characteristics to the ego and to the shadow and that their variation in and of itself is significant."[23]

To put all of this in terms of the Jungian psychology, it may be argued that the Sevres syndrome prevents Turks from encountering their shadow entirely and coming to terms with it peacefully. Nevertheless, the necessary opposition to the conspiratorial web of the Sevres syndrome is evolving more strongly than ever and the mental resistance to the idea of ethnic diversity in Turkish society is weaker than ever.

The Alevi renaissance and the Kurdish and Islamist activities abroad have had identity-disclosing effects on the Turkish collective awareness and public debate and helped Turks come to terms with the collective shadow cast by the Sevres syndrome. Turkey is not a closed-off society anymore and is particularly exposed and vulnerable to what happens abroad. While the bid for the European Union membership is a significant exogenous source of pressure for self-criticism, some important work in the trenches is also done by migrant networks.

THE EXPANSION OF CIVIL SOCIETY IN TURKEY

A columnist from the *Milliyet* daily summarizes the trajectory of the civilianization of Turkish politics in the 1990s as follows:

> When Turkey was a society composed of "ruling bureaucrats" on the one hand and "ruled peasants" on the other, political thought had a "statist focus." We, the right-wing youth, would only think of capturing the state. So did the revolutionary left. As urbanization, individualization, bourgeoization, integration with the world and similar social dynamics developed, "the individual," "civil society," and "liberal values" gained in importance. (*Milliyet*, 9 June 1999)

Indeed, there are important changes in the traditional patterns of state-society relations in Turkey. The contraction of the state's outreach into the economy and society through neo-liberal Özalist policies of the late 1980s, the relaxation of military-civilian relations, and the privatization of the media in the early 1990s facilitated the expansion of the public sphere of civil society. With this expansion, the state's monopoly over information and deliberation about major existential and constitutional issues was broken. Turgut Özal's policies also have set off a discussion on Turkey's transformation into a *second republic*, thereby making him break more fundamentally than any politician before him with the official ideology and relegating strict adherence to Kemalism to the so-called *first republicans*."[24]

However, whether or not *statism* has ceased to be a significant part of Turkish political thinking is a different question. The unity of the state or polity in the Turkish collective mind and practice eschews the logic of the doctrine of the separation of powers. The military, the bureaucracy, the cabinet, the parliament, and the courts all make up the state, which continues to be a holistic, grand "idea" worthy of respect even though there are serious signs of its implosion (except for its military component) in practice.[25]

Statism (*étatisme*) in Turkish political culture, particularly in the 1960s, 1970s, and early 1980s has resulted in the exact opposite of the Habermasian understanding of the public sphere. Similar to the practices of *Jacobinism* in France that excluded the "enemies of the regime" from public debate, "[b]ehind a faction of a unified, authoritative public opinion, an anonymous oligarchy thus prefabricated consensus in the form of an ideology that acted as a substitute for the nonexistence public competition of ideas."[26] Although diminishing in strength, statism as a "first principle" and the state as a paternalistic entity (*devlet baba*) in Turkey are still alive and continue to render the unitary nature of Turkish polity sacrosanct in important sectors of the newly fledgling civil society as well.[27]

Nonetheless, the expansion and the politicization of the non-state arena had the observable consequence of creating politically more active and better-organized social forces. The now more assertive non-state arena in Turkey manifests itself not only in the numerical explosion of civic associations.[28] The expansion of the civil public sphere also manifests itself in the expansion of the realm of public debate on broader political questions such as political religion and ethnicity, two issues that present the biggest constitutional challenges in modern Turkey.

Debates about the proper role of Islam in politics and the revival of Alevi identity raise serious questions about the secular nature of the Turkish state. Debates with regard to Kurdish rights and the recognition of the Alevi as well as the Kurdish identities raise questions about the neutral state thesis, national unity, and sociopolitical integration. Such developments indicate that ideological and normative appeals made by the state elite to the legitimacy of the Turkish state are increasingly failing to elicit compliance in larger segments of the population.[29]

One way of measuring the expansion of the public sphere of civil society is to take a closer look at anti-status quo discourses in effective print and broadcast media. In the specific case of the Kurdish question the Persian Gulf War in the summer of 1990 and its chronological coincidence and interaction with privatized media in Turkey had an important liberalizing impact.[30] The very acknowledgment of the Kurds *abroad* was also an implicit acknowledgment of the Kurds *within*.[31]

In 1991, Mehmet Ali Birand, a prominent columnist for the left-liberal daily *Milliyet*, wrote, under the title "*Finally We Discovered the Kurds. However…,*" that the Pandora's box, feared by so many for so many years, had been opened and that the Kurdish question in Turkey had reached a point where it could no longer be ignored.[32] However, he added reassuringly that there would not be much to be afraid of if the problem were handled with the principle of territorial integrity in mind. In other words, without condoning separatism, Birand was calling for coming to terms with all aspects of the Kurdish question with courage.

In another daily, Duygu Sezer, under the heading *"We're Making Peace with Kurdish Identity,"* was pointing out that there was a difference between respecting Kurdish identity and championing a Kurdish state. According to Sezer,

> [p]olitical developments abroad affect the political balance of power, movements, and approaches inside, and domestic developments affect international approaches and policies vis-à-vis Turkey. The stage that Turkey has arrived in the last couple of years with respect to the Kurdish question is a good example of the close interaction between this country's inner and outer worlds. The pioneering role that Western countries give to democracy and human rights in the new world order, the upsetting influence of the gulf war on the regional balance of power, the fact that American and European forces, which establish themselves on Turkish soil, have become protectors of Kurdism, and that nationalism has re-emerged forcefully in Europe all hand in hand and in varying degrees have been influential in assuring that demands for Kurdism attain

a legitimate place in the Turkish political system. (*Cumhuriyet*, 25 November 1991)

More recently, following the Kurdish leader Öcalan's arrest, Şükrü Elekdağ, the former Turkish ambassador to the United States and now a prominent columnist, wrote an article on the necessity of acknowledging the Kurdish identity and making good use of the window of opportunity that arose following the military and diplomatic victories against the PKK without raising any eyebrows.[33] Raising eyebrows would have been the most benign form of official reaction a journalist could receive to such suggestions in public forums in the late 1970s and early 1980s.[34]

Most recently, the former president of the Constitutional Court and the current president of the republic, Ahmet Necdet Sezer, sharply condemned the restrictions on freedom of speech and urged the parliament to repeal a series of such restrictive laws and constitutional provisions, including lifting the ban on the teaching of Kurdish language in schools.[35] Sezer's call for political liberalization was preceded by the request of the European Human Rights Court, in its decision of March 1999 with respect to the Öcalan trial, that the composition of the state security courts be changed. In June of 1999 a parliamentary commission indeed voted to dismiss military judges from state security courts and in August 2002 a law permitting teaching in minority languages passed the parliament as part of a larger liberalization packet required by the Copenhagen criteria for European Union full-membership.

THE COMMERCIALIZATION OF THE MEDIA

The privatization of the broadcast media has been a catalyst in the discursive liberalization of Turkish politics. The link between this development and the Turkish presence in Europe may be traced back to the very genesis of satellite broadcasting in Turkey in the early 1990s.

The privatization, and hence the commercialization, of Turkish television began with a pirate venture by Turkey's first private TV channel *Star 1*, beaming out of Germany via EUTELSAT into Turkey.[36] The initiator of this liberalization was the Özal administration, since Özal's son was a partner of the Swiss-based company Magic Box, which also owned the station Star 1.[37] Thus, not unlike the early development of the bourgeois public sphere in Europe as chronicled by Habermas, the initial motive in forcing the state to share the airwaves with the private enterprise was profitability. According to some analysts, it was also part of Özal's election strategy to hold the [state owned] TRT and [the first] private channel in his own hands." As a result, the unconstitutionality of the pirate undertaking was tolerated initially.[38]

However, this venture had tremendous implications that surpassed electoral politics. "The example set by this 'pirate' venture [from Germany] was quickly followed by others. In the subsequent three years, the number of companies renting satellite transmission space to beam into the Turkish market has rapidly increased. What started as 'pirating' rapidly became accepted as de facto reality, with TRT competing with the new commercial channels for advertising revenue and audience ratings. Thus the underlying logic of broadcasting has progressively shifted away from serving 'the needs of the public' towards 'consumer choice.'"[39]

In her interpretive analysis of the Islamist utilization of commercial media for political campaigning shortly before the 1990 general elections, Ayse Öncü discusses the significant political implications of private mass media. In her inquiry on how commercial television has served to construct a distinctive knowledge of Islam, Öncü makes the following remarks:

> In the context of the Middle East, Turkey is the first country, so far, to reconcile itself with domestic private broadcasting — via satellite from Europe. 'Homegrown' commercial channels, beaming into Turkish markets via satellite have managed to evade European regulations over content of broadcasting, and amidst raging political controversy at home they have enjoyed de facto freedom from state controls. In barely three years, Turkey has moved from a scarcity of images directly controlled by the state, to an abundance of them, fueled by the competition among increasing numbers of commercial channels. (Öncü 1994, 13)

Until 1993 there was no attempt made in the parliament to adjust the legal situation to social reality. In March 1993, the SHP-DYP coalition directed that all private radio and television stations broadcasting from within the country close down. They could not do much to intercept broadcasting from abroad. But a huge popular protest followed, with taxicabs and private automobiles tying black ribbons around their antennas. The closed-down stations started planning to get together and form a "Radio Speaking Turkey." Due to strong public pressure, the parliament passed an amendment to Article 133 of the constitution on August 7, 1993 and ended the state monopoly in broadcasting formally by liberalizing and legalizing private radio and television networks.[40]

As a combined result of the eventual removal of legal barriers, profitability, and the "threshold effect" that made private radio and television irreversible phenomena, in the late 1990s commercial channels proliferated in Turkey.[41] Due to these developments in the broadcast media, the state no longer dominates public political discourse. It is the challenge to this monopoly from the European hinterland that was the initial grand facilitator of political liberalization and the expansion of the public sphere in Turkey.

Following privatization, the media became a major vehicle of accountability in the Turkish political system. In some instances, the media started performing the functions of the parliament in the sense of responding to constituency needs and demands. Political talk shows on television exposed the government more effectively to the people than any opposition in parliament could have done. The media forced the government to be more accountable by taking citizens' side when their houses were flooded, when they engaged in acts of civil protest like demonstrations and boycotts, when they were treated unfairly, or ran into a bureaucratic or political snag with the state.[42] In addition to their role in issue advocacy, the media also enabled people to find out what the different sectors of the society thought about various public issues. Thus, it enabled ideas to interact and clash with each other on the air and thereby allowed people to learn from each other.

New talk shows like *Siyaset Meydani* (Political Arena) provided unlimited deliberation (with no time limit, which made the show go on to early morning hours of the next day), facilitated participation by citizens from different backgrounds, and enabled their interaction with experts and politicians with respect to a variety of issues. The moderator of this highly popular political program, Ali Kirca, would shoulder the difficult task of calming frequently rising tensions during emotional discussions of hot topics. During one such tense moment on the air Kirca said "we and our parliament will learn gradually how to deliberate," indicating the important function of his show and others as a public exercise in debating issues rationally. Another popular political show was *Kirmizi Koltuk* (Red Chair). Whoever sat on it would be subject to free, honest, and harsh questioning with regard to hot button issues of the day.

By giving practical force to the concept of accountability and by being a substantial source of critique, the media became the propelling force of civil society in Turkey and the main determinant of the implosion of the state and the erosion of the principle of statism. In the aftermath of this Turkish "glasnost," led by the privatization of the media in the 1990s, ethnic identities have acquired new salience in public thinking as well as in academic research.[43] A new assertion of religious identities also took place in the public arena.[44] In place of the old imagined unity, there was now a new awareness of the complexity and diversity of Turkish identity.

In this respect, the Alevi case deserves special attention: Until very recently the existence of the Alevis and their special belief system had been a taboo in public discourse in Turkey. For a long time, the make-believe was that the Turkish society was culturally homogenous and that, from a spiritual point of view, a single Islamic community existed. But with changes in world politics and the cautious democratic opening in Turkey since 1989 the ethnic and religious make-up of the Turks became the subject of an extraordinary discussion. "With the slogan 'we won't be silent anymore' in 1990 the Alevis broke through the wall of silence."[45]

The late 1980s and 1990s also witnessed published articles on the Alevis in Europe as well as in Turkey, heralding, endorsing, and enabling the re-entry of these identities back into public light.[46] In May 1993, a sociopolitical talk show on a private broadcast network played a particularly significant role as both a manifestation of that breakthrough and as a cause of further awareness of Alevi existence in Turkey. This was the HBB-TV's show called *Yüksek Tansiyon* (High Tension). *Hürriyet* daily had the following comment to make before the broadcast: "High Tension, prepared and moderated by Erhan Akyildiz, brings this week to the screens the debate on 'Alevism' that never has failed to occupy the agenda in the last couple of years. Alevism, that has been a taboo in the press and on television for many years, will be discussed from two opposing perspectives represented by writer and researcher Cemal Şener on behalf of the Alevi community and their demands and by Hasan Ali Buldan a former *vaiz*."[47] The program generated a major controversy when Buldan, a Sunni religious figure, called the Alevis "heretics." Never before on national television had the opinions of a certain section of the Sunnis regarding the Alevis been aired in such clear terms.[48]

Following the show, not only HBB-TV but also the offices of many newspapers received hundreds and hundreds of angry mail and telephone calls, particularly by Alevis and Alevi friendly Sunnis protesting Buldan.[49] Twenty Alevi associations published an advocacy ad calling for an end to state-sponsored Sunnism in Turkey. One Alevi protester described her feelings in the following way: "More than the nonsense by a brainwashed ignorant on TV, what hurts us most is the fact that the state prepares a supportive legal and economic environment that facilitates the upbringing of such people."[50] The fracture of state monopoly over televised broadcasting was the triggering factor of this national debate.

This awareness also became apparent, in distinct ways, among Turkish communities in Western Europe.[51] The irruption of Turkish media into Europe reinforced the forces of cultural and ideological dynamics there, thereby contributing to continuing identification with the homeland. "Images of daily events in Turkey have served to strengthen the importance of Turkey as a cultural and political reference point."[52] "All these stations provided innovative coverage of Turkish society and contributed towards representing the multiple dimensions of it. Through the 1990s, these channels also sought actively to make their programmes available to the Turkish populations in Europe, through satellite links, but also by means of deals with cable operators. Programming to Europe has now become integral to their scheduling practices. The state broadcaster has also gone transnational, with its new channel, TRT-INT."[53]

TURKEY AND THE INTERNET

The cyberspace is an arena where "[i]ssues relate or hyperlink to each other without any reference to actual geographical locations."[54] As such, the cyberspace is the exemplary transnational sphere.

The cyberspace is also a superb arena of dissent. One interesting analysis of the homepages of Saudi resistance groups shows how opposition groups share the cyberspace with governments on equal footing. A homepage created by a single college student can compete with the homepage of an entire regime.[55]

What is revolutionary about the cyberspace is not that the content of the material it contains is more subversive than what is on satellite television broadcasts or published in books and pamphlets. The Kurds on the net are not discussing anything different than what is on MED-TV or in the library of the Kurdish Institute in Paris. What is revolutionary about the cyberspace is that it is the genuine common good: no one can be excluded from its benefits; even those who do not partake in the making of its content. The very constitution of the cyberspace revolutionizes access and exposure to rebellion, not the content of its material.

How something is said in the anonymity of digital communication affects what is said and what the ramifications of that written word would be. The following excerpt is taken from an on-line article by a young computer consultant who discusses the development of the Internet in Turkey since 1993:

> [I]n Turkey it is very hard to be rude to someone when you are face to face, because this can start a fight very easily between the hot-blooded Turks. So, when you read some messages on a hot subject, for example in a Turkish newsgroup, it is rather more direct than everyday life and a bit rude. I think humanity is gradually learning how to use this new toy. Therefore, one could make the simple assumption that the Internet opens up new and polite, or, in other words, controlled ways to communicate. (Yurderi 1997)

Indeed, the Internet may have a civilizing effect on human communication. We cannot physically harm anyone, although we can be freely offensive. "People in virtual communities do just about everything people do in real life, but we leave our bodies behind. You can't kiss anybody and nobody can punch you in the nose, but a lot can happen within those boundaries."[56]

Whether or not the physical security achieved by the cyberspace will lead to a more civilized conversational mode is yet to be seen. What is important however is that the distancing from the object of the critique achieved this way is functionally equivalent to the physical and intellectual distance that can be achieved in the transnational sphere.

At the time of this writing, it was rather difficult and premature to say that access and exposure to the transnational critique in the cyberspace was a widespread Turkish phenomenon. As of May 1997, four years after April 1993 when Turkey was first connected to the Internet via the Middle East Technical University in Ankara (METU), only one percent of the Turkish population (600 thousand people) was connected to the Internet.[57]

However, tatistics in this area are bound to be anachronistic very rapidly. There is a steadily growing Turkish presence on the Internet, originally led by Turkish governmental organizations, universities, and banks but no longer confined to them.[58]

All Turkish government consulates and embassies are on an *intranet* (*http://www.turkey.org*). That is to say, that the Turkish embassy in Berlin has the same links to parliaments, government agencies, other embassies and consulates, schools and universities, the banking system, the Securities and Exchange Commission (SPK), the cabinet, the media, including radio, television, newspapers, magazines and political parties, as other Turkish diplomatic representations around the world.

There are virtual forums such as http://www.demokratik.net, http://www.guncel.de, and *http://www.turkishforum.com*, where issues ranging from the Kurdish question, Islam in politics, military democracy, human rights, the Cyprus issue, the Armenian question constitute the main hot-button issues of all times. These issues are debated with utmost passion and with explosive language. But, unlike in its counterpart on the ground, in this digital extension of Turkish civil society the spoken (or written) word gets no one into trouble.

The following chapters will contain brief analyses of the cyber-presence of each of the four diasporic groups and of the discursive fields they have created where critical assessments of Turkey and Turkey-related issues dominate their agenda.

NOTES

[1] For the philosophical argument on behalf of the neutral state, see Katherine Fierlbeck, "The Ambivalent Potential of Cultural Identity," *Canadian Journal of Political Science* 29:1 (1996) and Rhoda E. Howard, "Cultural Absolutism and the Nostalgia for Community," *Human Rights Quarterly* 15 (1993), 300-323.

[2] Ismail Cem, "Ottoman-Turkish Interpretation of Islam on Ethnicity," interview by *L'Express*, Ankara, 15 December 1998.

[3] Emin Çölaşan, "Şer Yuvalari," *Hürriyet*, 25 March 1999. Emphasis added.

[4] For a detailed account of about 47 ethnic groups in Turkey, see Peter Alford Andrews, *Ethnic Groups in the Republic of Turkey* (Wiesbaden: Dr. Ludwig Reichert Verlag, 1989).

[5] Mustafa Kemal, at the onset of the Turkish War of Independence (1919-1923), obtained the blessings of all Alevi leaders and some powerful Kurds like Bediuzzaman Said-i Nursi, the founder of the *Nurculuk* movement.

[6] Zentrum für Türkeistudien, *Das Ethnische und Religiöse Mosaik der Türkei und seine Reflexionen auf Deutschland* (Munster: ZFT, 1998).

[7] Ayşe Kadioğlu, "Milletini Arayan Devlet," *Türkiye Günlügü* 33 (March –April 1995), 91-101. For the idea of a state in search of its nation, also see Rogers Brubaker, *Citizenship and Nationhood in France and Germany* (Boston: Harvard University Press, 1992).

[8] Betigül Ercan Argun, "Universal Citizenship Rights and Turkey's Kurdish Question," *Journal of Muslim Minority Affairs* 19:1, 85-103, (April 1999), 91.

[9] "The National Pact" on the existing national borders of Turkey, passed by the First Congress in Erzurum on July 23, 1919. It declared that foreign intervention should be rejected totally and that national borders of Turkey, as they exist today, are indivisible.

[10] The Constitution of 1982, which is the current constitution of the land, was designed by the military junta headed by General Kenan Evren. The constitution is lengthy and repressive with respect to some citizens' rights and duties. However, it was approved, under the conditions of the early 1980s by 90 percent of people at a nation-wide referendum. This high approval rate was a reflection of a massive sense of relief following the coup that ended the authority vacuum within which the daily terror of armed political factions fighting each other rocked the country. This sense of relief had long coattails, extending, albeit in a diminishing fashion, legitimacy to the constitutional order created by the junta up to date.

[11] The MGK is composed of the president, the prime minister, the chief of general staff, ministers of defense, interior, and foreign affairs as well as the heads of the army, navy, air force and the gendarme.

[12] *Anayasa, 1995 Değişiklikleriyle*, art. 118 (Istanbul: Alkim Yayinlari, 1996).

[13] Sabri Sayari, "Migration Policies of Sending Countries: Perspectives on the Turkish Experience," *Annals of the American Academy of Political and Social Sciences* (May 1986), 96.

[14] Vamik Volkan and Norman Itzkowitz, *Turks and Greeks: Neighbors in Conflict* (Cambridgeshire, England: The Eothen Press, 1997), 187.

[15] Naomi Quenk L., *Beside Ourselves: Our Hidden Personality in Everyday Life* (Palo Alto, California: CPP Books, 1993), 8.

[16] Johnson, Robert A., *Owning Your Own Shadow: Understanding the Dark Side of the Psyche* (San Francisco: Harper, 1991), 31.

[17] The Sevres Treaty of 1920, following the Ottoman defeat in the First World War, was the peace treaty, which stipulated detailed provisions with regard to the territorial disintegration of the Ottoman Empire and the colonization of its geography among Britain, France, Italy, and Greece. Also foreseen in the treaty was the establishment of an Armenian state, the boundaries of which were to be determined by President Wilson of the United States, and the foundation of a Kurdish state in the Southeast of Anatolia. The spirit (or the ghost rather) of the Sevres Treaty, which was rendered invalid by the Lousanne Treaty of 1923, is considered the ultimate "other' of Turkey's national unity and territorial integrity. For an account of the effects of the Sevres syndrome or the *beka sendromu* on the Turkish political psyche in general and on the approach to the question of ethnic minorities in particular, see Tanil Bora, *Milliyetçiliğin Kara Bahari* (Istanbul: Birikim Yayinlari, 1995).

[18] Carl Gustav Jung, *Aion: Researches into the Phenomenology of the Self* (Princeton, New Jersey: Princeton University Press, 1968), 61.

[19] Naomi L. Quenk, *Beside Ourselves: Our Hidden Personality in Everyday Life* (Palo Alto, California: CPP Books, 1993), 9, 11.

[20] Robert Johnson, "On the Teeter-Totter of Ego," interview by *Parabola*, (Summer 1997).

[21] Anthony Storr, *The Essential Jung* (Princeton: New Jersey: Princeton University Press, 1983), 91-93.

²²Nazi Germany is depicted as a collective neurotic outburst resulting from the suppressed dark side of a culture. Certain religious practices and rituals are also portrayed as mechanisms to deal with the shadow in a "benign" manner.

²³Robert A. Johnson, *Owning Your Own Shadow: Understanding the Dark Side of the Psyche* (San Francisco: Harper, 1991), 6.

²⁴ Turgut Özal became Turkey's first prime Minister following the restoration of civilian politics in 1983 through elections and the lifting of the martial law in 1984. He left a substantial legacy in Turkish politics. In 1993 he died as the president of Turkey. Özal frequently rocked the boat by saluting the armed forces in his warm-ups or by entertaining the possibility of a federated Turkey with an autonomous Kurdish region.

In contemporary Turkish political parlance the term "first republic" is used to describe the revolutionary roots of the statist, populist, and secular regime of the early republic, whereas the term "second republic" is used to distinguish the neo-capitalist and neo-liberal regime that followed the 1980 takeover, which broke the state's monopoly over a variety of areas in public life and therefore allowed for more room for pluralism, including and most controversially for political Islam and for Kurdish nationalism.

²⁵J.P. Nettl, "The State as Conceptual Variable," *World Politics* 20:4 (1998), 559-592.

²⁶Banjamin Nathans, "Habermas's 'Public Sphere' in the Era of the French Revolution," *French Historical Studies* 16, (Spring 1990), 620-646.

²⁷According to *Piar-Gallup* survey results, 81.3 percent of those questioned in 1997 continue to believe that the state is responsible for the welfare of its citizens. For the role of the state and statism in Turkish politics, see Metin Heper, *State Tradition in Turkey* (Beverly Hills: The Eothen Press, 1985); Serif Mardin, "Center-Periphery relations: A Key to Turkish Politics," *Daedalus* (Winter 1973), 169-190; Ilkay Sunar, "State, Society, and Democracy in Turkey," in *Turkey Between East and West: New Challenges for a Rising Regional Power*, ed. Vojtech Mastny and Craig R. Nation (Boulder, Co and Oxford: Westview Press, 1996), 141-155.

²⁸Between 1990 and 1995, not only did the number of civic associations mushroom in Turkey, but their membership expanded as well. The formation of an Information Center for Non-Governmental Organizations in 1995 and its publication of a guide, encompassing more than 1500 NGOs nation-wide, is quite telling in this regard. What is even more telling is the existence of 18 or more watch groups such as the Committee for the Supervision of Parliamentarians from Istanbul and Political Ethics (ISTMIKOM) and the like. According to the guide of civic organizations, as of 1995 there were 2700 foundations, 50 thousand associations, 1200 trade unions and professional organizations in Turkey. Most of these civil society institutions came into being in the late 1980s and 1990s.

²⁹Ian Lustick, *Hegemony and the Riddle of Nationalism: The Dialectics of Political Identity in the Middle East* (unpublished paper, 1996).

³⁰In March 1991, the leaders of the two warring Kurdish factions in Northern Iraq, Mesut Barzani and Celal Talabani, met secretly in Ankara where the Turkish premier Turgut Özal played a mediating role. This meeting generated rumors of a possible Turkish-Kurdish-Arabic federation in Northern Iraq endorsed by the United States and Turkey.

[31] For example, in 1991, 95 intellectuals singed a text written by Murat Belge about the Kurdish question, stating that "in order to be from Turkey, one does not have to be a Turk."

[32] *Milliyet*, 13 March 1991.

[33] *Milliyet*, 14 June 1999.

[34] This author's personal experience as a journalist in 1986 attests to the once problematic usage of the term "Kurd." A report on the clashes between the PKK and the army in the Southeast came back from the editor of the section with a note: "Do you want to go to jail? It's not 'Kurds'; the correct term is 'separatists.'"

[35] *The New York Times*, 30 April 1999. Turkey is a parliamentary democracy, which makes the prime minister the chief executive. The president has symbolic powers as the head of state and projects the image of being above all partisan divisions. However, the 1982 Constitution does give the president relatively more political power such as the ability to veto legislation and the power to preside over the National Security Council. The scope of the president's powers also depends on the strength or the weakness of the prime minister and the personality of the president himself. The two latest presidents Özal and Demirel were active presidents and gave a substantial political boost to presidency. Sezer has so far proven to be a liberal-minded leader, favoring and affecting political change, through his veto power and by consensus building, in the direction of conformity with international norms.

[36] Other examples of private broadcasting through EUTELSAT are the Kurdish television MED-TV or the fundamentalist HAKK-TV broadcasting from the "exile caliphate state in Cologne" to Europe and Turkey.

[37] Vedat Demir, *Türkiye'de Medya ve Özdenetimi* (Istanbul: Iletişim Yayinlari, 1998)

[38] Uğur Mumcu, *Cumhuriyet* 11 October1991. Also, relevant are Piar-Gallup statistics on Turks' relationship to broadcast media (1997): 43.2 percent watch TV regularly, 91.8 percent watch the news, 53.4 percent listen to the radio regularly. Only 33.2 percent read a daily newspaper regularly. 84.1 percent own a color TV and 94.1 percent report that they follow political events from the television.

[39] Ayşe Öncü, "Packaging Islam: Cultural Politics on the Landscape of Turkish Commercial Television," *New Perspectives on Turkey* 10, 13-36 (1994), 19.

[40] Vedat Demir, *Türkiye'de Medya ve Özdenetimi* (Istanbul: Iletisim Yayinlari, 1998), 101.

[41] Now the main ones are Interstar, Kanal 6, Show TV, ATV, Kanal D, and religious channels like Samanyolu, Kanal 7, and TGRT.

[42] An example would be the broadcast media coverage of "Saturday mothers." This group of women continues to meet in a visible public place called *Galatasaray* every Saturday to protest the government through sit-ins and interviews with the media. Their sons are missing and believed to have been kidnapped, detained, or killed by the state or with the knowledge of certain sectors in the state apparatus. The coverage has gathered considerable popular support for the mothers' cause and had been pressuring the authorities for the last two years.

[43] Kurdish, Laz, Bosnian, Caucasian, and so on. See Peter Alford Andrews, *Ethnic Groups in the Republic of Turkey* (Wiesbaden: Dr Ludwig Reichert Verlag, 1989).

[44] Sunni and Naqshbandi Islam with its many denominations have surfaced into public light. Alevis also came out of hiding and opened cultural centers and their own places of worship, namely *cemevis*. However, these traditional Alevi institutions continue to face legal chal-

lenges from state authorities because they continue to be perceived as a threat to secularism and to religious and ethnic homogeneity.

[45] Karin Vorhoff et al., *Wie der Phoenix aus der Asche: Renaissance des Alevismus* (Cologne: AABF Publications 1998), 13.

[46] Some of these are documented and analyzed in chapter seven.

[47] *Hürriyet*, 12 May 1993. Also see Cemal Şener, *Alevi Sorunu Üstüne Düşünceler* (Istanbul: ANT Yayinlari, 1994).

[48] In the show Cemal Şener was arguing that the Islam practiced today by the Sunnis is the *Ummayyad* Islam that has been selectively altered. He said that the Alevis considered the Koran as a living text, not just God's word where everything stops but a text that talks back.

[49] Cemal Şener, *Alevi Sorunu Üstüne Düşünceler* (Istanbul: ANT Yayinlari, 1994).

[50] *Cumhuriyet* and *Milliyet*, 20 May 1993.

[51] Kevin Robins, *Negotiating Spaces: Media and Cultural Practices in the Turkish Diaspora in Britain, France, and German*, available from http://www.ncl.ac.uk/ctrans/spaces.html; Internet; accessed in June 1999.

[52] Ibid., 3.

[53] Ibid.

[54] Ingrid Volkmer, "Universalism and Particularism: The Problem of Cultural Sovereignty and Global Information Flow," in *Borders in Cyberspace: Information Policy and the Global Information Infrastructure*, eds. Brian Kahin and Charles Nesson (Cambridge, Massachusetts and London, England: The MIT Press, 1997), 48-84.

[55] Mamoun Fandy, "CyberResistance: Saudi Opposition between Globalization and Localization," *Comparative Studies in Society and History* 44:1 (1999), 146, 147.

[56] Howard Rheingold, *The Virtual Community: Homesteading on the Electronic Frontier* (Reading, Mass.: Addison-Wesley Publishing Co., 1993), 3.

[57] Available from http://www.nua.ie/surveys/how_many_online/europe.html; Internet.

[58] Currently there are 50 Internet Service Providers (ISPs) offering services via Turkish Telecom's Internet backbone TurNet. TurNet is a monopoly with international connectivity to the U.S. Sprint. According to the Istanbul chapter of the Internet Society (ISOCTR at www.isoctr.org), there are four other companies that are trying to override TurNet's monopoly, but that the Turkish Telecom would not let them. "Monopoly kills the Internet!" is their motto on their web site. "Some dark forces are telling us that we should keep our hands off the Internet. We say No! We will not keep our hands off the Internet. We will not let these forces take the country to the dark ages." ISOCTR also blames the Telecom monopoly for the slowness of connectivity, which makes the use of the Internet in Turkey quite difficult. See Tolga Yurderi, *Internet Development in Turkey: A Case Study* (Canada: SoftCom Technology Consultancy, 1997).

VII
The Alevis

THE BUILDING WAS AN OLD CHURCH IN KREUZBERG. IT WAS RECENTLY SOLD to Anatolian Alevis, who not only did not mind conducting their rituals (*cem*) in a church, but who were utterly pleased to have an entire building of their own as the embodiment of the revitalization of their long hidden identity. It was a time of glorious self-expression and this building, with its tall ceilings, stained-glass windows, and its awesome altar was the perfect architectural manifestation of that re-emergence.

Dedes were invited all the way from Turkey so that young people could learn about the old ways and traditions.[1] Knowledgeable *dedes* were scarce commodity here in Deutschkei. There was much display of unity and self-confidence. Soon, however, the traditional was bound to clash with the modern.

Sitting arrangements during *cem* had become a thorny issue in the Alevi diaspora. There was a lot of dissatisfaction among older and more traditional Alevis with regard to the fact that some groups were conducting *cem* by sitting on chairs in rows facing the altar, as opposed to sitting in a circle on rugs, as it was done in the past. The Turkish *dedes* did not know what they were getting themselves into when they called on everyone to take off their shoes and sit on carpets like it was supposed to be done according to tradition. They were taken by surprise when most Alevis present simply ignored the wise men and remained seated on their chairs. A silent, but adamant conflict could be sensed between modernity, in this instance, represented by sitting on chairs, and the traditional way of attending *cem* by sitting on the floor. A few did do what they were told by the elderly, but there was a thick air of dissent in the room, heralding a new generation of Alevis and much difference in the interpretation of this Islamic heterodoxy.

ALEVISM AND THE POLITICS OF STATE REFORMATION

From the perspective of Alevi groups in Deutschkei Turkey's problems require substantive political reforms that include, primarily but not exclusively, a clearer institutional separation between religion and politics and a constitutional recognition of Turkey's religious diversity.

Simply stated, an Alevi is a person who loves and follows Ali, the son-in-law of the prophet Mohammed.[2] The love for Ali constitutes a common denominator for all Alevis. Even agnostic or atheist Alevis, who reject the proposition that Alevism is an off-shoot of Islam or that it is at all a religion, revere Ali at least as a historical figure who has always been a defender of the disadvantaged and as a symbol of social justice, who himself had experienced the biggest of all injustices.[3]

In Alevi thought, the deification of Ali as the most perfect human being and thus his approximation to God goes hand in hand with the relative deification of humans. Unlike the radically monotheistic orthodox Islam with an abstract notion of God at its center, Alevism contains pantheist and humanist properties that presuppose that God could be found in nature and in human beings.[4] The injustice done to Ali by Sunnis and the persecution of Hasan and Huseyin in Kerbela add a strong emphasis to the twin Alevi principles of *social justice* and *equality*. These principles not only have defined the political preferences of most Alevis up to date, particularly of young Alevis who have generally been attracted to the philosophy of the political left. But the principle of equality also manifests itself in the progressive social status of women in Alevi communities. The relative equality, freedom, and power enjoyed by Alevi women in their communities have been one of the main sources of strategic stereotyping of the Alevi minority as heretics.[5] Indeed, the Alevi stance with respect to secularism and the social status of women constitute the major divide between Sunni Islamists and Alevis.

Another reason for Alevis' persecution by Sunnis has been the fact that Alevis do not recognize and observe the five pillars of Islam.[6] The fact that Ali was killed in a mosque while praying has prevented the public institutionalization of Alevism in architectural sites like mosques or churches. Safety concerns due to the fear of persecution and the emphasis on the individual have also contributed to the maintenance of Alevism as a belief system in the private rather than the public sphere. For centuries Alevis have gathered for *cem* privately and discretely in their homes. In part, the story of Alevi resurgence is the story of

Alevism's entrance into the public sphere through the institutionalization of *cem* rituals, among other initiatives, to increase Alevi visibility in public.

The particular interpretation of Alevism they adopt divides Alevis along political lines. While those who understand Alevism as a religion tend to be affiliated with the more socially conservative political right, those who see it as a way of life, a culture, a philosophy, or a worldview tend to be oriented towards the political left in their support and voting behavior.[7] Having said that, the majority of Alevis, both in Turkey and Germany, continue to support social democratic and left-of-center parties, although in Turkey in the last decade, Alevi votes have become relatively more fragmented along the left-right continuum.

The lack of consensus on what Alevism is and its specificity as a Turkish religion also distinguish Alevism from Kurdish ethnonationalism and from Islamism in terms of its political resonance. In this sense, Alevism appears to be an ethno-religion and raises interesting questions about the ethnic as well as the religious makeup of Turkey.

Anatolian Alevis see themselves as the genuine Turks. The fact that almost all, with the exception of a few, Alevi prayers, rituals, and religious hymns are held in Turkish is a unique characteristic that distinguishes Anatolian Alevis and the *Bektashis* of the Balkans and the Asia Minor from Muslims elsewhere in the world.[8] Many Alevis take pride in the historical Alevi contribution to the preservation of the Turkic ways of life in the face of "danger" presented by Arabized Sunni rulers of the *Umayyad, Seljuk,* and *Ottoman* dynasties. In this respect, and particularly in recent years, the Turkish state had been endorsing this Alevi self-perception by promoting Alevism as the Turkish brand of Islam against Islamic fundamentalism, which is seen as stemming from Arabic rather than "Turkish" roots.

Alevis have an ambiguous relationship to the Turkish state. They, and to a lesser extent Kurds, tend to be more tolerant and flexible in their approach to the culture of destination. On the one hand, Alevis are highly critical of violations of democratic principles in Turkey. On the other hand, they have an important stake in two first principles, which legitimize Alevi revival in the eyes of the Turkish political establishment: the territorial integrity of Turkey and its secular system. Alevis are sensitive to the first existential problem, since they do not aspire for an Alevi state and think of Anatolia as an embodiment of unity in diversity. As far as the principle of secularism is concerned, almost all Alevis see a secular state as their only defense against a possible tyranny of the Sunni majority.

Alevis have long been critical of religion-state relations in Turkey. They do so, not only by sharply distinguishing their ways from Sunni Islamists, but also by questioning the legitimacy of the statal Directorate for Religious Affairs

(DIB) and its sponsorship of the Sunni sect. Through this latter critique, they problematize the very nature of Turkish secularism. Some prominent Alevi figures, like Izzettin Dogan, the head of CEM Foundation, have demanded a percentage of the directorate's budget to be allocated to Alevis.[9]

Since Alevis do not pose a territorial threat and since they support secularism, they enjoy a certain state sponsorship not felt by Kurds and by Islamists.[10] On the other hand, however, by asserting their identity and culture and by fighting for the recognition of their group name, Alevis are challenging the illusion of ethnic homogeneity in Turkey forcefully.

ALEVI REVIVAL IN TURKEY: POLITICIZATION, FRAGMENTATION, AND RADICALIZATION

Unlike Islamists and Kurds, Alevis have benefited, initially, from the nation building efforts of the Ottoman/Turkish military bureaucrats at the turn of the century. In particular, secularization has had an emancipating effect on Alevi collective existence, since it was and still is seen as a check on Sunni dominance. Yet, what is particularly noteworthy about Alevis is that, despite their apparent alliance with the founding philosophy of the Turkish state, they continue to represent a *counterculture* in modern Turkish polity, as they have done so in Ottoman times.

The marginalization of Alevis in Turkish society was, in part, a result of their resistance to sedentarization. Alevis tended to preserve their semi-nomadic ways of life because it helped them, for centuries, to maintain their seclusion and to understate their Alevi-ness. It was almost as if Alevi culture in contemporary Turkey has hibernated until 1990s when the Alevi "revival" or "renaissance" came to mean the *disclosure* and the cultivation of Alevism.

The long history of Alevi persecutions has prepared the early favorable conditions for Alevis' politicization. Throughout the 1980s there were overt government attempts to assimilate Alevis by building mosques in Alevi villages against the wishes of their inhabitants. There were revisionist publications claiming that many Alevi poet-philosophers of the Anatolian middle ages were actually Sunnis.

The main turning points in Alevi self-assertion and self-organization, however, were the incidents in *Sivas* in 1993 and *Gaziosmanpaşa* (Gazi) in 1994. These are sites where Sunni attacks against the Alevis took place and where the state has either seemed to have condoned or reacted slowly to the brutalities. These events have played a formative role in Alevi collective consciousness. Indeed, Alevis from all walks of life would agree that with Sivas and Gazi a new chapter in Alevi presence in Turkey and Europe has been opened.

The relative liberalization of the state's approach to the quintessential ethnic issue in the country, namely to the Kurdish question, and the 1991 repeal of the law that discriminated against the Kurdish language in publishing have also helped the resurgence of Alevi identity.[11] "The Alevis, a heterodox religious minority, began manifesting themselves very much as yet another ethnic group. All over the country, as well as among the migrant communities in Europe, Alevi associations sprang up. Alevi intellectuals and community leaders set out to define Alevi identity, Alevi tradition, Alevi history. Both the Kurdish movement and the government courted the Alevis, and both did their utmost to prevent the other from making inroads among them."[12]

Broadcast media, in no small way, played a role in unveiling the latent Alevi-Sunni tension in Turkey and in bringing it right into people's living rooms. One particular event demonstrated Alevis' increasing sensitivity to their public image as well as their power in numbers in a non-violent but effective way:

In 1995, a popular host of a television show made a comment using the term *Kizilbash*, which was meant to be a joke.[13] To non-Alevi ears the joke was a little more than tasteless. But the Alevi uproar and crowds that surrounded the television station in Istanbul within less than two hours following the show as well as hundreds of protest calls to the station demonstrated that Alevis were particularly sensitive about the biases apparently underlying the Turkish collective subconscious. They had the clout to force the host to apologize publicly from all news broadcasts for his comment. The spontaneous protests his remarks engendered not only caught the TV host himself off guard, but perplexed non-Alevi viewers as well. Immediately, the incident set a public debate about the place and the treatment of Alevis in Turkish society.

Similar reactions from Alevis were witnessed to the blunder by the minister of justice in 1997. That year, secular-minded Turks all across the country engaged in a collective protest of the anti-secular activities by the Islamist/center-right coalition government, known as "Refahyol," by turning off their lights in the evening for an hour during an entire month. The minister of justice, a member of the parliament from the Islamist party concerned, described this massive civic protest as "mum söndü" (blowing out the candle). This description, in the intricacies of the Turkish language, made an immediate reference to the well-known stereotype, with no factual background, about Alevi spiritual gatherings, where allegedly incestuous acts would take place in the dark after the candles were blown out.[14]

Although Alevis seem to be drawn away from their traditional alliance with the political left and are more fragmented in their party identifications, Alevis' importance in Turkish politics is growing, as more and more Alevis are coming out expressively with their identity and as more Alevi votes are up for grabs in electoral competition.

With respect to the new political capital and clout Alevis now seem to be enjoying, Turgut Öker, the head of the Federation of Alevi Organizations in Germany (AABF), had the following to say:

> There are Alevis whose status has changed due to internal migration and emigration from Turkey. As a result a tendency among some Alevis has developed to rely on the state for certain favors and perks. They borrow from state banks. They vote for conservative parties. From the perspective of their self-interest this is a normal tendency. There are also rural Alevis. There are intellectual Alevis. Naturally they all have different political preferences. It is no longer possible to talk about Alevis who vote as a bloc for one political orientation as it was the case in the past. But most are still poor, still laborers, still live in shantytowns. Their preferences will naturally be similar. There are and will be wealthy Alevis. But they are in minority. There will be those who look at Alevism in religious terms and will become Sunnis to some extent. Clearly, those Alevis will organize and vote differently.[15]

While a fragmentation of Alevi votes along the left-right continuum can be observed, the Alevi resurgence in Turkey and Europe also corresponds to the radicalization of Alevi youth, signaling a change of course from the pacifist philosophy of Alevism.

"I am very concerned," said an Alevi youngster in Germany in an interview. "The leftists, Kurdish nationalists, and Kemalists are trying to use us. The fundamentalists and the fascists, on the other hand, are simply trying to butcher us."[16] "You have to respond to violence with violence," interjected one of his friends. "We won't engage in massacres out of the blue, but when they kill Alevis we won't remain silent, we'll defend ourselves," said another participant in the interview. "We don't expect anything anymore from the state. ... After each massacre Alevis take their *saz*, sing their *deyiş*, and dance their *semah*" said another, referring to the traditional Alevi ways of expressing opposition by singing and dancing in ritual gatherings.[17] "Okay, we are Alevis too. Yet, you can dance the *semah* all you want, but you cannot stop massacres with that."[18]

The military's active promotion of the Turkish-Islamic synthesis as a version of Sunni Islam since the early 1980s forced a renewed interest among Alevis in Alevism as a religion. "Whereas in the 1970s most of the young Alevis had rejected religion and taken pride in Alevism as a democratic social movement, the failure of the leftist movement in Turkey made many reflect on Alevism as a cultural and then as a religious identity."[19]

Parallel to the shift among Alevi youth to left radicalism, some Alevis' sympathy for the Marxist/Leninist PKK and the existence of Kurdish-speaking

Alevis complicate the matter even further. "The growing influence of the PKK among Turkey's Kurds, and by the late 1980s increasingly also among Alevi Kurds, gave the authorities another incentive to allow and even stimulate the development of Alevism as an alternative 'ethnic' identity."[20]

Indeed, the Turkish government has been trying to use Alevism as an alternative both to Islamic fundamentalism and to Kurdish nationalism. This not only alienates Alevis from the state and stimulates Alevi-Sunni tensions, but also creates an Alevi-Kurd divide, even though alienation from the state have brought some Alevis closer to the PKK.

THE ALEVI BRIDGE BETWEEN GERMANY AND TURKEY

It is estimated that about 30 percent of the Turkish nationals in Germany are Alevis.[21] The 1960s and 1970s witnessed large numbers of Alevi immigrants to Europe as guest workers. In the early stages of Turkish migration to Europe, several Alevi villages reported heavy emigration, while the nearby Sunni Muslim villages experienced relatively fewer exits. Villages from which half or more of the adult men emigrated and often did not return were frequently Alevi rather than Sunni. According to some analysts, being a minority in the society of origin seems to increase the propensity to emigrate and not to return.[22]

In a once highly active magazine put out by young people in Turkish and German, Halil Can wrote the following in his introduction to an interview with Alevi youth: "Alevism is not a phenomenon confined to Anatolia but is beginning to become a reality in Europe as well."[23] Can interviewed a group of young Alevis who had formed the Association of Independent Alevi Youth (BAGD). The underlying theme in their responses to the questions about their thoughts on the "Alevi revival" was that Alevis should no longer hide their identity and that they should work for themselves rather than for any other nation, class, or ideology. "I didn't learn about Alevism from my mother. My parents used to hide it so nothing would happen to me at school. 'Don't tell anyone that you're an Alevi, they'll beat you up' they would say."

Why did Alevis not defend their identity earlier?

"I think that those Alevis who took part in the student movement of 1968 made a big mistake. They fought for other people's problems at the expense of their own. This has buried Alevism to silence. Then the incidents in Sivas took place and they woke up. ... For many years Alevis have carried other people's briefcases. In the 1970s they served the left, in the 1980s the Kurds. Today they are trying to serve the Kemalists. But neither Kemalism, nor the Kurdish nationalist movement, nor the left serve Alevism now."

These young Alevis in Germany also argue that Alevis should be less indexed to Turkey: "Devoting all of your mind's energy to Turkey is like not having your feet on the ground. You live in Berlin but your mind lives in Turkey. We have to react to events here as well, like to the fascist attacks for example."[24]

In the initial phases of their immigration to Germany, Alevis were at a disadvantage in engaging in effective collective action. Not only did they have little experience of organization in their homeland, but the decentralized and egalitarian nature of Alevism itself, as well as Alevis' centuries-long self-imposed distance to politics, also hindered their institutionalization in hierarchical structures and under a unified political leadership. Although Alevi associationism in Europe in general and in Germany in particular continues to be handicapped by the mostly informal nature of Alevi networks, Alevis nevertheless have made progress in these areas and gained significant experience in associationism. This experience has, under favorable conditions and from time to time, been transferred to the Turkish political arena, especially in the form of sharing organizational skills and leadership between Europe and Turkey.

The Federation of Alevi Organizations in Germany (AABF), which is located in Cologne, has been the bulwark of Alevis' organizational success in Europe. The AABF played the leading role in the establishment of the Confederation of Alevi Organizations in Europe (AABK) on June 18, 2002, bringing together 165 member associations, including Alevi federations in Germany, France, the Netherlands, Austria, Denmark, Switzerland and Alevi cultural organizations in Sweden and Belgium and thus shouldering, according to their own accounts, the representation of around one million Alevis.[25] The federation in Germany, which used to represent the European Alevis before the confederation came into being, is now called the Federation of Alevi Unions in Germany (the acronym "AABF" has been maintained).

The AABF has received extensive coverage in the Turkish press. The Federation's endorsement of a particular political party affects the direction Alevi votes will go. The AABF supported the creation of the Peace Party (BP), an Alevi party that participated in the 1999 national elections in Turkey.

The organization has also contributed to and presided over the formation of the first federation of Alevi associations in Turkey and the Union of Alevi-Bektashi Organizations (ABKB) in 2000, which was legally challenged by the Interior Ministry for its declared goal to foster the proliferation of Alevi prayer houses (*cemevis*) in Turkey.[26] The AABF leadership has been continuously lobbying for constitutional changes in Turkey to have Alevis recognized as an ethnic and religious minority and to bring an end to the state's official support of Sunnism.

Another important and relatively recent Alevi formation in Europe is the Alevi Academy of Europe (AAA), founded in 1997 in Cologne to promote research and teaching of Alevi history and culture.[27]

The introduction of the founding document of AAA contains the following paragraph:

> Alevis, who wanted and supported a genuinely democratic republic more than anyone else in order to escape from the *sharia* order and its *caliphate* and to be free, were disappointed soon. Suppression and prohibitions continued. The Turkish Republic preferred Sunnism. Alevism was outlawed and those who said 'I'm an Alevi' were treated like criminals. Bloody attacks, massacres, and burnings followed one another. Today, the Alevi community, along the lines of its initial expectations, continues to fight for a genuinely democratic and secular order.

Alevi presence in Europe has historical foundations. Alevis have been in constant dialogue with great European thinkers and, even today, they are most familiar with the Enlightenment philosophers. Humanism has always been in harmony with the values of Alevism in general and Bektashism (urban Alevism) in particular.[28] Especially in the Balkans (for instance, in Kosovo), the Bektashi orders have remained intact and have been in frequent contact with Alevi formations elsewhere in Europe.

Irene Melikoff writes that when in 1826 the Ottoman Jannissary (*Yeniceri*) army, which was in solidarity with the Alevi-Bektashi orders, was disbanded, many sympathizers established a good dialogue with Europe. They re-discovered the *Geist* of the French revolution.[29] Together with the Yeniceris, the Bektashi order was also banned. As a result of the socioeconomic divide between urban Bektashis and rural Alevis, the Bektashis became more familiar with the masonic lodges in Europe. The *Franc-Maçonnerie* with its supra-confessional, liberal, non-conformist, and anti-clerical qualities have overlapped with and appealed to the Bektashi/Alevi values.[30]

The Young Turks, with the funding and support from masonic lodges, spread masonry in Turkey. In a sense, Turkish free masonry at the time was a natural extension of the Bektashi orders. Some of the most prominent Turkish nationalists of the era who were in extensive dialogue with the West, like Namik Kemal, were members of these lodges. With the 1908 Young Turk revolution the lodges opened and remained open until 1925 when they were closed down with all public institutions of folk Islam in Turkey.[31]

Anatolian Alevis first came to Europe as laborers following the Second World War. Initially, they were highly invisible in European societies since they did not have special clothing, beards or publicly discernable rituals. They held their spiritual gatherings in private homes. Alevis became members of German-Turkish friendship organizations, labor unions, and culturally oriented Turkish associations.[32]

The first European-Alevi cultural centers were established in the 1980s. In the 1960s, Alevis who worked in and for the left-of-center Turkey Unity Party (TBP) in Turkey formed Patriotic Unions in Berlin, Hamburg, Hamm, Munich, and Ulm. These were later united under the Federation of Patriotic Unions. They continued their close ties with the TBP, by inviting its leader Mustafa Timisi to their meetings and by informing their base in Germany about the activities of the party in Turkey.[33]

In June 1990, in Mainz, the Federation of Alevi Communities (Alevi Cemaatleri Federasyonu) was established, which later, in 1993, became the Federation of European Alevi Organizations (AABF) in Cologne. 1993 was also the year of the Sunni attacks on Alevis in Sivas. As mentioned before, this event accelerated Alevi politicization and unity in Europe. The number of Alevi associations mushroomed in Europe that year as a reaction to this calamity. In 1995 there were 130 member associations of the AABF. By this time Ali Riza Gülçiçek was the head of this umbrella organization. The organization moved from Mainz to Cologne and, until 1995, all its activities revolved around reacting to the events in Sivas and the fight for the official recognition of Alevi identity in Turkey.

Following extraordinary incidents, such as the events in Sivas and Gazi, the AABF offered spiritual and financial help to the victims' families and as such they gave, and continue to give, moral support "to the Alevi organizations in Turkey which feel the internal political pressure much more."[34] But the activities of the AABF go beyond that.

Article 2.9 in the founding document of the AABF includes the following formulation:

> The AABF works towards the just and humane resolution of problems, resulting from Turkey or from the country they reside in, of Turks, Kurds, Laz, and Circassians who come from Turkey. It supports all initiatives geared towards the establishment of a modern forum where our citizens can express their problems together. It supports social, cultural, and political activities of migrant and cultural associations, and particularly member associations who work for the resolution of social problems.

According to article 2.11 "[t]he AABF develops friendly relations with the representatives of Alevi-Bektashi culture and belief. It is in solidarity with institutions and organizations that contribute to Turkey's democratization. It works towards bringing the Alevi community under unity."

Only from 1995 onwards did the Alevi political elite start thinking about what they can do for Alevis in Germany, "instead of trying to save Alevis in Turkey." According to Öker, "because we had Turkey on our agenda for so long, we neglected institutionalizing ourselves here. After the Sivas incident we visited Turkey quite often. We supported the organization of Alevis in Turkey. They couldn't use the name Alevi in their institutions. For that reason we would give speeches as the true representatives of Alevis. Thus, we neglected our task here in Germany for too long. In 1998, when my team and I submitted our candidacy for the leadership of the federation we said that we would no longer focus exclusively on the salvation of Alevis in Turkey. We will turn our attention more to the problems of Alevis here."[35]

When explaining the personal reasons for his active involvement in the organization of Alevi identity in Germany, the AABF president Öker mentions the "S.O.S Rassismus," a multiculturalist movement of Algerian students in 1985 as his source of inspiration. "France does not belong only to the French. The nation-state is a thing of the past. Many nations may live on the same soil. A new political structure is needed, within which all can express themselves freely. A multicultural, multinational project of coexistence is needed," says Öker and in doing so he directs criticism not only to Turkey but to Germany as well.

> Without Alevis living their faith freely, there could be no democracy in Turkey. They say that in Turkey the state does not have an official religion. But since in practice the state is institutionalizing itself as if it were Sunni and since this is nothing that can be defended in this day and age, people are organizing themselves. ... The Alevi revival gave relief to those who were afraid of the power of the *sharia* proponents. Many people of Sunni background now join Alevi organizations. At the same time Alevi revival also taught Europe that there are differences among people who come from Turkey. It used to be that everyone here would associate Islam with Sunnism. Alevis have little problems with integration and with approaching Germans. Our *kabe* (the holiest Islamic site in Mecca) is the human being. Our faith teaches us to treat all nations the same way. The Germans don't have the experience of living with different people. What they don't know turns into prejudice. In Anatolia, on the other hand, a multiplicity of nations and ethnicities has been living together for centuries and continues to do so. Alevis can bring this experience and wisdom to this country.[36]

Öker argues and laments that the state in Turkey has adopted a policy to make everyone Turkish and Sunni.

> Alevis' revival demonstrates the bankruptcy of that project. Similarly, the emergence of the Kurdish movement also shows that with this policy there is no

peaceful coexistence among peoples in Turkey. Alevis who express themselves freely in the democratic environment in Europe can contribute to the emergence of a new project of coexistence by supporting and encouraging Alevis in Turkey to express themselves just as fearlessly. That would be a contribution.[37]

Öker points out that in Europe a *cemevi* can exist next to a mosque or a church, that school textbooks include Alevism next to Islam, that European universities have courses on Alevism, that Alevi cultural weeks are celebrated. "Gains such as these have encouraged Alevis in Turkey," he says.

> When we go to Turkey we can meet the president or the prime minister *as Alevis*. All of this is very encouraging. We call for the legal recognition of Alevis. We say we are Alevis. The president participates in Alevi activities. But in doing so everyone violates the law that prohibits the usage of the term 'Alevi.' Because *tekkes* and *zaviyes* were closed down in 1924, Alevi *dedes* are looked upon as charlatans. There is only one Alevi association in Turkey that has the adjective 'Alevi' in its name: in Izmir, the Narlidere Alevi-Bektashi Cultural Association. And that was because of an oversight on the part of the ministry of interior. We want school textbooks to include Alevism. We want them to stop building mosques in Alevi villages. We want the Directorate for Religious Affairs to be abolished. Its budget should go to building roads, schools, and hospitals. Religious organizations should finance themselves on their own. The state's duty is to open schools and hospitals. Look at how it's done in Germany.[38]

Following the events in Sivas, Alevi self-organization in Turkey also gained a strong momentum. Particularly, the idea to establish umbrella organizations for more effective interest articulation and advancement has gained strength. In 1993, the representatives of various Alevi and Bektashi organizations in Turkey got together in the Haci Bektash district of the province Nevsehir and formed the Council of Alevi-Bektashi Representatives (ABTM). However, this group could not gain official status because of the ban on organizations based on confessions in the law of associations. In order to gain strength and effectiveness, the AABF chair in Europe was elected the president of the ABTM and remained so until 1996.[39]

The leadership of European Alevism also participated in the formation of an Alevi political movement in Turkey, which later became a political party. Under Ali Haydar Veziroğlu the Democratic Peace Movement (DBH) was formed in 1995.[40] The European leadership took part in the DBH congress in 1995 in Turkey. But they later withdrew their support because of organizational disagreements.[41] In 1996, the DBH was threatened with closure, because the party's program included the demand that the Directorate of Religious Affairs should no longer exist as a state institution. The party reacted to this threat by establishing another party, the Peace Party (BP). The BP leadership stressed that they did not want to be an exclusive Alevi party, but a mass party with a focus on peace. They demanded that ethnic and confessional belonging should be articulated freely and in that way the potential for conflict in society should be diminished.

In the months preceding the 1999 general elections in Turkey, there was a heavy traffic between Alevi leaders in Europe and Turkey. In January 1999, Ali Kiliç, the president of the AABF at the time, came to meet with Alevi leaders in Turkey to discuss the infrastructural issues about the prospective Alevi confederation. Their new slogan was "wherever is our name, there is our address." By this, they meant that they would support parties that recognize Alevis' tangible demands and identity. "We don't want Alevi votes to be fragmented. As citizens living abroad we want the Peace Party (BP) to overcome the 10 percent parliamentary threshold and establish a democracy front."[42]

When asked at an interview with the liberal daily *Hürriyet* whether they were not getting too involved with business in Turkey, Kiliç said the following: "There is no other Turkey! Therefore, it is our duty to address the problems of this country. We don't mean that Alevis should govern Turkey. We just don't want divisions like Turk versus Kurd, Alevi versus Sunni. ... Turkey has changed. We no longer can debate about 'who is more leftist.' There is an immediate need for a secular, democratic front in the parliament against religious fundamentalism. If this can be realized, it will receive support from all of us."[43]

A consultation meeting also took place between the BP leader Veziroğlu and Kilic, to determine the electoral preferences of Alevi groups prior to the 1999 elections. The task was to determine which of the two social democratic parties, the Republican Peoples' Party (CHP) or the Democratic Left Party (DSP), the Alevis should endorse. The two groups also determined, together, the list of candidates from the BP.[44]

The BP also created "peace volunteers" in Europe to campaign on behalf of the party in Turkey. Kiliç was later transferred as the vice president of the BP, leaving federation leadership to Öker. On the other hand, the former federation leader Gülçiçek declared his candidacy from the social democratic CHP. He also formed an association in Cologne to support the CHP.[45]

The BP was one of 21 parties that entered the elections. However, due to the minimal electoral support they received, far below the parliamentary threshold, the party closed itself down on May 11, 1999. This initiative, which came from the party itself, was considered a most civilized and model withdrawal from the political scene, unaccustomed to in Turkish politics.[46]

ALEVIS IN CYBERSPACE

The Alevi presence on the World Wide Web has gained in strength in the last couple of years. The site *http://www.alevibektasi.com/dostlar.htm* includes 25 organizational websites and 30 personal websites by mostly European Alevis that were functional at the time of this writing.

Two noteworthy homepages are *http://www.alevi.com* (which hosts the AABF) and *http://www.alevi-institut.de*. These, like other Alevi sites, are designed to introduce the Alevi culture and religion to the world. The following passage from the website of the Alevi-Bektashi Cultural Institute, founded in 1997 in Bonn, describes the focus of the Alevi cyber presence:

> We want to collect and transfer to the new generations whatever is left from the suppression, denial, and cultural destruction of 750 years. We will use the Internet, engage in research, we will establish an international communications web, starting with libraries and universities. We call particularly Anatolian intellectuals, but also those who believe that these unique cultural values are also a part of the universal culture, to come and support our project. Let us say 'stop' to attempts to bury the Alevi culture and traditions because of political calculations.

The following is an excerpt from an exchange on Alevism from a chat room on *http://www.demokratik.net*, which illustrates the content and the mode of cyber-discussions in this area:

> Participant Yilmaz writes: "The debate around the issue of Sunnism versus Alevism is brought to the agenda constantly by the existing system and by former leftists. This latter group has set aside their favorite dictum 'religion is the opium of the masses.' Instead, they are now looking for Alevism to cover up their clumsy leftism. So far one sect (Sunni) had been upheld by the state. Now another sect is being upheld by these leftists of the past and America is being rediscovered."

The response follows: "Alevi-Bektashi culture has existed in Anatolia for centuries. It is ridiculous to interpret it as the latest political fashion. Marx has never been a rigid religion hater. He also said that 'one cannot conduct surgery without opium.' At this point, I think Marxists think differently than Marx himself."[47]

THE ALEVI VIEW OF KEMALISM

"We were having a hard-time trying to calm down the Alevi youth in Turkey. Who would have thought that the military, which did so much injustice to Alevis in the past, was going to do us a favor one day."

These words belong to an Alevi writer in Germany and the reference is to the February 28, 1998 moratorium by the military, which eventually led to the closing down of the Islamist party by the Constitutional Court. My interviewee was telling me that had the military not interrupted the Sunni ascendance and domination in Turkish politics in 1998, the Alevi youth would have been ready for clashes with their Sunni counterparts. He said that the Alevis were preparing and arming themselves for such a conflict. "There was going to be much blood shed," he added nodding his head. It was another way of saying that when it comes to protecting secularism, Alevis would even side with the military, if necessary.

Throughout the history of the modern Turkish republic Alevis have been, in part by default, in a natural alliance with the original philosophy of Kemalism and its partisan manifestation, namely, the Republican People Party (CHP) founded by Ataturk. In this respect, Mustafa Kemal's (Atatürk) visit to Alevi spiritual leaders on December 22, 1919, shortly after the Turkish war of independence had started, was a turning point. This visit was thoroughly engrained onto the Alevi collective consciousness and its effects continue to prevail today, albeit in a mythical form. Mustafa Kemal, during this visit to seek Alevi support in his fight against foreign occupation and in his plans to create a secular republic, was embraced by Alevi leaders as "the other Ali!" "Today it is customary to have in many Alevi households, next to Ali's portrait the portrait of Mustafa Kemal. Not infrequently, it is argued that Mustafa Kemal himself was an Alevi, but had to hide his identity for security reasons. It is believed among the Alevis that even his spiritual development was influenced by the Bektashi ideology, since he had a lot of Bektashis around him when growing up. Because of this admiration, the fact is forgotten that not even during Mustafa Kemal's lifetime did Alevis receive official recognition as a community of believers in their own right. They had to continue practicing their religion in seclusion. Nevertheless, the myth of Alevi friendly Atatürk prevails and the utility of secularism is seen as more important than freedom of religion."[48]

Along these lines, Markus Dressler looks at how Atatürk is treated in the two prominent Alevi journals *Cem* and *Nefes* as a de facto Bektashi, a *mehdi*, a savior, and the other Ali.[49] Dressler argues that by linking Ataturk inextricably to their tradition and by linking secularism to their existence, Alevis were able to protect themselves against Sunni aggression.[50]

But the particular applications of Kemalism throughout the republic's history and particularly the *neo-Kemalism* of the 1980s and the 1990s have often been disappointing for the Alevis.[51] Indeed, starting with the gradual process of re-Islamization of politics in Turkey as early as 1950, Alevis' alienation from the new regime, to which they have given full support initially, has grown. The initial but brief idea of making Alevism the official religion of the state at the time of the founding was discarded for full-blown secularism. The Sunnis after Atatürk got their mosques and religious holidays back, whereas the sites of Sufi folk Islam remained closed, leaving little room for the rituals of decentralized heterodox belief systems to express themselves.[52]

For contemporary Alevis, it is the principle of secularism, rather than Kemalism per se, which has become a public cause. European Alevis demand a stricter separation of church and state than their cousins in Turkey. They are adamant in their criticism of some Alevi demands for state funding of Alevi religion. Because of their internalized social liberalism, they also embrace the idea of multiculturalism much more thoroughly than other groups treated in this study. In this respect, they see cultural diversity as a fundamental building bloc of Turkey's democratization.

European Alevis' greatest institutional contribution to the revival of Alevism in Turkey lies in the organizational support and transfer of leadership that they offer. Furthermore, by advocating the withdrawal of the state from the self-organization of religion in civil society and by emphasizing the ethno-religious diversity of Anatolia, European Alevism keeps the traditional role played by Alevi heterodoxy and dissent in Turkish politics alive. While they articulate Alevi interests and a rational critique of Turkish politics, they remain within the pro-West, universalist orientation of early Kemalism.

NOTES

[1] *Dedes* are wise religious men who are believed to have prophetic lineage. *Cem*, a derivative of the term *cemaat* (community), describes religious, spiritual gatherings where Alevis play their string instrument *saz*, sing, and dance the *semah*.

[2] Alevis are not related to the Alawites in Syria.

[3] The reference here is to the killing of Ali and his sons Hasan and Huseyin by Sunnis.

[4] "Aynaya baktim, Ali'yi gördüm." (I looked in the mirror and I saw Ali). This reiteration contains not only the deification of Ali, but also the deification of all ordinary humans.

[5] Woman's status in society is the main fault line that separates Islamists from secularists and Sunnis from Alevis.

[6] Those five pillars are *namaz* (daily prayers), *oruç* (fast), *zekat* (almsgiving to the poor), *hac* (pilgrimage to Mecca), and *sahadet* (reiteration of the oneness of God and the prophecy of Muhammad).

[7] Mustafa Düzgün, interview by author, Aachen, Germany, March 1998.

[8] Karin Vorhoff et al., eds., *Wie der Phoenix aus der Asche: Renaissance des Alevismus* (Cologne: AABF Publications, 1998), 15. According to Vorhoff, a prominent scholar in this area, in the 12th and 13th centuries, Ahmed Yesevi's Sufi mystic

Islam came to Anatolia with the help of dervishes who fled Mongol invasions. Under these influences a syncretism of Islamic mystic and pre-Islamic substance called *Bektashism* was born of the meeting between Alevi, Zoroastrian, Shamanist, Helenistic, and early Christian belief systems in Anatolia under the leadership of Haci Bektash Veli (1209–1272)—Vorhoff, *Wie der Phoenix* 1998.

[9]The acronym CEM both corresponds to the name of Alevi ritual gatherings and stands for the Republican Education Center, indicating an alliance with the state. By claiming a share from the state's budget for the official cultivation of Alevism, Dogan is accused by most Alevis with promoting "the kind of Alevism that the [Turkish] state wants," according to Metin Mat, from the Cultural Center of Anatolian Alevis. From an interview conducted with Mat in Berlin, on March 28, 1999.

[10]In the 16th century Alevis sided with the Persian Empire against the Ottomans, which became the precipitating factor of their persecution by the Ottoman sultan Yavuz Sultan Selim and his successors.

[11]Martin Van Bruinessen, "Kurds, Turks, and the Alevi Revival in Turkey," available from http://www.let.ruu.nl/oriental_studies/mvbalevi.tml; Internet; 1999.

[12] Ibid., 2.

[13] Kizilbash literally means "redhead." The term is sometimes used derogatorily to describe the Alevis.

[14]This reference was the same as the joke above and the stereotype comes from the co-ed nature of Alevi collective rituals.

[15]Turgut Öker, interview by author, tape-recorded, Cologne, March 1999.

[16]*Kau Yaz*, 1996, 40.

[17]Ibid.

[18]Ibid.

[19]Martin Van Bruinessen, "Kurds, Turks, and the Alevi Revival in Turkey," available from http://www.let.ruu.nl/oriental_studies/mvbalevi.tml; Internet; 1999, 4.

[20]Ibid., 5.

[21]Ertekin Özcan, *Türkische Immigrantenorganizationen in der Bundesrepublik Deutschland* (Berlin: Hitit Verlag, 1989), 59.

[22]Philip Martin L, *The Unfinished Story: Turkish Labour Migration to Western Europe* (Geneva: ILO, 1991), 45, 60.

[23]*Kau Yaz*, 1996, 39.

[24]Ibid.

[25]There are also other Alevi groups that are not members of the confederation.

[26]As of February 2002 this lawsuit was in the appeals stage.

[27]There are also efforts under way to create an international center in Europe to research Alevi culture and history.

[28]Karin Vorhoff et. al., eds., *Wie der Phoenix aus der Asche: Renaissance des Alevismus* (Cologne: AABF Publications, 1998).

[29]Irene Melikoff, *Haci Bektaş: Efsaneden Gerçeğe* (Istanbul: Cumhuriyet Kitaplari, 1998).

30 Ibid.

31 Ibid.

32 Sinan Erbektaş, "Die Aleviten in Europa," in *Wie der Phoenix aus der Asche: Renaissance des Alevismus*, ed. Karin Vorhoff et al., (Cologne: AABF Publications, 1998), 103.

33 Turgut Öker, the president of AABF, interviewed by author, tape-recorded, Cologne, March 1999.

34 Sinan Erbektaş, "Die Aleviten in Europa," in *Wie der Phoenix aus der Asche: Renaissance des Alevismus*, ed. Karin Vorhoff, et al., (Cologne: AABF Publications, 1998), 104.

35 Turgut Öker, the president of AABF, interview by author, tape-recorded, Cologne, March 1999.

36 Turgut Öker, interviewed by author, Cologne March 1999.

37 Ibid.

38 Ibid.

39 Zentrum für Türkeistudien, *Jahrbuch*, (Essen: ZFT, 1998), 107–109.

40 Ibid.

41 Ibid. Not to be confused with Democracy and Peace Party (DBP), under the leadership of Refik Karakoç.

42 Bayer, Yalçin, "Yeter, Söz Milletin," *Hürriyet*, 23 January 1999.

43 Ibid.

44 Yalcin Bayer, "Yeter Söz Milletin," *Hürriyet*, 17 January 1999.

45 Ibid., *Hürriyet*, 11 February 1999.

46 "A Model Withdrawal in Democracy," *Hürriyet*, 11 May 1999.

47 Available from http://www.demokratik.net; Internet; accessed in March 2000.

48 Text available from http://www.uni-duisburg.de/JUSO/EMRE/alevismu/tc-alevi/3-2.htm; Internet.

49 Markus Dressler *Vom Ulu Önder zum Mehdi-Zur Darstellung Mustafa Kemal's in den Alevitischen Zeitschriften Cem und Nefes* (Istanbul: Orient-Institut der Deutschen Morgenlandischen Gesellschaft, 1996).

50 Ibid., 24.

51 Kemalism, in its inception, was a progressive worldview. By emphasizing the role of the state in the economy and by upholding the principle of equality in society it was a leftist political force. It was composed of six principles: Republicanism, nationalism, secularism, statism, revolutionism, and populism. *Neo-Kemalism* may now be considered the conservative ideology of the urban middle classes with emphasis on secularism and nationalism at the expense of all other Kemalist tenets.

52 Karin Vorhoff et al., eds., *Wie der Phoenix aus der Asche: Renaissance des Alevismus* (Cologne: AABF Publications, 1998).

VIII
The Kurds

IN THE GERMAN PRESS THEY WERE PRESENTED AS "GOOD KURDS." IN CONTRAST to the supporters of the Marxist-Leninist PKK, the sympathizers of the Socialist Party of Kurdistan (PSK) and its auxiliary, the Association of Kurdish Workers from Kurdistan (KOMKAR), appeared to be moderate Kurdish nationalists, fighting with pens rather than guns and within the political party system.[1]

The young activist at the Berlin division of KOMKAR greeted me in German and spoke German all the way through the interview even though he was fluent in the Turkish language and knew where I was coming from. Between a Turk and a Kurd, Turkish seemed to have become an awkward lingua franca, especially when discussing Kurdish nationalism. So, for purposes of neutrality and practicality, we tacitly agreed to replace Turkish with German.[2]

"Turkey cannot become democratic unless it solves its Kurdish question" was the overarching theme of his comments. He said he came to Germany when he was a young boy and has not visited his relatives back home for five years. "Turks and Kurds here get along well until politics comes up as a topic of discussion. Turks here are just as misinformed about the reality in Kurdistan as Turks in Turkey are. They don't even know that there are groups, other than the PKK, representing Kurds."

The PSK/KOMKAR wants either a federal system in Turkey with a separate Kurdish parliament or a unitary state where the equality of Turks and Kurds is established constitutionally. Considering the fact that there are so many Kurds scattered in all regions of Turkey, a separate Turkish-Kurdistan, they say, is not feasible. They also renounce violence as a method of achieving minority rights and other political goals. "We want a peaceful and democratic solution to the Kurdish question," the young KOMKAR member said at the onset. "We want Kurds to speak and write in their own language and have their own television, radio, and political parties."[3]

The KOMKAR member was careful in the way he discussed the responsible forces in the Turco-Kurdish dispute. He did not blame the Turkish people, or Turkish governments, or even the state. Rather, he singled out the military. "It is in the interest of the Turkish army to equate the Kurdish question with a single organization like the PKK" he said. "How else are they going to justify their continuing political influence?"

KURDS AND THE POLITICS OF STATE FORMATION

The ultimate political goal of the Kurdish diaspora is Kurdish *self-government*, be it the form of a separate state or local government in a federal structure.[4]

While the ultranationalists, and lately even the Islamists and Alevis, have obtained state sponsorship from Turkey, Kurds do not enjoy the privileges of such a backup. That makes their case substantively different than the other groups.[5] This difference is also a source of the radicalization of the Kurdish diaspora. The fact that Kurdish nationalism has a regional-territorial basis, with claims to nativity on the part of Kurds, making them the indigenous peoples of a particular geography divided among four states, contributes to this radicalization and adds a significant international dimension to its problematization.

Substantial Kurdish resistance in the Ottoman-Turkish history can be traced back to the middle of the 19th century when the centralization of the Ottoman state apparatus, in order to combat imperial decline, began and attempted to penetrate into regions of Kurdish autonomy.[6]

Gunnar Weissner writes that the tribal structure of the traditional Kurdish society, left intact by the administrative autonomy granted by the Ottomans for centuries, was a determining factor in the preservation of a distinct Kurdish identity over time.

> [t]raditional Kurdish society divides itself into tribes in which family and political authority is combined and through which any direct influence from the outside is made more difficult. Rivalry between the tribes, however, hinders national unity while providing external forces with possibilities for indirect influence. The shattering of the de facto independent Kurdish principalities in East Anatolia in 1847 did not lead to a political controlling of the population, since the tribes, in consequence of their basic family structure, remained. As a result, Turkish administration has been similar to a moderate form of indirect rule since then. (Weissner 1997, 289)

The Ottoman-Turkish bureaucratic centralization reached its peak with the foundation of the Turkish nation-state in 1923. Previously, the Treaty of Sevres, which divided the remnants of the Ottoman lands among the British, French, Italians, and Greeks, had promised an independent Kurdish state in the Southeast. Its overturning by the new Turkish "nation-state" was upsetting not only for the occupying forces but for minorities as well.[7]

In 1924, with the abolition of the *caliphate*, Kurdish schools, publications, and associations were also banned in Turkey.[8] Religion was replaced with Turkish nationalism, which was equally upsetting to the Kurdish *shaikhs* who had been losing political and social power. Kurdish *shaikhs*, who were not only spiritual leaders, but political figures and warriors as well, have played an important role in mobilizing Kurdish resistance against the center throughout the Ottoman-Turkish history.

As much as rupture, however, there was continuity as well in the relations between the new Turkish state and the Kurdish tribes. The Turkish state, like in the Ottoman times, generally cooperated with Kurdish tribes rather than altering or replacing them with other structures. The symbiosis between Turkish administrators and Kurdish tribal leaders was legitimized with the advent of the multi-party system in 1946 that led to the election of tribal leaders to political positions.[9]

PKK AND THE INTERNATIONALIZATION OF KURDISH NATIONALISM

As a Marxist-Leninist Kurdish movement the PKK emerged during Abdullah Öcalan's college years in Ankara in the 1970s. The group was established officially in 1978 and started its full-blown war against the Turkish state in 1984. Shortly before the 1980 military coup, Öcalan fled to Syria. PKK attacks continued, directed from the Bekaa Valley in Lebanon, until in late 1998 Syria, under heavy pressure by the Turkish military, "asked" Öcalan to leave.

One significant turning point in the internationalization of the Kurdish issue was the Kurdish Conference in Paris on October 14 and 15, 1989. This meeting was organized by the France Liberties Foundation and the Kurdish Institute in Paris.[10] It was decided at this forum to call for a special meeting on the Kurdish question at the General Assembly of the United Nations, to ask for an observatory status for Kurds in the organization, and to form a common Kurdish organization where all Kurds can be represented. The fact that the immunities of seven parliamentarians from the Social Democrat Populist Party (SHP) were later taken away by the Turkish government, because they attended this meeting, also contributed to the internationalization of Turkey's Kurdish problem.[11]

Another important turning point in the process of internationalization was the Persian Gulf War of 1990. This war and the de facto Kurdish government it created in the northern part of Iraq put the Kurdish question as a permanent issue on the Turkish agenda and made Turkey more aware of this matter within and outside of its borders.

The first mainstream Turkish political party that committed itself to the recognition of the Kurdish question was the SHP. The SHP council endorsed a report on the Kurdish issue in July 1990. In 1991, important reforms passed the parliament with the backing of the president at the time, Turgut Özal. The Law on Publications and Broadcast in Languages other than Turkish (#2932) of 1983, which prohibited the use of any language, other than the official languages of countries that recognize Turkey, indirectly targeted the Kurdish language since the Kurds did not have a state of their own. This law was annulled in 1991 and the dissemination and public consumption of a variety of cultural material became free in the aftermath of this development.[12] Articles 141, 142, and 163 of the Turkish Penal Code, prohibiting the propagation of communism, separatism, and religious regimes were also repealed. This development paved the way for the legal formation of Kurdist and Islamist political parties.

In October 1991, president Özal made a promise to solve the Kurdish problem: "A flat refusal to discuss concepts such as a Kurdish federal solution meant abandoning the field of debate to the PKK without a fight" he said.[13] Never before had any Turkish politician been able to deviate from the mainstream Turkish political thinking about the Kurdish question to such an extent. A group of intellectuals started debating the possibilities of a federated solution and the legalization of the PKK.

In this atmosphere of such détente, in March 1993 PKK leader Öcalan offered a unilateral cease-fire that only lasted for two months. Despite the fact that the Özal administration had pioneered liberalization in this area, it did not and could not go as far as engaging in legal negotiations with PKK. The cease-fire was broken with a PKK setup in Bingöl that killed 30 Turkish soldiers. The complex set of underlying causes of the end of detente ranges from Özal's death in 1993 to the Turkish military's enduring rigid posture vis-à-vis this issue.

In 1993 Germany joined the ranks of countries like the United States and Britain in condemning PKK as a terrorist organization. The same year the German government issued an international arrest warrant for Öcalan following a heavy campaign of PKK attacks targeting Turkish establishments on German soil and in European cities.[14] When Öcalan left Syria in 1999 this German warrant played a significant role in the rejection of Öcalan's plea for political asylum by European countries.[15]

THE KURDISH DIASPORA IN EUROPE

The desire to establish one's own state and becoming a political refugee, exile, or asylum seeker as a result of it makes exit from the host society much more difficult and renders the transnational condition almost permanent.[16] Being *locked* in the transnational space alienates Kurds further from the country of origin and enhances the vigor of their efforts not only to get to know the host society and its resources better, but to craft a *virtual Kurdistan* with the help of transnational technologies like satellite broadcasting and the Internet.

Perhaps more than any other group studied here, Kurds live and thrive in the transnational space. The virtual consulate of the Federal Republic of Kurdistan solely exists on the World Wide Web, but it offers almost all services a consulate can offer ranging from information on passports and visas, language classes, links to the Kurdish Parliament in Exile (KPE), the Kurdish Institute in Paris, and so on.[17] Kurdish satellite broadcasting from Europe to the Kurdish parts of Turkey are discussed by some analysts in terms like "extra-territorial nation-state," "sovereignty in skies, allowing dissident voices and non-state peoples a forum," "denying the state a single coherent sovereign presence," "satellite dishes as national flags," and "viewers as citizens rather than just an audience."[18]

PKK activities among migrant workers in Europe have started informally around 1978. By the end of 1981, these activities were reorganized under the group's so-called "Europe Bureau." The duties of the bureau included recruiting guerillas from the ranks of young workers, sending them to Lebanon for training, collecting money through various methods, sending those funds to the administration in Damascus, conducting public and media relations, exerting influence on workers, and publishing books, newspapers, pamphlets, handouts and so on to raise awareness of the Kurdish issue.[19]

According to Ahmet Aydin, Öcalan, who was residing in Damascus, Syria, and visiting training camps in Bekaa, would only send those people to Europe that he trusted the most. Most PKK functionaries who went to Europe were members of the organization's Central Committee. Öcalan knew that those who would be active in Europe would have the opportunities to think more freely and critically. The costs of leaving the organization would be lower for them because they could easily apply for political asylum. But Öcalan had to take that risk, since Europe was the goose that laid the golden egg. The European theater was indispensable for PKK operations in Turkey.[20]

When Öcalan decided to start the campaign to infiltrate into Turkey in the summer of 1983, most of his European cohorts disagreed with the timing and the methods of the plan. They argued that the campaign should be delayed until the civilian government in Turkey is restored. When Öcalan called them to Damascus to discuss the situation, they remembered what happened to Resul Altinok, whose dissent against Öcalan in Europe ended silently with a call to Damascus. Several of these dissenters then left the organization.[21]

Europe has also been a fertile source of human resources for PKK. Metin Dalman and Ismail Tabak from the German-Turkish Press Agency (DTPA) have documented extensively how Turks as well as Kurds, who were in fact economic migrants rather than political refugees, were smuggled from Turkey into Germany and then were subjected to intimidating recruitment strategies by the PKK. A documentary prepared by the DTPA and the German television networks WDR and SDR, titled *Wanted: The Con Artists of Asylum*, showed false legal documents being presented to German authorities about political persecution back home and witnesses talking about counterfeited passes and visas. The feature also showed PKK's extortion activities such as poll taxes, forced attendance in protest marches, forced purchases of the organization's newspapers, t-shirts, buttons, cassette tapes and other paraphernalia with the ERNK's (PKK's political wing) emblem on them to raise extra money for the group.[22] According to the German *Verfassungsschutzbericht* of 1997, functionaries of PKK have also been taking teenagers from Kurdish parents in Germany and sending them to camps in Bekaa Valley and in Greece for training to fight the war in the southeast of Turkey. Smuggling of drugs also contributes to bankrolling the activities, military or otherwise, of the PKK. PKK networks are believed to be responsible for about 20 to 30 percent of all heroin traffic into Europe via Turkey.[23]

It is estimated that the PKK has about 11 thousand sympathizers in Germany. The group engages in propaganda activities (particularly during *newroz*, the Kurdish new year's celebrations), raises money, recruits and trains new members for the movement. When the Turkish army entered northern Iraq on May 14, 1997 to pursue PKK guerillas, there were numerous protests and solidarity demonstrations organized by the PKK all over Europe. At the end of every campaign, donation, and pledge year, double figures of millions of DM were collected by the PKK, sometimes coercively, sometimes voluntarily, and sometimes through smuggling of weapons and drugs.[24] The organization has an active youth branch (YCK) and a women's organization YAJK. The Federation of Kurdish Associations in Germany (YEK-KOM) is also a roof organization encompassing sympathizing associations of PKK.

The PKK's main publications are *Serxwebun* (Independence) and *Özgür Politika* (Free Politics). In 1993, when the group was banned in Germany, its auxiliaries such as the publishing companies Berxwedan-Verlags GmbH, Kurdistan-Komitees e.V., and the Kurdish News Agency (KURD-HA) were also banned. The broadcasts of MED-TV, the PKK broadcast medium beaming via EUTELSAT from London to the Middle East, were also suspended by Britain in the spring of 1999.[25]

Despite occasional setbacks, politically active members of the Kurdish diaspora, in and outside of the PKK, have been gaining strength in their transnational activities towards Turkey. Because of its genuinely deterritorialized nature, the Kurdish movement cherishes its existence in the transnational space. The Kurdish diaspora in Europe has become a more important lifeline for Kurdish nationalism, financially, intellectually, politically, and socially, than ever before. Particularly noteworthy is the shift in influence from political refugees to settled Kurdish intellectuals in the diaspora who are relatively more moderate in their rhetoric and style.[26]

"If the Kurdish grievance is not eradicated by economic development, political democracy and the rule of law, Kurds will create another organization with more modern leaders who are closer to Europe and better adapted to the European style of politics. That would be quite a problem for Turkey."[27] These words belong to Doğu Ergil, the head of the Foundation for Research of Societal Problems, who has prepared one of the first comprehensive reports on the Kurdish question under the title *The Eastern Report* in 1995.[28] Ergil's comments reflect a certain truth about the political future of Kurdish nationalism: that it lies right in the heart of Europe, rather than in Turkey proper.

Indeed, it may be argued that the real Kurdish nationalism is in the making in Europe. Statistics may vary and may not be fully reliable, but as of 1984 approximately one third of the 1.5 million migrants from Turkey were estimated to be of Kurdish origin. As it is the case in Turkey, the PKK is the most organized Kurdish formation in Europe—although it is not the only one and, more importantly, it is not the politically most significant one. Rather, the PKK now represents, primarily, the military wing of the Kurdish movement, although it is hard to separate the movement's military and political dimensions. The ERNK, the Kurdish Parliament in Exile (KPE) in Brussels, and the Kurdish Institute in Paris do most of the lobbying and the politicking on behalf of the PKK. The annual meetings of the KPE regularly become a thorny diplomatic issue between Turkey and the countries that host them.[29]

Because of German government policies and the fact that ethnic conflict in Turkey has its extension in Germany, an ethnic differentiation between Turks and Kurds has found its early and articulate expressions in Germany. The observations made by Suzanne Schneehorst from the Nuernberg Public Library, for example, point out perhaps to the first empirical signs of this differentiation.

Germany reflects the political and social conflicts of Turkey. The Kurdish conflict or the strengthening of nationalistic and fundamentalist movements in Turkey, for example, does exist in the Turkish population in Germany as well. So, in the last few years, growing demand for literature about Kurds or the Islamic religion in Turkey can be noticed in public libraries. (61st IFLA Conference-Conference Proceedings-August 20–25, 1995)

Some students of the Turkish community in Berlin have suggested that the Kurds' experiences of their ethnic minority status in Turkey (not an official, but a sociological, political, and psychological one) might manifest themselves in a prolongation of "us and them" feelings towards other migrants, facilitated by the pattern of chain migration. Prior experiences in Turkey, combined with such communal closeness provided by self-segregation and ghettoization, offer a favorable environment for the development and maintenance and cultivation of ethnic identity.

In a similar vein, Martin Van Bruinessen writes that among Turkish guest workers who had migrated to Western Europe since the late 1950s, there were many who discovered, in the course of the past few decades, that they were not Turks, but Kurds. As a result, since the 1970s and especially in the 1990s, contacts between Kurds from different nation-states have increased, while the gap between them and their non-Kurdish compatriots has widened. Van Bruinessen argues that this trend is in good part explicable by the "dramatic improvements in the means of transport and communication, resulting in a dramatic increase in the ability of people and ideas, which can only to a certain extent be controlled by state governments, the presence of large Turkish and Kurdish immigrant communities in Western Europe, and a political climate there favoring minority cultures."[30]

Van Bruinessen draws attention to the transnational aspects of nationalisms, their deterritorialization, elite-drivenness, and the influence of extra-territorial public spheres on home country politics. In the specific case of the Kurds he observes that the Kurdish diaspora in Europe has, over the last decades, acquired central importance for the Kurdish movement in Turkey (to a much lesser extent for those in Iran and Iraq) and that the separatist movement, headed by the PKK, enjoys strong support from the Kurds in the diaspora, even though few of them express intention to return to an eventual independent or autonomous Kurdistan. As it is the case with other political diasporas such as Jewish, Cuban, Palestinian, Chinese, and Armenian, large sums of money are raised abroad to support activities back in the homeland. Young men and women are socialized not only into positions of fighters, but also of organizers, diplomats, teachers, and technicians.

But most importantly, Van Bruinessen draws attention to the visible fact that the center of political (as opposed to military) activities of the Kurds directed towards Turkey has shifted to Europe. It is in the European diaspora that the significant aspects of Kurdish nationalism, namely, political mobilization, linguistic development, and intellectual activities realize themselves to their fullest extent. In major migrant-receiving European countries, the *Kirmanci* dialect of most Kurdish tribes in Turkey is in the process of transformation into a literary "high Kurdish." This development is deterritorializing Kurdish-ness even further and generating a linguistic nationalism that was previously primarily territory-based. In particular, the Kurdish migrants in Sweden, who were, unlike those in Germany, highly politicized before they reached that country (and therefore less susceptible to military recruitment than their compatriots in other countries) find a much more stimulating environment for developing Kurdish into a modern language than they would have found in Turkey.[31]

As for the emergence of a Kurdish intelligentsia as the vehicle of linguistic nationalism and political thought, Van Bruinessen writes the following:

> Kurdish has been enriched and sufficiently developed to serve as a vehicle for modern political and literary discourse. ... Journals and books in Kurdish were published in Germany, France, Belgium, the Netherlands, and especially in Sweden. The number of these publications gradually increased in recent years, reaching an annual production of 40–50 Kurdish books in Sweden alone. ... Books that had earlier appeared in Europe were reprinted in Turkey and several Kurdish journals moved their offices from Europe to Turkey. New Kurdish journals were also established, and there was a veritable boom in Kurdish publishing. (Van Bruinessen 1998, 47)

In addition to the websites, discussion groups, and other instruments provided by the Internet, which Kurdish nationalists have been utilizing successfully, the PKK had, until recently, a highly effective private broadcast medium at its disposal that also has helped their movement to develop away from a strictly territorial mode of nationalism.

In this respect, Amir Hassanpour interprets MED-TV, a private media institution launched by Kurdish nationalists, which would broadcast from 1995 to 1999 via satellite from Europe, as an *extra-territorial Kurdish nation-state with sovereignty in skies*. This interpretation demonstrates how globalized communication networks enable ideas to flow without being confined to national boundaries and how the notion of "sovereignty" might be re-conceptualized without a nationally appropriated geographical territory.

According to Hassanpour, the case of the Kurdish diaspora in Europe illustrates how satellite broadcasting has allowed dissident voices and non-state peoples a space in the global village and how it denied the state a single coherent sovereign presence. MED-TV, he writes, demonstrated the extra-territoriality of state power by making national flags out of satellite dishes and by establishing relations with viewers not as members of an audience, but rather as citizens of a sovereign state in skies. Thus, Kurdish access to satellite television has contributed, simultaneously, to the relative dissolution of the Turkish nation-state and to the formation of Kurdish nationhood and "statehood."

MED-TV enjoyed the support of the Kurdish business sectors across Europe. It also received financial assistance from the Kurdish Foundation Trust, which is funded through private and individual donations, and from advertising and program sponsorship.[32] According to MED-TV officials the station's daily 18–hour cultural and political broadcasts could be viewed in Europe and in southeast Turkey by 15 million people and, according to *Turkish Daily News*, by 90 percent of the population in southeast Anatolia.

Hassanpour argues that during the time of its operation, until its license was taken away by the British Independent Television Commission (ITC), MED-TV established state-like sovereignty in skies.

> ... it is clear that every second of MED-TV's broadcasting seriously undermines Turkish sovereign rule. The logo "MED-TV," which is always present in the upper left corner of the screen, is an assertion of Kurdishness (the Kurds are Medes not Turks). It also asserts Kurdish rights to statehood. ... The daily menu begins with a grand orchestral performing of the Kurdish national anthem, *Ey Reqib* (O Enemy!). The ever-presence of the Kurdish national flag and anthem means that MED-TV has the power to treat the Kurds not as audiences but as citizens of a Kurdish state. This is therefore more than a war of meanings and identities. It is a conflict between two nationalisms—one that has achieved state power and one that struggles for statehood. (Hassanpour 1998, 59)

KOMKAR: A KURDISH CIVIL SOCIETY IN EUROPE?

In contrast to PKK, KOMKAR is a non-violent, non-military Kurdish nationalist umbrella organization with its headquarters in Cologne. According to some accounts it is the largest Kurdish organization in Germany.[33] Its member associations support the Socialist Party of Kurdistan (PSK), headed by Kemal Burkay, a prominent Kurdish intellectual in exile.

The weekly newspaper *Hevi*, which means "hope," is a pro-KOMKAR publication with its center in Wuppertal, Germany, and is distributed to approximately three thousand subscribers in Europe and Turkey. It voices the views of KOMKAR, embraces rational argumentation and a relatively sophisticated anti-systemic critique towards Turkey that uses the Kurdish question as an instrument of such a critique rather than as the target of the critique itself. A content analysis of *Hevi* as well as personal interviews with KOMKAR members demonstrate the scope of an emerging Kurdish civil society in Europe with an eye on the homeland and only peripherally on host country politics.

At the time of research for this work, the last four issues of *Hevi* had been banned in Turkey. The newspaper has a long history of disappearing and reappearing under different names. The main reason for changing names, even though the newspaper could be published without interruption in Europe, is to maintain readership in Turkey. Ziya Laçin, a publisher of and writer for *Hevi*, argues that because the climate in Turkey for the circulation of this newspaper is not a "natural" one, the paper could not become a commercial enterprise, but remains strictly a political undertaking. Moreover, Laçin adds that *Hevi* offers a forum for Kurdish nationalists of all persuasions in Europe. "Where else can they go?" he asks. The implication is that the content of the coverage sometimes becomes inevitably political in the subjectively selective and emotional sense of the term. But the paper, by being inclusive, also offers an arena where different interpretations of Kurdish nationalism can clash.

The newspaper covers issues such as the lack of economic independence of Kurdish intellectuals, their unemployment, their statelessness and how these conditions affect Kurdish political writing. Nonetheless, there is confidence in the fact that there are now Kurdish political parties and a Kurdish political movement in Turkey and in Europe. The newspaper endorses the PSK platform and the Democratic Peace Movement (DBG), a political party headed by Refik Karakoç and active in Turkey. In fact, the DBG's vice chairman himself writes regular comments for the newspaper.

There is comfortable usage of terms like "Turkish people" and "Kurdish people" in the paper's columns. In other words, there is a tendency to essentialize both Turkish and Kurdish ethnicities and to cultivate a so-called "anthropology" of Kurdish-ness. But the solutions sought to Turkey's Kurdish problem are peaceful, consensus based, and political. *Hevi* supports the internationalization of the Kurdish issue through the organization of an international conference on Kurdish identity, a diametrically opposed position to that of the Turkish government.

A strong tendency in the paper is to interpret most of Turkey's political, economic, and social problems as derivative of the Kurdish question. The idea is that the settlement of the Kurdish question would also solve all other problems Turkey is facing internally and internationally, including those in the areas of democratization and human rights. Having said that, however, what distinguishes the combined perspective of *Hevi*, PSK, and of KOMKAR from that of

PKK and its print media is that the position voiced by *Hevi* contains a deliberate effort to launch a *comprehensive* critique of the political system in Turkey, rather than a simple discussion of the Kurdish question per se. Human rights, the functioning of the justice system, the relations between the press and the military, academic freedom, ultra-nationalism, and violations of democratic rules all are directly or indirectly tied to the Kurdish problem. But overall, *Hevi's* critique is structural and systemic, rather than parochial and emotional.

There is a strong renouncement of violence, regardless of which side it emanates from. *Hevi* is cautiously defensive vis-à-vis PKK and its tactics, implicitly calling it an ethnocentric and undemocratic organization. Moderate nationalist writers for the paper argue that the Kurdish question cannot be represented by a single person or organization, but that it is a freedom movement that belongs to an entire group of people.

KURDS IN CYBERSPACE

More than any other group treated in this study, Kurds have the most substantial web presence, ranging from virtual public spheres of critical debate to web-based consulates. At the time of this writing, Kurdish sites on the web included the Kurdish Parliament in Exile (KPE), the Kurdish National Liberation Movement, historical documents on Kurdistan, Kurdish mailing lists, the Kurdistan Committee of Canada, Kurdish Information Network, Ataturk's Children the Kurds, American Kurdish Information Network, Kurdish Academy of Science and Art, Kurdistan Web (Kurdish Information and Documentation Database), Kurdish Library and Museum in New York, Voice of America Kurdish Program schedule, and the Kurdish Studies Program at Florida State University.

This list is by no means all-inclusive. Moreover, there are other groups with web presence like *http://www.ozgurbakis.com*, *http://www.ozgurpolitika.org*, *http://www.vatan-online.com*, and *http://www.kurtulus.com* that are leftist, pro-Kurdish groups and who launch a substantive critique against the Turkish state. These sites are linked to each other and to publications in Turkish, Kurdish, and English such as *Serxwebun, Özgür Politika, Kurdish Observer, Azadiya Welat,* and *Pine*. These groups call Turkey a "counter-guerilla state" that co-operates with the CIA and the local oligarchies against its own people. The National Security Council (MGK) that represents the military's influence in Turkish politics and the Turkish media, which is accused of having become particularly bourgeois in recent years, are the main targets on these sites. "Are we going to continue to be the country of coups, moratoriums, and massacres?" asks the journal *Vatan-Online* and calls, in an open letter to the public to resist. Popular topics are polit-

The Kurds

ical scandals in Turkey, civil disobedience acts such as the vigil of "Saturday mothers", fascist Gray Wolves and the ultranationalist party (MHP), prisons, torture, human rights and the like.

KOMKAR's site *www.komkar.org* greets visitors in German. Its focus, however, is unambiguously on Turkey.

> The largest part of Kurdistan is within the borders of Turkey and makes up one-third of the entire land. In this area, there live about 20 million Kurds who have been calling it home for centuries. They have their own language, a rich culture that differentiates them from Turkish, Arabic, and Persian cultures. ... The Turkish state, which is trying to establish a monolingual and cultural society, has been trying for 75 years to destroy the multiplicity of cultures in this land. ... We appeal to the peace loving people of Germany. Please help us to realize our wish for a peaceful and democratic solution to the Kurdish problem in Turkey. Reject the sale of Leopard tanks to Turkey. Exert pressure on the German government, so that it would engage itself actively for the democratization, human rights and the solution of the Kurdish problem in Turkey.[34]

This site has links to other Kurdish groups on the web, including the Kurdish Parliament in Exile (KPE).

> The KPE greets and salutes "all residents and travelers in cyberspace." We take no joy in the relative counts of corpse and empathize with all Turkish, Arab and Persian mothers grieving for their fallen sons as much as we emphasize with Kurdish mothers. We hold intellectuals, columnists, editors, politicians and opinion leaders far more responsible for the ongoing death and destruction than the conscripts. We are delighted that in spite of the efforts by some quarters, there is no ethnic hatred between the overwhelming majority of the Kurds, Turks, Arabs, and Persians.[35]

By including other groups like Persians and Arabs, the group tries to draw attention to the multiethnic character of Anatolia and the Middle East and moves away from the nation-state construct.

The elections of the KPE members, they say, are democratically organized by the political parties, communities and socio-cultural groups in countries where the Kurdish exiles live, but not on the "occupied" territory of Kurdistan. Quotas are allocated to the organizers country by country, following the guidelines drawn by a special preparatory committee.

The main purpose of the KPE, they argue, is to secure a cease-fire in the Turkish Kurdistan that would lead to a political solution of the Kurdish question through peaceful democratic means. This, they say, can only be achieved with international support and help from democratic institutions such as the European Union (EU).

> Our parliament is not, in principle, against Turkey's joining of the customs union. [But] in our opinion, Turkey has not, up to now, fulfilled the conditions set up by the European Parliament in its resolution of June 13, 1995. These were freedom for the Kurdish imprisoned members of the Turkish parliament and acknowledgment of the rights of the Kurdish people. We wish that the European Parliament would remind Turkey of these conditions, because we believe that its intervention would play an active role in the democratization process.
>
> We also demand the implementation of a specific Parliamentary Inter-Group about the Kurdish question and a round of Turco-Kurdish meetings under the auspices of the group's. We would like to see a modification of the Turkish constitution in order to include the recognition of the Kurds as a separate nation. We demand an end to all legal discrimination against Kurds, the release of all Kurdish and Turkish political prisoners. We want to see a general amnesty law, the outlawing of all racist and fascist groups, the legalization of all Kurdish political parties, including the PKK, and Turkey's transformation into a democratic federal state and a federation consisting of Turkish and Kurdish republics, like Belgium. Kurdish should become one of the official languages of the new federal state. In order to realize these democratic achievements, the democratic governments of the United States, the industrialized world, and third-world countries should put an end to the flow of financial and military aid to Turkey.[36]

This open letter was written by Yaşar Kaya, the president of KPE. These proposals have also gained support from some European governments and it is yet to be seen how they will affect Turkey's EU candidacy in the years to come.

Finally, the following is a sample debate between Turks and Kurds on the web about Kurdish identity. It is an illustrative instance of cyber-chat that shows how ethnic identities thoroughly color the positions taken in a seemingly sophisticated debate on the Kurdish question.

This particular discussion revolves around Yilmaz Güney, a famous Turkish-Kurdish film director, who died in exile in Paris where he fled after having been accused of killing a judge and engaging in anti-state subversion. The debate is sparked by the controversy when the Greek film director Costa Gavras expressed his intention to make a film of Güney's life.

According to the Kurdish participant in the debate with the username "diyarbekirli" "the white Turk" was now upset.[37]

"As you know, Yilmaz Güney's life is becoming a film. That is why the hell is breaking loose. Because a film like this will bring the Turkish Republic's 80 years long Kurdish policy into light. In this movie it will be seen that Güney is a Kurd and not a Turk. In the movie *Yol* he wrote his country's name in capital letters: Kurdistan. ... It's unbelievable! The Turkish Republic has made such a taboo out of the Kurdish issue that had Ataturk himself gotten out of his grave and said "I'm not a Turk, I'm a Kurd" the police would have arrested him right then and there, the state prosecutors would have called for the death penalty or he would simply disappeared into the ranks of the missing."

In response, the Turkish participant in the debate with the username "dumrul," talks about his interview with Güney on behalf of the German *Der Spiegel* in Paris in 1983.[38] "Let me first make it clear: Contrary to what the media had been projecting, Yilmaz Güney did not have much to do with the PKK. At the time, the PKK wasn't around much. Rather, Güney was cooperating with ASALA [the Armenian ultranationalists], which really is the precursor of the PKK, sharing the same goal and strategy to divide Turkey. He came to our appointment with a well-educated French speaking ASALA activist as his escort.... I asked him about the sudden 'discovery' of his Kurdish-ness immediately after he fled to Europe. He said that his dad was Kirmanco and his mother was Zaza, that they could understand each other only in Turkish, and that Turkish is the only language he speaks. As far as his socialism was concerned, he was quite confused. Rather than being a socialist, he had a feudal mind interested in social issues. I cannot imagine a socialist who beats up his wife and makes her wash his feet!"

KOMKAR AND PKK ON KEMALISM

Öcalan has traditionally been keen on comparing the military and nationalist aspects of his movement with Turkish nation building by Ataturk. His sometimes overt and sometimes covert admiration for the military identity of Ataturk also colors his ambiguous stance vis-a-vis the Turkish military. On the one hand, in the past he called for guerilla action against the military, on the other hand he expressed hope that the army, as a progressive institution, may be the one to frame the Kurdish question in the most attractive way. In a previous article in the journal *Özgür Halk Dergisi,* under the alias Ali Firat (March 15, 1997), he wrote about his thoughts on the military and claimed that the Chief of Staff is the only Kemalist political party that has remained in Turkey.

Öcalan thinks that under the conditions of the time, it was inevitable for Mustafa Kemal to rely on Turkish nationalism as a social project. However, he is critical of taking Kemalism out of his historical context, de-historicizing Ataturk, and making him the entirety of Turkey, its past, present, and future.

Oral Calişlar, a prominent Turkish journalist from the left-of-center daily *Cumhuriyet* interviewed Öcalan, the leader of PKK, and Kemal Burkay, the leader of PSK, in the summer of 1993, when the Turkish state's approach to the Kurdish question was at its liberal peak. Calişlar was later prosecuted for the interviews that he published in a book.[39] Some excerpts are taken from these interviews to illustrate the nature of the critique that these two socialist Kurdish groups launch against Kemalism from abroad.

> This exaggerated glorification of Kemalism as being everything for Turkey is disrespect to the diversity and reality of Anatolia. .... If Turks don't rethink Kemalism, no single problem in Turkey will be resolved. The debate between the First and the Second Republicans shows that there is indeed a problem. Your only hope is to criticize Kemalism. This critique has to take place realistically. His approach to religion, secularism, history, all should be subject to criticism. Constant glorification is in fact a disservice to Kemalism. The critique of Kemalism should also not be constrained with arguments about territorial integrity. Kemalism has value to the extent that it uplifts us to another level of social project. ... If I had had Mustafa Kemal himself at the other end of the table today, we could have solved our differences through analyses, criticism, and mutual interaction. But the dwarfs of Kemalism are hindering any solution. Such criticism may enrich Turkey and may make the Turkish people possible to live with. The real model of unity for Turkey requires respect for the Anatolian reality, that is, respect for what was historical and socially real. (Calislar 1993, 69–72)

Similarly, according to Kemal Burkay, the state structures of the Turkish Republic have never been compatible with social realities in Turkey. "Unitary government is not realistic for Turkey," says Burkay. He puts forward the "dual nationality thesis," which stipulates that there are two nations, Turkish and Kurdish, living in Turkey.

> There is no doubt that there are two nations in Turkey. *Misak-i Milli* [national pact on borders] has acknowledged this. But the republic that followed this pact turned out to be mono-national. Any prospective solution has to recognize this social duality. ... However, Turkey's problems with democracy exceed the nationality question. Kemalism, at the onset, was, as a bourgeois revolution, a progressive force. Even though Kurds did not achieve equality, women's rights, secularism, the abolition of the Sultanate and the Caliphate are some examples of Kemalism's progressivism. But this social force later became a dogma and therefore a conservative force. The state was never sufficiently secular. Alevis for example were excluded. (Calişlar 1993, 130–134)

As leftists, both Öcalan and Burkay interpret nationalism in general and Kemalism in particular, from the perspective of historical materialism. Both being Kurdish, they see in Kemalism first and foremost an exclusive Turkish nationalism. The common denominator in their interpretation is the *historical specificity* of Kemalism, rather than its *universalism* as understood by Alevis for instance. And this reading is radically critical of the dominant and widespread thinking in Turkey about Kemalism.

NOTES

[1] KOMKAR supports PSK under the leadership of Kemal Burkay, who currently lives in Europe.

In May 2002 PKK was placed on the European Union's official list of terrorist organizations. The EU has decided to freeze all PKK assets and forbid all financial dealings with the organization. PKK now operates under the name Kurdistan Freedom and Democracy Congress (KADEK).

[2] The great irony about the PKK-led Kurdish ethno-nationalist movement in Turkey is that its leader Abdullah Öcalan could not speak Kurdish. Öcalan conducted all his business and his interviews in Turkish. According to Öcalan, even after the creation of the new Kurdish state, Turkish would continue to be the official language until Kurdish is revived and taught publicly. By contrast, linguistic nationalism permeates KOMKAR much more than it does the PKK. PSK/KOMKAR has been quite active in the development of a written Kurdish language. Their newspaper *Hevi* regularly contains Kurdish articles and news, in addition to text in Turkish.

[3] Interview by author, tape-recorded, Berlin, March 1999.

[4] This goal has, in part, been realized by Iraqi Kurds in northern Iraq under the security umbrella provided by the United States and its military forces. Although internationally not recognized, there seems to be a functioning political infrastructure of a Kurdish state with two centers of power: one located in Erbil, controlled by Mesud Barzani and his Kurdistan Democracy Party (KDP) and the other one centered in Suleymaniyah, controlled by Jalal Talabani and his Patriotic Union of Kurdistan (PUK).

[5] From a conversation with Ayşe Çağlar, professor of ethnology at the Free University in Berlin, March 1999.

[6] For a good account of the origins of the Kurdish question with respect to the Turkish state, see Mesut Yeğen, "The Turkish State Discourse and the Exclusion of Kurdish Identity," *Middle Eastern Studies* 32:2 (1996), 216–274.

[7] The so-called *Sevres syndrome* had a tremendous and lasting impact on Turkish political psyche in general and on Turkey's approach to the Kurdish question in particular. The spirit (the ghost, rather) of the Sevres Treaty is considered the ultimate "other" of Turkey's national unity and territorial integrity. Since Sevres, Turkey's territorial unity has been perceived by the elites and the masses as being under constant conspiratorial threat.

[8] Nicole Pope and Hugh Pope, *Turkey Unveiled: A History of Modern Turkey* (Woodstock and New York: The Overlook Press, 1997).

[9] Gunnar Weissner, "Grundfragen Aktueller Politischer und Militärischer Entwicklungen in den Kurdischen Provinzen der Türkei," *Orient* 38, (Deutsches Orient Institut, 1997), 289.

[10] The Kurdish Institute in Paris, under the leadership of the exiled Turkish-Kurdish scholar Kendal Nezan, works like a think tank with the input of Kurdish intellectuals from across Europe and Turkey.

[11] Rafet Balli, *Kürt Dosyasi* (Istanbul: Cem Yayinevi, 1991).

[12] To some extent Article 8 of the Anti-Terror Law and Articles 26 and 28 of the 1982 Constitution have replaced the abolished language law. Nevertheless, liberalization in this area

had irreversible effects on Kurdish language and its place in the public sphere in the form of the production and sale of journal articles, books, music cassettes and the like.

[13]Nicole Pope and Hugh Pope, *Turkey Unveiled: A History of Modern Turkey* (Woodstock and New York: The Overlook Press, 1997), 270.

[14]Yojana Sharma, "Fear of Violence in the Wake of Kurdish Deaths in Berlin," *World News*, (February 1999).

[15]Öcalan was captured in Kenya the same year. After a trial that was closely watched by the European Union and the international media, Öcalan received the death penalty. He is currently awaiting execution, which first needs to be approved by the Turkish parliament.

[16]It must be added that not all Kurds are political migrants. In fact, most Kurds, like Turks, migrate mainly for economic reasons. However, once they arrive in the country of destination it is very difficult for ordinary Kurds to resist politicization. They are constantly subjected to recruitment, mobilization, or harassment by the PKK.

[17]Zagros Madjd-Sadjadi, Consul General, the Virtual Consulate of the Federal Republic of Kurdistan, Los Angeles: "The Virtual Kurdish Consulate exists for the needs of Kurdish citizens everywhere. At this site, one can access news, pictures, and other information regarding the Kurdish struggle for statehood. Plans for the site include visas, passports, tourist information, immigration and naturalization, foreign investment, cultural outreach"; available from http://www-bcf.usc.edu/~madjdsad/kurdish.html; Internet.

[18] Amir Hassanpour, "Satellite Footprints as National Borders: MED-TV and the Extraterritoriality of State Sovereignty," *Journal of Muslim Minority Affairs* 18 (1998): 53–72.

[19]Ahmet Aydin, *Kürtler, PKK, ve Abdullah Öcalan* (Ankara: Kiyap 1992), 70, 71.

[20]Ibid., 85, 86.

[21]Ibid.

[22]Metin Dalman and Ismail Tabak, *Avrupa'da Insan Ticareti ve PKK* (Istanbul: Türk-Alman Basin Ajansi-DTPA, 1995), 125.

[23] *The Geopolitical Drug Dispatch* 40, February 1995.

[24] *Verfassungsschutzbericht*, 1997.

[25] *Verfassungsschutzbericht*, 1997. The reason given for the closure was incitement of violence in Turkey. The action followed a bomb that exploded in Istanbul and, apparently, the call for it came, a couple of days prior to the explosion, on the airwaves of MED-TV.

[26]Rafet Balli, *Kürt Dosyasi* (Istanbul: Cem Yayinevi, 1991).

[27] *The New York Times*, 17 February 1999.

[28]See Doğu Ergil, *Doğu Sorunu: Teşhisler ve Tespitler, Özel Araştirma Raporu* (Eastern Question: Diagnoses and Observations: Special Research Report), (Istanbul: July 1995). Also see Ümit Cizre Sakallioğlu's critical discussion of this report in "Historicizing the Present and Problematizing the Future of the Kurdish Problem: A Critique of the TOBB Report on the Eastern Question," *New Perspectives on Turkey* 14, (Spring 1996), 1–22. Ergil's report was the first detailed study of its kind of the issue, sponsored by the Turkish Union of Chambers and Security Exchange (TOBB). Other reports by the Social Democrat Populist Party (SHP), the Welfare Party (RP), and the Turkish Association of Industrialists and Businessmen (TÜSIAD) have left an impression on the public.

[29] The 65-member assembly was established in The Hague on April 12, 1995. The KPE held annual congresses in cities like Moscow, Copenhagen, and Rome. In the summer of 1999, when the Basque parliament in Spain wanted to host a KPE assembly, another diplomatic uproar led to Spain's Constitutional Court suspending the move on grounds that it violated the central government's right to conduct foreign policy.

[30] Martin Van Bruinessen, "Shifting National and Ethnic Identities: The Kurds in Turkey and the European Diaspora," *Journal of Muslim Minority Affairs* 18 (1998): 41.

[31] Ibid.

[32] Amir Hassanpour, "Satellite Footprints as National Borders: MED-TV and the Extraterritoriality of State Sovereignty," *Journal of Muslim Minority Affairs* 18 (1998): 53–72.

[33] Nermin Abadan-Unat, "Ethnic Business, Ethnic Communities and Ethno-Politics among Turks in Europe" in *Immigration into Western Societies: Problems and Policies*, ed. Emek M. Uçarer and Donald J. Puchala (London and Washington: Pinter, 1997), 244.

[34] Text available from http://www.komkar.org; Internet; accessed December 10, 1999.

[35] Ibid.

[36] Text available from http://www.ariga.com/peacebiz/peacelnk/kurd.htm#few; Internet.

[37] Diyarbakir is a province with a large number of Kurdish inhabitants. In fact, the city of Diyarbakir is considered by Kurdish nationalists the capital of the independent state of Kurdistan. The choice of the username, therefore, is indicative of ethnic belonging.

[38] Deli Dumrul is a hero in the ancient Turkic epic literature. Again, the username corresponds clearly to the position taken.

[39] Oral Calişlar, *Öcalan ve Burkay'la Kürt Sorunu* (Istanbul: Pencere Yayinlari, 1993).

IX
The Ultranationalists

THE BERLIN TURKISH HEARTH (*BERLIN TÜRK OCAĞI*), A LOCAL MEMBER association of the Federation of Democratic Idealist Turkish Associations in Europe (ADÜTDF), was not easy to locate in the city. But it turned out that finding them was the easy part of the whole attempt to interview some die-hard Turkish nationalists in the midst of Europe.[1] The first suspicious question was "who's sent you here?" Being affiliated with an American university certainly did not help. It took some convincing to reassure them that I was an innocent student of politics rather than a spy looking for trouble.

They were not supposed to have any organic partisan connections to Turkey.[2] While the members would deny having any relationship with "any" party, we were all sitting in a room entirely decorated with the paraphernalia of the Nationalist Action Party (MHP), including little pieces of gray wolves carved out of wood scattered around and the stern face of the party's leader Alpaslan Türkeş looking down upon us from the wall of the poorly lit room.[3]

ULTRANATIONALISTS (IDEALISTS) AND THE POLITICS OF STATE CONSERVATION

Thanks to its experience from 1975 to 1977 as a coalition partner in the administration, the MHP was able to place its own members in important positions in the bureaucracy, the police, and the secret service in the Turkish state apparatus. This situation continued, with some interruptions, up to date.[4]

Although the basic tenets of Turkish ultranationalism is oriented primarily towards preserving and enhancing the existing power relations in Turkey, this political tradition has indeed gone through substantive changes in its understanding of the contents of the Turkish national culture and in its relations with the state. These changes, however, cannot be understood without taking the vast European hinterland of the Turkish idealists into account.

Throughout the 1970s, the MHP militants clashed with left-wing radicals both in Turkey and in Europe. Civil-war-like conditions created by this left-right polarization and violence ended with the military takeover in 1980 and with massive purges in both camps. Following the coup, MHP leader Turkeş, like other prominent politicians prior to 1980, was banned from active politics. In 1983, the Nationalist Work Party (MÇP) succeeded the closed-down MHP and continued the same political tradition.

In 1987, an amnesty and a popular referendum that lifted the political ban on all former politicos also relieved Turkes from his prison sentence. With this development, Türkeş became the leader of the MÇP. In the 1991 parliamentary elections, the MÇP received 4 percent of the popular votes. In 1992, the party acquired its old name, MHP, and in the 1995 general elections the party increased its electoral support to 8 percent.

The 1999 elections resulted in an apparent popular reaffirmation of state nationalism. Pollsters had doubted whether the MHP would even be able to pass the 10 percent barrier to capture seats in the parliament, since in the 1995 general elections they remained outside the national legislature. Four years later, to everyone's surprise, the party received 18 percent of the popular votes—more than double their share in 1995.[5]

The party has also managed to broaden its electoral base beyond traditional alliances to include corporate and swing votes.[6] By skillfully avoiding substantive commentary on the most controversial national issues, the MHP, under a new leadership, presented itself as the reformed, clean, and untried alternative.[7] In Turkey's highly fragmented party system, the MHP emerged as the second party and in 1999 became a coalition partner in a government led by democratic socialists.

GRAY WOLVES IN EUROPE

Europe, and particularly Germany, has served as a "withdrawal zone" (especially through asylum applications) for MHP activists and for MHP's paramilitary commandos, the Gray Wolves, since the beginning of the labor migration from Turkey.[8] Germany has also been a major source of financial and political support for the Gray Wolves.

Turkish ultranationalists have been frequently contacting like-minded German groups and parties to garner support for their activities in Deutschkei.

For example, they have established close relations with the German Christian Social Union (CSU). The friendship between Franz Josef Strauss and Türkeş was a well-publicized relationship.[9] According to Gunther Wallraff, in the 1970s, Strauss told Türkeş at a secret meeting in Munich that the Bavarian government would provide a suitable political climate for the Gray Wolves and their propaganda in Germany.[10]

Turkish right-wing extremists also have cultivated relations with the German intelligence services and with neo-Nazi groups.[11] Türkeş wrote a letter on July 28, 1977 to his associates, stating that their party "is developing in Turkey. It is necessary that these developments also affect our citizens living in Germany. We need to speed up the work and get organized. In order to achieve the desired results, it is necessary to improve relations with the German National Socialist Party (NSPD) to benefit from their experiences and methods."[12]

Throughout the 1970s and 1980s the Gray Wolves were not only active in Europe, but they also participated in the political process in Turkey from abroad, both in conventional and in non-conventional ways.[13] The MHP (at the time MÇP) was the first Turkish political party to have party organizations abroad, starting with local chapters in Kempten in 1973. In 1976, the Turkish Constitutional Court prohibited foreign organizations of Turkish political parties and called all parties to close down their foreign organizations. The main target of that call was MHP. But MHP denied that it had any foreign auxiliaries.[14]

The party has also managed to overcome the constitutional ban establishing a variety of associations such as the Greater Ideal Association (*Büyük Ülkü Derneği*), the Turkish Community (*Türk Cemaati*), and Turkish Students and Youth Associations (*Türk-Genç*).[15] In 1978, when the center-left led government came into power in Turkey, several MHP members, who were being pursued for their violent activities, fled to Germany, received asylum, and further contributed to the formation of the foreign arm of the Gray Wolves. Later, in 1978, these organizations came under the roof of the Federation of European Democratic Idealist Turkish Associations (ADÜTDF), also known as the Turkish Federation.[16]

The Turkish Federation is particularly active in the area of educating and socializing second and third generations in Europe into their culture of origin. The group's self-proclaimed goals are to protect and strengthen the national identity of Turks living abroad, particularly that of young people, to establish sports clubs and cultural organizations for this purpose, to support the "mother party" MÇP/MHP in Turkey, and to build and maintain mosques in Germany. The *imams* for the federation mosques are in part provided by the Directorate for Religious Affairs (DIB) from Turkey and in part from the Federation's own resources in Germany.[17]

The ADÜTDF continues to cooperate closely with the MHP. According to a former MHP member, there are two different types of directives and disclosures in the party, in order to cover tracks. One type of directive is an official disclosure of activities, prepared for the press, courts, and the public. The other one is a secret directive that would come directly from the *başbuğ* (the leader of the party) from Ankara and would go to the ADÜTDF in Frankfurt, which would then be relayed to the rank and file and the so-called member "cultural associations."[18] This lack of transparency and introversion continue in the ultranationalist establishment in Europe as well as to some extent in their counterparts in Turkey.

Similar to the cases of Alevis and Islamists, the European hinterland has also been an important recruitment ground for ultranationalists' political aspirations in Turkey. Late Uğur Mumcu, a prominent Turkish journalist, had written extensively about ultranationalists abroad, who have run on various occasions as candidates for the Turkish parliament.[19]

It has also been documented that the finances of the ultranationalists were in part linked to drug and weapons smuggling throughout Europe, and between Turkey and Europe. The Gray Wolves were also linked to the Liberation Army of Turkish Prisoners (ETKO), which allegedly trains its guerillas in Germany. Koran schools all over Germany have also been a fertile recruiting ground for ultranationalist militancy.

Regular, less sensational political contacts have been commonplace between groups in Europe and Turkey. These contacts are heightened in periods preceding Turkish elections. In September 1994, the Turkish Federation held its "On the Way to Victory" conference, in preparation for the 1995 general elections. Representatives from the MHP were invited.[20] Türkeş, the former leader of the MHP, frequently visited his party's parallel organizations in Europe in the early 1990s. The 18th general assembly of the ADÜTDF, held in Frankfurt on April 11, 1995, was attended by Türkes and the Turkish ambassador to Germany. A congratulatory telegraph from the Turkish prime minister of the time was one of the highlights of the meeting.[21]

When green light came from Turkish authorities with respect to the "possibility" of voting by mail in the 1999 general elections for Turkish citizens abroad, the news, just like in 1995, once again mobilized Turkish organizations in Europe. "We are MHP sympathizers abroad. We will do our part of the work to make sure that our party comes out of the next general elections with victory!" said the vice president of the Turkish Federation at the Federation's general assembly in Frankfurt, where the motto question printed on banners read: "Are we ready for the next general elections?"[22]

The MHP was particularly active in the "electoral tourism" geared towards the 1999 elections. The party mobilized migrant voters through meetings and information campaigns. Flights were chartered from cities like Frankfurt and Dusseldorf to Kapikule on the Turkish border where voters from abroad could cast their votes. In an interview before the elections, the president of the Freidberg Idealist Hearth told a journalist that "[i]t's time for change in Turkey. The MHP will emerge as a very strong party from these elections. At least, it will become a coalition partner."[23] He was right.

THE IDEALIST PHILOSOPHY IN FLUX: THE ISLAMIST NATIONALISTS

Initially, the tendency among ultranationalists was to look for the roots of Turkish-ness in pre-Islamic times. Islam was considered the religion of the Arabs. The meaning of Islam for the MHP was less of a religious nature. Rather, Islam was derivative of and secondary to national identity. The main question asked was "to what extent is Islam a characteristic of Turkish-ness?"[24]

However, the successive electoral victories of Islamic parties in Turkish politics have forced the MHP, like every other party except the radical left, to adopt Islamic themes in varying degrees throughout the 1970s and 1980s. Islamization and the concomitant concoction of the Turkish-Islamic synthesis by the ultranationalists were, in a way, electoral survival strategies. However, Islamization was not understood by all in the party in such instrumentalist and pragmatic terms. Particularly in the 1980s, both in Turkey and in Europe, a group of ultranationalists who adopted Islam more substantively separated themselves and founded their own parties. The Big Unity Party (BBP) in Turkey and the European Turkish-Islamic Union of Cultural Associations (ATIB) in Europe represent these relatively recent formations and they maintain contact with each other.

Tanil Bora and Kemal Can have researched extensively the trajectory of the ultranationalist/idealist movement in Turkey. They write that even before the 1980 military coup, there was already a division between the grassroots, the Idealist Hearths, and the party leadership in the MHP movement. In the early 1970s, the idealist movement, which was a cadre doctrine limited to intellectuals and the political elite, began to popularize itself, thanks to the efforts of Türkes who wanted to turn the doctrine into a political party.

In the middle of the 1970s, the movement adopted Islamic overtones with a distinctive anti-Alevi stance. While the party adopted Islam only stylistically, the hearths would take it substantively and more seriously. Moreover, the rejection of both socialism and capitalism (again taken more seriously by the rank and file and the hearths than in the party's higher echelons) as alien systems left Islam as the only genuine, authentic language for the fight against oppression and poverty. Idealism versus pragmatism, downstairs versus upstairs—these cleavages found their accentuation in post-1980 jail-time experience of many idealists. There were rumors that those "upstairs," namely those in the leadership, were transferring the monies collected in Deutschkei to their personal accounts in Turkey. With this split between the more Islamized rank and file and the relatively more secular-minded party leadership, the period between 1980 and 1983 witnessed a turning point in party ideology.[25]

In 1987, it finally came to the so-called "great divide" in Europe. In June 1987, when Türkes visited Europe, he visited the Gray Wolves' camps exclusively (the more pre-Islamic, rather than Islamic, wing of the movement) and used an accusatory tone in his speeches toward Musa Serdar Çelebi and Ali Batman, who represented the Islamist dissenters against the hard-core, pro-Türkeş Gray Wolves.[26]

All of this accelerated the imminent rupture and hurt Türkeş and his party both financially and in terms of other sources of support.[27] Around 70 organizations split from the ADÜTDF in 1988 and formed, under the leadership of Çelebi and Batman, the European Turkish-Islamic Union of Cultural Associations (ATIB). The divide had been forming for some time in Europe between the younger Islamists and the more traditional, older, Turkist Gray Wolf camps. According to Bora and Can, this divide was also a reflection of the larger trend in the movement that manifested itself in terms of a division between the base and the leadership. In Europe the divide was even more obvious and visible, while in Turkey the respect for a common past and for the leader continued to be important values until the death of Türkeş in 1997.[28]

The partisan manifestation of the great divide among the Turkish ultranationalists is the BBP in Turkey. In the words of its leader, Muhsin Yazicioğlu, the BBP is a defender of the civil society against encroachments by the state and the military. Emphasis on civil society is accompanied by the rhetoric of multiculturalism and diversity that makes odd bedfellows with ultranationalism. The repeated motto of the party and its leader is "we are all patterns on the same *kilim*," whereby *kilim* means colorful Anatolian Turkish rug. Here is how Yazicioğlu describes BBP's political philosophy:

> The Big Unity Party espouses a more native, more open-to-change, more civilian, and a more democratic ideology. It also has a high level of dynamism and enthusiasm. Even though it appears to put Islam to the forefront, it rejects arti-

ficial distinctions like Turk and Kurd or Alevi and Sunni. We do not argue that we are the sole representatives of either Islam or the nation. These are natural values for us. We all are patterns on a *kilim*. We, the Kurds, the Turcomans, the Alevis, the Circassians, the Bosnians are the members of a family called "Turk." We don't consider the term 'Turk' in racial terms, but see it as encompassing all people who live on this soil. When I go to the southeast and talk about the "Turkish nation" no one is bothered by it. When you ask a woman in Agri, who cannot speak Turkish, whether or not she wants her son to undergo his education in Turkish or in Kurdish, she just says "I just want him wear a tie like you do." She doesn't care about divisions like Turk versus Kurd. She is looking for results. These are artificial distinctions. The question whether religion or nation comes first is also a meaningless one for us. We want to rescue nation and religion from being competing terms.[29]

The BBP maintains ties with the Turkish Federation. In 1993, for example, Yazicioglu, visited the Grand Idealists Association, which is affiliated with ADÜTDF. However, its functional equivalent in Europe is ATIB, which also came into being as a result of the great divide between the Turkist Gray Wolves camp and the Islamically oriented nationalists.

THE EUROPEAN TURKISH-ISLAMIC UNION (ATIB)

In 1988, ATIB, now with 122 affiliates, emerged as a splinter group from ADÜTDF. While ATIB is more extroverted, ADÜTDF has become a more secretive organization over the years.

Compared to ADÜTDF, ATIB's brand of Turkish national identity is intricately intertwined with Islam. Islamist nationalists use the language of Islam not only to achieve political rights, assert their presence, and to influence multicultural policy outcomes, but also to delineate clear ethnic boundaries.[30] They see multiculturalism as an opportunity for such delineation and non-integration. At ATIB's second Congress in June 1989 in Iserlohn, the leader of the organization, Musa Serdar Çelebi, said the following: "We want Islam to be recognized as an official religion [in Germany]. We want voting rights and the right to open our own schools to raise and educate our children within our own system. ... How can we preserve our national identity in countries that consider getting rid of their own flags? The answer lies in establishing our own religious and national institutions."[31]

In 1992, in Wuppertal, at the 5th convention of ATIB, Çelebi proudly announced the emergence of the "European Turk," and gave the following speech:

> We want our state [referring to the Turkish state] to acquire new structures that these new conditions require. How is this going to happen? First of all, the

state structures need to acquire an identity appropriate to the beliefs and cultural values of the Turkish people whom they are representing. If this doesn't happen, then every ten years more time will be wasted with quests for a new regime and for a new constitution. But our people have no tolerance for wasting and losing! We must realize the richness of our history and the values emanating from our beliefs with a consideration for new realities. We owe this much not only to our people, but also to other peoples in the world who have been suffering under man-made secular systems and who have been disoriented and fallen into a void because of the bankruptcy of those systems.[32]

The ATIB leadership may appear to take pride in being "European Turks," but the adjective "European" refers not to acculturation of any kind, but rather simply to physical and economic presence of Turks in Europe. There is no desire on the part of ATIB to see Turks integrate into European societies. Integration is understood as losing one's national identity, that is, as assimilation. It is actively discouraged through the maintenance of close ties with Turkey, sending kids on cultural tours to designated religious and national sites in Turkey, teaching them the Turkish language and the Islamic religion. ATIB's brand of European Turkish-ness is strictly indexed to mainland Turkey. The group considers the European Union an imperialist initiative against Turkey's interests. Turkey, Çelebi argues, should be "rebuilt on its own historical foundations with entirely local material."[33]

The following excerpts are taken from a speech given by the leader of ATIB at its 8th annual convention in Aachen:[34]

> The preservation of our national identity is an issue that is inextricably linked to our future in Europe. ... If we don't pursue this goal, then we will end up with generations neither Turkish, nor German, nor Christian, nor Muslim. Unfortunately some of the members of our second and third generations in Europe are lost in this sense. ... We need to have our own radio and television. We need to be more organized and more connected as a community. ... It is obvious that we will obtain better positions in every area by acquiring citizenship in the countries we live. However, there are questions about our future, which are of some concern. If, in 10 or 15 years, all Turkish citizens convert to German citizenship, what would happen to the cultural problems of these German citizens of Turkish descent? Would the Turkish courses that are taught to Turkish children in schools today be given to Turks who are German citizens? Under 'new citizenship' or 'new identity' how is the national identity to be protected? These questions lead us to the issue of 'minority rights' as a potential solution. We believe that in order to remain a community well-adapted to the societies they live in, yet preserve our national culture, we need to be recognized as a minority like the Turkish minority in Western Thrace or the Danish minority in Schleswig–Holstein.

The speech shows a highly pragmatic understanding of citizenship and the non-integrationist stance of the ultranationalists. Turkish organizations of this political persuasion in Europe are unambiguously indexed to Turkish politics, culture, and life, and as such, they are also unambiguously against letting Turkish children become "like Germans."

Turkey's outreach in Europe was also subject to a strong critique:

> ... We are Turkish citizens. In all our endeavors we need the backing and the support of the Turkish state. Unfortunately, Turkey is being governed by narrow-minded, bickering rulers, disconnected from their people. The Turkish state is unable to protect those who live in Turkey, let alone us living in Europe. ... They don't value their own people there or abroad. The best example for this is the attitude of Turkish governments about our voting rights. ... We keep telling them that our inability to participate in Turkish elections affects our struggle to obtain voting rights in Europe adversely. Voting rights would strengthen our people's connection to homeland. If those in Europe could enter the Turkish parliament as members, they might bring with them the experiences that they had abroad along with new perspectives, styles, and approaches. This may be fresh air for the system that has difficulty breathing. But Ankara doesn't hear us. They don't want to listen to people's voice.

The group calls on Turkish governments to establish a ministry for "national culture" and a ministry for "Turks abroad." In 1988, during their visit to Turkey, ATIB's regional representatives from northern Germany explicitly stated this demand with a letter to the Motherland Party (ANAP). The conventions of the organization regularly attract state ministers and party officials from center-right Turkish political parties. They organize student trips (for the children of Turks born in Germany) to cultural and religious sites in Istanbul and other parts of Turkey. An interview with 50 such kids appeared in the papers under the title "The silent scream of Turkish children born in Germany: We long for *ezan*. When we here the church bells we cover our ears."[35]

TURKISH IDEALISTS IN CYBERSPACE

ATIB, ADÜTDF, and the two major ultranationalist parties in Turkey are present on the Internet. There is a direct link from MHP's site to ADÜTDF (*http://www.turkfederasyon.com*) in Germany and its counterpart in the Netherlands.

ATIB's web site, *http://www.atib.org* greets visitors in Turkish and in German. The group presents its primary objectives as the preservation of the Muslim-Turkish identity and the strengthening of the cultural ties among Muslim-Turkish people, motherland Turkey, other Turkic states, and Islamic countries. "No matter how good their intentions may be, people who are brought up in a foreign culture cannot think like a native. It is also a known fact that someone who cannot preserve his culture cannot adapt to a foreign society. At this point, the importance of education becomes clear."[36]

On this homepage, one sees pictures of Turkish politicians visiting ATIB forums. ATIB's activities include Koran courses, folklore, theater, sports, German, Turkish, religion, and history classes, trips to Turkey, festivals, services to facilitate pilgrimage (*hac, umre*), almsgiving (*zekat*), sacrificial meat (*kurban*), burial information (*cenaze*), earthquake relief fund, and other charitable campaigns.

ATIB's cooperation with the International Academic Studies Information and Coordination Center (Inter-Akademi) is another point of emphasis on the site. Inter-Akademi, formed by academics and students from Turkey working and studying at European universities, works in cooperation with ATIB.

As of 1995, there were 15 thousand students from Turkey studying at German universities alone. Around 5 thousand college graduates work in German companies and organizations. "Inter-Akademi wants to take advantage of this brain power in solving the problems of our communities living in Europe. It also wants to see that scientific and technical expertise gained in Europe is carried over to Turkey." To further these causes, ATIB and Inter-Akademi sponsor joint projects and organize trips to Turkey.

THE ULTRANATIONALIST VIEW OF KEMALISM

As a general rule, Atatürk is revered by ADÜTDF and ATIB as a good nationalist and a military genius. However, his secularism is perceived as atheism and therefore criticized by ATIB.

By the turn of the 20th century, when the Young Turks of the Committee of Union and Progress (CUP) were looking for the ideological bases of alternative social projects to the crumbling multi-ethnic Ottoman Empire, there were three choices that were in the process of formulation: Islamism, neo-Ottomanism, and Turkism. The latter ultimately became the underlying principle of the new nation-state that followed the empire.

However, from its inception, there were two strands of thought in Turkish nationalism. The first one was the irredentist Turkism of the immigrants from Russia to the Ottoman Empire. It was "an expansionist philosophy which sought the unification of the Turkish race."[37] The second line of thought was led by Ziya Gökalp, which was a non-irredentist variant that sought to unify the Turkish culture. Indeed, after the foundation of the republic, "the priority of securing new national frontiers meshed well with Gökalp's Turkism."[38]

The tension between these two different conceptions of the Turkish nation became a permanent characteristic of Turkish nationalism. This tension has been generating periodic oscillations between Turkism's civic and ethnic variants discussed in chapter five, whereby the civic understanding reflects Gökalp's ideas.

Ideologically, the ultranationalist partisan tradition of CCMP/MHP/MÇP/MHP has developed a platform derivative of the irredentist and ethnic school of thought.[39] This line of thinking conceptualized Turkish history, from its very beginning to the present, as an uninterrupted epic whole.[40] Since this whole included the pre-Islamic as well as Islamic periods of Turks, religion was just as important a building bloc of Turkish-ness as pre-Islamic and secular elements. This thinking prepared the conditions for the later officially sanctioned merger of religion and nationalism under the rubric of Turkish-Islamic synthesis discussed earlier, even though Islam, originally, was not an item on the ultranationalists' list of principles.

Among all groups examined here, the ultranationalists are least critical of the Turkish state. The exception is the BBP, which presents itself as a formation independent of the state. The party's leader boldly states that "the military is not a civil society institution."[41]

The relations between Euro-Turkish ultranationalists and the official representatives of the Turkish state in Europe have generally tended to be collegial.[42] Consulates and embassies generally do not see the need to distance themselves publicly from these formations. In fact, according to some accounts, the Turkish National Intelligence Agency (MIT) was involved in the very organization of the Turkish extreme right in Germany. Türkeş appointed Enver Altayli, a MIT agent since 1968, at the end of the 1970s as the leader of the party's organization in Germany. His successor was Musa Serdar Çelebi, the current leader of ADÜTDF.

Nevertheless, the idealists' relations with the Turkish state have undergone changes. Following the 1980 coup that crushed both the political left and to a lesser degree the political right, feelings of resentment vis-a-vis the state and the Turkish military were rampant in ultranationalist camps. Some of the their leaders like Türkeş and Yazicioğlu were jailed and served sentences for several years. It is around this time that the Islamized elements split, first ideologically then physically from the rest of the movement.

In the late 1980s and the 1990s, thanks to Kurdish ethnonationalism and the Turkish military's monopoly over the Kurdish question, the ultranationalists made amends with the state. Idealist commandos collaborated with the state in the fight not only against Kurdish separatism, but also against the common ultimate "other," namely, the radical left. The PKK, as both Kurdist and leftist, was a natural target. Campaign slogans like "every vote for MHP is a slap against the PKK" and "either you like this country or you leave" carried MHP to power.⁴³

NOTES

¹The Idealist Hearths (*Ülkü Ocakları*) are the grassroots organizations of the Turkish ultra-nationalist movement. They are strongly institutionalized in Europe, particularly in Germany. The focus of their activities abroad is on countering neo-Nazi attacks on Turks, fighting the PKK and the leftists, socializing migrants into Turkish culture and religion, and mobilizing support for ultranationalist causes in Turkey.

²Article 69 of the Turkish Constitution of 1982 and Articles 66, 79, and 92 of the Law on Political Parties prohibit Turkish political parties from receiving contributions from associations and groups foreign countries, as well as from organizing and engaging in activities abroad.

³ The "gray wolf" is the symbol of Turkish ultranationalists and the MHP. The name comes from an ancient Turkic epic story in which an entire Turkic tribe in Central Asia is led by a gray wolf away from danger.

⁴ The MHP was formed in 1968–69 from the ranks of the Republican Farmer and Nation Party (CCMP).

⁵The Democratic Left Party (DSP), a nationalist-leftist formation headed by the incumbent prime minister Bulent Ecevit, received, with 23 percent, the plurality of the votes. The DSP was followed by the MHP. The Islamist Virtue Party (FP) came third with 15 percent of the votes. While the center right, composed of the Motherland Party (ANAP) and the True Path Party (DYP), could only extract a percentage slightly more than 10 percent, which is the national threshold, the social democrats could not make it to the parliament. While the Kurdish-nationalist People's Democracy Party (HADEP) experienced a historical victory in the southeast, the Peace Party (BP) and the Big Unity Party (BBP) remained around one percent.

⁶ Traditionally, the MHP's voter profile consisted of artisans, craftsmen, small farmers, shopkeepers, young marginals, and a sector of the Anatolian big bourgeoisie.

⁷Following the death of its charismatic leader Türkeş in 1997, Devlet Bahçeli, an economics professor, became party leader. After Türkeş's death and prior to the latest national elections, reforms were undertaken in the organization and in the party doctrine. Leadership was relegated to the background. Bahçeli purged the party from extremists, recruited a host of academics, and brought the party closer to the mainstream. Not least because of the ultra-nationalists' victory, the results of the 1999 Turkish elections reflected the Kurdish conflict's fault lines in Turkish politics. The Islamist RP lost its "borrowed" votes to the MHP in central Anatolia. It also lost to the Kurdish party (HADEP) in the southeast. The HADEP, although receiving 4 percent nation-wide, won mayoral seats in six important southeastern cities.

⁸*Insiyatif* 7, 1994.

⁹Franz Josef Strauss was the leader of the West German Bavarian Christian Social Union (CSU) from 1961 to 1978. He was also the premier of Bavaria between 1978 and 1988 and an influential conservative politician in German federal politics.

¹⁰Gunther Wallraff, *Ganz Unten* (Cologne: Kiepenheuer & Witsch, 1985), 26.

¹¹Enver Altayli's (a Turkish intelligence officer and the head of ultranationalists in Europe) letters to Türkes show that he was also connected to the German Secret Intelligence Agency (*Bundesnachrichtendienst*). These letters were documented by the late Turkish journalist Uğur Mumcu in 1988.

¹²Yücel Yeşilgöz, "The Turkish State and Racist Violence," in *Racist Violence in Europe*, eds. Tore Bjorgo and Rob Witte (St Martin's Press, 1997).

¹³The Gray Wolves are no longer mentioned as an extremist organization in the German *Verfassungsschutzbericht*.

¹⁴*Milliyet*, 1–5 July 1976.

¹⁵Nermin Abadan-Unat, "Ethnic Business, Ethnic Communities, and Ethno-Politics Among Turks in Europe," in *Immigration into Western Societies: Problems and Policies*, ed. Emek M. Uçarer and Donald J. Puchala (London and Washington: Pinter, 1997), 243.

¹⁶The Federation was established in 1978 in Frankfurt under Lokman Kundakçi and has 180 affiliated associations today. By 1995, it had six thousand members. Its current president is Mehmet Erdoğan. Its publication is *Türk Federasyon Bülteni*.

¹⁷Their ideology is based on Islam and the Turkish nation. The spin-off group ATIB, which will be discussed in the following section under the "nationalist-Islamists," is more Islamic than ADÜTDF in its orientation, but relatively more interested in operating within the parameters of the German political system.

¹⁸*Insiyatif* 8, 1994.

¹⁹*Cumhuriyet*, October 13 1980.

²⁰*Insiyatif* 5, 1994.

²¹*Insiyatif* 10, 1995.

²²*Sabah*, September 29, 1997.

²³*Hürriyet*, 19 April 1999.

²⁴*Insiyatif* 8, 1994.

²⁵Tanil Bora and Kemal Can, "1980'li Yillarda Faşist Hareket," *Birikim* 10 (February 1990): 37–49. Also see *Cumhuriyet*, 8 August, 1992.

²⁶One additional reason for this distancing was the fact that Celebi was being charged with involvement in Mehmet Ali Ağca's assassination attempt on Pope John Paul II.

²⁷Tanil Bora and Kemal Can, "1980'li Yillarda Faşist Hareket," *Birikim* 10 (February 1990), 45.

²⁸Ibid.

²⁹Muhsin Yazicioğlu, the leader of BBP, interview by author, tape-recorded, Ankara, August 1998.

³⁰"Islam is equality, Islam is freedom, and Islam is the free, equal, and prosperous coexistence of people," quoted in *Türkiye*, September 11 1990.

³¹*Türkiye*, 20 June 1989.

³²*Türkiye*, 4 May 1992.

33 Ibid. Emphasis added.

34 *Insiyatif* 10, 1995. The meeting took place on December 11, 1995. Among the participants were the mayor of Istanbul from the Islamist party, the head of the Hearth of Intellectuals, Islamic businessmen and owners of conservative newspapers in Turkey.

35 *Türkiye*, 29 March 1989. *Ezan* is the Islamic call to prayer.

36 Text available from http://www.atib.org; Internet; accessed in April 2000.

37 Ayşe Çağlar, "The Greywolves as Metaphor," in *State and Society in Turkey*, ed. Nükhet Sirman and Andrew Finkel (London: Routledge, 1991), 83.

38 Ibid.

39 The philosophical underpinnings of this type of thinking came from the so-called "*Thirteen Lights*" theory of Huseyin Nihal Atsiz. The party's founder Alpaslan Türkes developed his "*Nine Lights*" doctrine in 1965 based on Atsiz's ideas compiled in this doctrine. Atsiz wrote numerous articles in journals like *Orhun* (1933), *Orkun* (1952), and *Ötüken* (1964).

40 This doctrine included the principles of nationalism, idealism, moralism, scientism, sociability, village-ism, liberalism and individualism, developmentalism and populism, industrialism and technocratism. Within the party a strict *fuhrer* principle was followed and this principle was also seen as a recipe for Turkey's redemption.

41 Musin Yazicioğlu, the leader of BBP, interview by author, tape-recorded, Ankara, August 1998.

42 *Insiyatif* 4, 1994.

43 *Hürriyet*, 20 March 1994.

X
The Islamists

ONE ENTERS THE LARGEST TURKISH INTEREST GROUP IN EUROPE THROUGH a parking lot, filled almost exclusively with Mercedes automobiles that are supposed to symbolize political and financial power. It is not until one sees the sign that indicates a separate "entrance for women" into the building that one puts two and two together. These are the headquarters of the European National Outlook Organization (AMGT) or, by its new name, the Islamic Community-National Outlook (IGMG) in Cologne—the largest Islamist network outside of Turkey.[1]

The "public relations and press official" of the IGMG would only answer questions under the conditions that the conversation not be recorded on tape and that the politically sensitive material remain off the record.[2] This secretiveness is indicative, yet not surprising, as students of the IGMG have long been aware of the difficulties of penetrating this network to get a clear picture of its goals and activities.

ISLAMISTS AND THE POLITICS OF STATE APPROPRIATION

The symbiosis between the IGMG and the partisan Islamist tradition in Turkey is well known, if not well documented. Necmettin Erbakan, the founder of and the most powerful figure in the partisan Islamic tradition in Turkey, himself spent time in Germany at a post-doctoral position at Aachen Technical University in the early 1950s.[3] Although he had an engineering background, rather than primarily a liberal arts education, his days in Germany were formative in establishing contacts with the future administrators of the IGMG and laying the groundwork for its foundation.

Erbakan's exposure to the German experience has also influenced his later emphasis on a "heavy industrialization" program for Turkey's development in the 1970s.[4] Islamist projects as late as the 1990s have assigned a large role to regulation and participation by state institutions not only in the economy but in social and political relationships as well.[5]

The deepest schism that cuts through Turkish society today has to do with the proper role for religion in politics and public life. Nuances here and there notwithstanding, from the general Islamist perspective, as far as the role of religious tenets is concerned there is no distinction between state and society. Secularists, on the hand, see a clear wall of separation.

One analyst formulates this cleavage as follows:

> The faithful countryside never had accepted the secularisation and Westernisation, which Ataturk dictated in big cities. The community (*Gemeinschaft*) of the tarikat offered consolation with the newly emerging abstract society (*Gesellschaft*). By means of the *tarikat*, religion became an alternative rural political culture (*Gegenkultur*): The secularised cities had their leftist intellectuals. The rural population still followed their preachers who date their presence back to pre-modern *dervishes*.[6]

To appreciate the meaning and the significance of the polarization between the Islamists and the secularists in Turkey, one has to understand the very nature of Turkish secularism. In this particular way of separating the "church" (organized religion) from the state, for which *laicism* may be a better term, the state is not a neutral actor but has its own brand of religion that it attempts to superimpose on society through its own institutions designed to deal with matters of religion.

The Directorate of Religious Affairs (DIB) is such an institution in Turkey which promotes a mild, enlightened form of "high Islam," essentially antagonistic toward the religious orders of traditional folk Islam (*tarikats*) as well as toward the orthodoxy of fundamentalist interpretations.[7] The Directorate has its own budget, which is larger than those of most state ministries, and these funds were used liberally in the last two decades to support the construction of mosques and religious schools all over Turkey.

Understood in this way, secularism, or laicism, is one of the main pillars of the official ideology and has become even more paradigmatic of Kemalism in recent decades as other Kemalist principles have undergone substantial change under new circumstances.[8] Religious political movements that questioned this principle have been looked upon suspiciously by the secular establishment, particularly by the military, and have been accused of using democracy instrumen-

ISLAM A LA TURCA IN EUROPE

The author of one of the most insightful inquiries written on an Islamist party in Turkey has once pointed out that the partisan Islamist discourse has a tendency to exclude Germany from its otherwise prevalent anti-Westernism.[9] The explanation for this omission lies in the fact that the IGMG, the deep hinterland of Turkish Islamism, is located in Germany. The IGMG has been functioning, for decades, as the auxiliary of the partisan Islamist tradition in Turkey. The close relationships between the IGMG and the German government became clearer when Ali Yuksel, the head of the IGMG, was declared, *Seyh-ul-Islam* by the *Islamrat* (Islamic Council) in 1990 and thereby the leader of all German Muslims.[10] Islamic parties in Turkey feel that they must have good relations with Germany, even if it is for the sole purpose of facilitating IGMG's operations in Europe.

Despite their primary focus on Turkey, the IGMG leadership, as part of their interpretation of the theoretical secondary-ness of nationalism to religion, publicly de-emphasizes the idea of nation-state: "Initially, we got together because we were Turkish. Then we started getting together because we were Muslims. We were nationalistic when we first came here, because that's how we had been taught in Turkey," explains the public relations official. IGMG's president Ali Yüksel and its secretary general Mehmet Erbakan, who is the nephew of Necmettin Erbakan, consider Turks in Germany and in Europe a "national minority," whereby the term "national" (*milli*) in fact means *umma* (religious community).[11]

IGMG officials claim that the organization has 740 affiliate associations in Europe, 514 of them in Germany, with 210 thousand members. Outside sources, however, quote the numbers as 26 thousand members and 262 member associations in Europe.[12] Around 80 percent of the affiliates are mosque associations.[13] The IGMG also owns a large variety of youth and women's organizations, web sites, Internet cafes, sports clubs, *imam-hatip* (preacher) preparation schools, and publications. The organization offers computer, language, and Koran courses. It has facilities in 270 places in Germany that are regularly used by 70 thousand people. The European Mosque Construction and Support (EMUG) works under the IGMG, to manage the large real estate holdings of the organization.[14]

IGMG's net worth is estimated to be around 250 billion dollars. It is believed that the organization owns more than 2 thousand pieces of real estate in Europe and Turkey.[15] Its wealth comes mainly from membership dues, Islamic financial institutions in the Middle East, and from the group's investment in real estate in Europe and Turkey. This list is by no means exhaustive of all of the organization's sources of economic power.

TRANSNATIONAL ISLAMIST EXCHANGES

It is among the second and third generations that one finds the most vibrant associational activity and an Islamic orthodoxy, which differs from their parents' traditionalist folk view of religion. Young German-Turks read the ideas of Islamist writers and theologians like Ali Bulaç, Abdurrahman Dilipak, Hekimoğlu Ismail, Necip Fazil Kisakürek, Mawdudi, Ali Shariati and the like and discuss political problems in Turkey on a daily basis in their leisure times.[16]

Although the myth of return is not as strong among the later generations as it is among their parents, surveys show that many would entertain the idea of living in Turkey if the conditions were favorable.[17] German citizenship laws have long deprived them of a sense of belonging and prevented them from resolving their identity crises. This fact, combined with the pervasive hostilities foreigners encounter from certain segments of the German population, enhances the continuity of interest in the affairs of the homeland.

The cultivators of political Islam have been particularly successful over the years in translating migrants' interest in the homeland into active participation in and influence on homeland politics. Indeed, there are detectable exchanges between the Islamists in Deutschkei and their counterparts and beneficiaries in Turkey proper.

While until the middle of the 1980s the Islamist organizations in Europe were largely funded by their ideologically related parties in Turkey or from sources in the Middle East, they now themselves financially support movements in Turkey. They are especially active in the field of religious foundations. In many cases, the construction of new mosques, student homes, residential and Koran schools in Turkey can be traced back to funds from the Turkish-Islamist community in Germany.[18]

> Many of these organizations started as offshoots from political parties and movements in Turkey, which could not freely organize there because of the political situation and religious policy in Turkey. Turkish political competition, official and underground, became reflected among the Turkish diaspora, and specifically in Germany. ... Most Turkish Islamic associations nowadays very much distance themselves from the political preoccupations of around 1980. The stronger focus on Islamic elements, as opposed to the earlier nationalist overtones, is connected to this distancing. Organizations are mainly concerned with being accepted as religious rather than political groups. Nevertheless, con-

nections with political strands in Turkey continue to exist and are indeed supported by Turkish politicians. (Karakasoğlu and Nonneman 1996, 256)

According to the Federal Office for the Protection of the Constitution, which in its reports has been consistently listing the IGMG as a foreign extremist organization on German soil, most of the extremist-Islamist groups of Turkish and Arabic origin "try to replace the more or less Western-oriented regimes in their homelands with *sharia* and Koran-based Islamic state systems. While the use of force seems to be an opportune means for most of the Arabic Islamists to achieve their political goals, the Turkish Islamists use political activities to change *social relations* in Turkey."[19]

According to the 1997 report by this office, IGMG's undeclared political objectives consist of overthrowing the secular regime in Turkey and the Islamization of, first, the Turkish society, and in the long run, of all societies in which Muslims live. To achieve these goals, IGMG supports political Islam in Turkey, both ideationally as well as financially. IGMG benefits particularly from the problems that arise in the course of Turks' integration to European societies. Difficulties in this area are taken up by Islamists as agitation themes and the solidarity of Muslims is proposed as a solution.[20]

Developments in Turkey affect the IGMG. For example, before the implementation of educational reforms in Turkey in 1998, designed to increase the mandatory primary schooling age from five to eight years, IGMG collected 38 thousand signatures to petition for the prevention of this reform.[21] Although the campaign was unsuccessful, it illustrates the scale of IGMG's grassroots lobbying.

It is also known that since the Welfare Party (RP) in Turkey was shut down by state security courts on January 16, 1998 and since Erbakan and other top party functionaries were banned for five years from active politics, there have been divisions forming within the IGMG among the older generation supporting Erbakan and his company and the younger activists aligning with the reformist wing.[22]

By the same token, developments at IGMG affect the form Islamism takes in Turkey as well as in Europe. Some observers, for example, see the seeds of a possible European Islam with Turkish foundations led by the IGMG. They point out to a trend among Islamic organizations to reach a consensus among each other and with European governments on issues important to migrants.[23]

Islamic organizations in Europe and their activities matter for Turkey in a variety of other ways ranging from financial support to channeling Islamic grievances from the Turkish political arena to European forums.[24] How Islam is understood among migrants from Turkey in Europe generates questions and debate about what kind of a role religion should play in society and politics in Turkey. Both Sunni Islamists and Alevis question the existing framework of secularism in Turkey, albeit from different angles. The organizational successes of Kurds and Alevis put pressure on what is dubbed here as "the illusion of ethnic homogeneity" that the official thinking strives to cultivate. In that sense, the Islamists challenge an important Kemalist tenet, namely, nationalism. Islamism also challenges republicanism, another Kemalist principle, by celebrating Turkey's imperial past. More and more fundamentalist groups denounce republicanism openly and categorically.

The IGMG has rather intricate political and economic ties with the main Islamist party in Turkey. Erbakan is admired as IGMG's spiritual leader. At the organization's fourth annual convention in Amsterdam on June 20, 1999, Erbakan was the guest of honor. At this forum, the head of IGMG, Ali Yüpksel, condemned the ban on the Islamist party and its leader Erbakan within the framework of a general critique of the Turkish political system and its understanding of secularism.

Some connections between Turkish Islam and its European hinterland are tangibly electoral in nature. At each parliamentary election, the Islamist party sets aside a certain number on its list of candidates for IGMG activists under the rubric the "Germany quota" (*Almanya kontenjani*). Within this framework, the former head of the organization, Osman Yumakogullari, for example, became a member of the Turkish parliament from the Welfare Party (RP) following the 1995 general elections. Ali Yüksel, the head of the IGMG at the time of this writing, on the other hand, tried to get elected to the national legislature from Turkey's Antalya province twice in 1991 and 1995. Both attempts were unsuccessful. Prior to the latest elections, two parliamentarians from the Germany quota of the party (now Felicity Party, SP), Şevki Yilmaz and Osman Yumakoğullari, campaigned vigorously in Germany for the elections in Turkey.

Since the 1986 elections the IGMG had been chartering cheap flights for the sole purpose of bringing religious votes to the voting stations at the border. IGMG functionaries also collect money at affiliated mosques for the Islamist party's election campaign in Turkey. Islamist party functionaries from Turkey have been able to defend their positions in numerous IGMG events and meetings in Europe. For instance, on June 14, 1997, the mayor of Istanbul (a member of the Islamist party) attended IGMG's annual meeting in Dortmund and praised the work done by the organization to prevent Turks from assimilating into the Christian culture.[25] The IGMG responded to the mayor's comments by saying that they are trying to build up a cadre of people, ready to be sacrificed for the Islamist party's cause in Turkey.[26] The party's publication *Milli Gazete*, printed both in Germany and Turkey, is also used by the IGMG regularly as a forum to disseminate its views.

The party in Turkey, its arm in Europe, and the Erbakan family also help each other financially. In addition to membership dues and investments in Europe and in Turkey, large donations to the organization are made during the holy month of Ramadan throughout Europe. Indeed, financial contributions to the IGMG increase around Ramadan, religious holidays, relief work for national disasters, and elections in Turkey. The findings of a special investigating committee of the Turkish parliament indicate that 2.9 million dollars, which had originally been collected as a special fund for the Bosnia-Herzegovina relief work, went to the private accounts of some members of the RP.[27]

Because the IGMG is under close surveillance by the Federal Office for the Protection of the Constitution, at times the organization continues its activities under surrogate groups that declare, officially, their organic independence from the IGMG, but in fact operate in an intricate web of relations with it. Ali Yildirim from AYPA-TV has documented that the Islamic Womens' Association, *Cemiyet-i Nisa*, had IGMG members on its executive board, despite the fact that the association had received permission from German authorities by convincing them of their independence from the IGMG.[28]

Another illustration of the intricacies of such connections, documented by the German journalist Eberhard Seidel in *Tageszeitung* in February 2000, is the tripartite relationship between the Islamic Federation, IGMG, and Erbakan. The Islamic Federation, which has recently been given the permission to offer Islamic religion courses in Berlin schools, was established as an independent organization with no obvious ties to IGMG. Seidel shows, with the help of contracts signed by parties involved as well as addresses of locations from which these groups operate, how the Berlin chapter of the IGMG, the Islamic Television in Germany (TFD), Islamic Federation, Islamic Foundation, and IGMG's central command in Cologne are connected to each other and how these groups acknowledge, in their internal affairs, the leadership and the arbitration of Erbakan's partisan formations in Turkey.[29]

Since 1992, IGMG also has been collaborating with the Islamically oriented Turkish employers association MÜSIAD.[30] In addition to enterprises that are members of this association, a variety of corporations became particularly active during the coalition government between the Islamist Welfare Party and the center right True Path Party (popularly dubbed as *Refahyol*) under the premiership of the DYP-leader Tansu Çiller in the mid-1990s. Most of these companies (their numbers are estimated to be around 43) are based in the conservative Anatolian province of Konya. *Jet Pa Holding* and *Kombassan Holding* are the most prominent ones with noteworthy links to Germany.

In Turkey, the so-called "green capital," dubbed by secularists to describe the ascendance of Islamic corporations in the 1990s, is accumulated primarily with monies collected from migrants in Germany and Europe. These companies target migrants' savings in German banks. Those savings are estimated to be around 74 billion dollars. Green capitalists contact migrants who are unhappy with the state of their investments in Turkey, collect money from them by offering "profit sharing," a non-interest-based kosher system of doing business according to Islamic law. They then channel this capital into Turkey.[31] The capital that has entered Turkey this way is estimated to be around 2.5 billion dollars. *Kombassan Holding* alone is responsible for one billion dollars entered so far into the country. It is argued that green capital has thus far created 100 thousand new jobs in Turkey and its contribution to Turkish export volume is measured around 100 million dollars.[32]

German Securities and Exchange Commission (*Bundesaufsichtsamt fur den Wertpapierhandel*) has been closely watching the activities of *Jet Pa International Marketing and Trading GmbH*, Jet Pa Holding's partner in Germany. In the meantime, the commission's functional equivalent in Turkey, the Capital Market Commission (SPK), has been warning the public of both Jet Pa campaigns and Kombassan stocks.[33] According to the SPK, Jet Pa has been collecting money from the public through campaigns, offering attractive deals on merchandise in order to pay off its existing debts, without backing it up with production. Kombassan stocks, on the other hand, had been sanctioned by the SPK on grounds that their public partnership offerings were misleading and that holding company stocks was not equivalent to becoming partners.

Moreover, according to the *Bundesaufsichtsamt*, Jet Pa, Kombassan, Air Alfa, Yimpaş, Endüstri Holding and similar green capital enterprises had been transferring money to Turkey, not through banks, but through private couriers. It is estimated that the capital that has entered Turkey in luggage this way is around half a billion dollars. It is also estimated that these activities became particularly vibrant in the months preceding the general elections of April 18, 1999.[34]

THE OFFICIAL TURKISH ISLAM IN EUROPE

The main reason why Turkish governments at all care about political Islam abroad lies in the potential and actual impact exerted by religious movements abroad on Turkish politics back home. The Directorate of Religious Affairs (DIB) has its institutional arm in Europe in the form of the Religious Affairs Turkish-Islamic Union (DITIB), with its headquarters located in Berlin.[35] DITIB's official objective is to fulfill migrants' religious needs abroad. But its

The Islamists 161

informal goals are to represent Turkish official Islam in Europe and to counterbalance the growing power of the non-official political Islam.

However, throughout the 1980s the relationship between official and non-official interpretations of Islam in Turkey became much more ambiguous than presented above. As Islamic symbols and overtones integrated themselves more and more into the official discourse and, thus, as the boundaries between official and extra-official Islam started to blur in Turkey, the Islamist Party and its political arm in Europe (IGMG) started penetrating the cadres of DITIB as well.

With the de-politicization of society in Turkey, following the 1980 coup, the appeal of extreme political organizations has somewhat diminished among Turks in Germany. The Turkish Islamic synthesis, discussed earlier as a doctrine to combat political extremism, not only found a good degree of acceptance among large parts of the population in Turkey, but its popularity also resonated in Deutschkei. In the initial phases following the coup, the Islamist parties increased their activities in Europe. To counter this development, the "synthesis" was propagated in Germany (and in Europe in general) through the state-sponsored vehicle of DITIB. The goal was to control more of the mosques, Islamic services and teaching than other organizations were able to do. DITIB is now by far the largest Islamic umbrella organization in Germany and continues to propagate the "moderate" Islam of the "synthesis."[36]

OTHER ISLAMIST GROUPS IN GERMANY

The Federation of Islamic Communities (ICCB), also known as the *Kaplancilar*, is the most radical Islamic formation in Europe that originates from Turkey. It split from IGMG in 1984 in Cologne and now has around 50 member associations. Its deceased founder and leader Cemalettin Kaplan was called the "Khomeini of Cologne." In the 1970s, Kaplan, who was a Muslim jurist in southern Turkey, sought and received political asylum in Germany.[37] When he died in 1995, his son Metin Kaplan took over. Kaplan Jr. declared himself the Caliph of Cologne and the head of the "caliphate state in exile."

The Federal Office for the Protection of the German Constitution has recently upgraded the ICCB as a terrorist organization. According to this office, since May 1998, Kaplan has been calling his sympathizers to topple the "puppet regime in Turkey" and to establish a *caliphate* state there.[38] It is known that Kaplan had declared Turkey *Dar-ül-Harb*, namely, a war zone, thereby legitimizing all violence against it in the name of God. In October 1998, during the 75th year anniversary celebrations of Turkey's independence and becoming a republic, the police arrested a group of ICCB sympathizers on grounds that they were planning to sabotage the celebrations with violence.

Kaplan Jr. was arrested on 25 March 1999 under the suspicion that he ordered, through a *fetwa*, the murder of an opponent who declared himself counter-caliph two years earlier. In a live broadcast for 1,5 hours from the Ulu Mosque in Cologne over HAKK-TV (their own station), transmitting to Turkey through EUTELSAT, Kaplan Jr. engaged in propaganda for *sharia* (Islamic law), claiming that "it is definitely stated in Koran that whoever goes against sharia will burn in hell. Anatolia belongs to the *umma* and should be given back to believers. April 23, May 19, and October 29 are dark days for the Muslims."[39]

The second significant fundamentalist group is the Union of Islamic Cultural Centers (VIKZ), also known as *Süleymancilar*. This group was established by Süleyman Hilmi Tunahan in 1973 in Cologne. It is now run by his son in law Kemal Kacar and is assumed to have command over 250 associations in Europe. The VIKZ strictly rejects secularism in Turkey. Their teachings stem from the conservative *Naqshbandiyya* order and they have supported center-right parties in Turkey like DP, AP, DYP, and ANAP, thereby increasing the *Naqshbandiyya* influence on these parties. They are also linked to the conservative newspaper *Tercüman* in Turkey, to the German Christian Democrats, and to Turkish organizations in Germany like HÜRTÜRK and ADÜTDF. The former mayor of Istanbul, the second man in the RP, and the leader of the new Justice and Development Party (AKP) Tayyip Erdogan, is believed to have close contacts with the VIKZ in Cologne.

Finally, the *Cemaat-i Nur*, or the *Nurcular*, is known to be the most radically anti-communist order in Turkey, with a substantial following in Germany. *Cemaat-i Nur* was the only religious group that openly criticized the 1980 military coup in Turkey and rejected the constitution that was crafted by it. The group exists, since 1967, in Cologne and is headed by Rustem Ulker. It is estimated that they own 30 schools (*medreses*) and have about 6 thousand members in Germany.

Cemaat-i Nur espouses a milder, more liberal form of Islam and embraces Mawdudi's idea of "theo-democracy" as a form of political organization. Its founder Beduizzaman Said-i Nursi (1877–1960) was a Kurdish *shaikh* who supported the founding of the Turkish republic in its initial stages.[40] He was then sent to exile to Western Turkey due to charges that he participated in the Kurdish-Islamist Shaikh Said rebellion in 1925. In exile he compiled his teachings under a series of books called *Risale-i Nur*.

The VIKZ and Nurcular are not as effective as the IGMG and the ICCB. Other Islamist groups organized in Europe are more marginal and their membership and influence have been in relative decline in recent years. Nevertheless, they all share the same political goal: to reunite Islam with the state apparatus—starting in Turkey.

TURKISH ISLAMISTS IN CYBERSPACE

As far as interest groups are concerned, the Islamist-Turkist ATIB and its web presence have already been discussed in the previous chapter. Here, I would like to turn my attention to the homepage of the IGMG.

IGMG's web site contains articles from the journal *Milli Görüş*, published by the organization. The journal's older issues are also available on line.[41] The focus of the journal tends to be on the Turkish state's weakness in dealing with Turkey's economic, social, and political problems. Articles generally contain a strong critique of the "official ideology" and how it oppresses the faithful with its radical secularism. Grievances include state licensing of mosque construction and imams' education, the state's involvement in the organization of the annual pilgrimage to Mecca (*hac*), the ban on headscarves in public offices, the ban on religious brotherhoods, and the exclusion of religious men from the military.

> Turkey is a chaotic country. At the heart of the chaos lies the official ideology that does not accept or tolerate any truth statements other than its own. ... The main characteristic of the existing system is that it co-opts Islamic concepts while suppressing and oppressing the Muslims. In doing so they sanctify the state. They enslave themselves to the state. They worship the state. But other than Allah there is nothing and no-one worth worshipping. Only true Muslims know whom to worship. They are not blinded by ideology.[42]

The official ideology and the state are blamed for issues ranging from sectarian divisions to the handling of relief work after natural disasters. In this regard, the visit to IGMG by the president of the *Ehl-i Beyt* Foundation, an Alevi institution, is highlighted as an indication that the conflict between Sunnis and Alevis is artificial and a fabrication of the Turkish state.

Turks and Kurds, it is written, have been brothers within the same faith. As much as Kurdish nationalist violence deserves sanctions, they say, those who violated the Kurds' human rights should also be brought to justice. As such, ethnic and nationalist separatism is denounced and Islam is presented as the only solution to all problems emanating from the Turkish state.

THE ISLAMIST VIEW OF KEMALISM

It should have become clear from the discussion so far that Kemalism represents the ultimate "other" of Islamism in Turkey. Over time, Kemalism has become a shorthand code for nationalism and secularism, two principles theologically not compatible with Islam. Despite apparent crossover liberal Islamists like Fethullah Gülen, who was, until recently, known as the "Kemalist *hodja*," the cloak of Kemalism should be seen as a survival tactic in a political environment permeated by an official discourse radically secularist, at least in its rhetoric, and a military establishment that signals its position in this regard by purging itself regularly and publicly from Islamist elements (*irticai unsurlar*).[43]

Similar to Alevis, Islamists also demand, a stricter separation of religion and state, albeit for different reasons. They demand that the state and the Directorate for Religious Affairs withdraw from matters of religion. Yet at the same time, unlike Alevis, the Islamists foresee and desire a larger role for religion in the affairs of the state and benefit significantly from the licensing and the employment opportunities in religious positions offered to them by the state.

The IGMG is also averse to republicanism, another Kemalist tenet. The glorification of the Ottoman imperial past by partisan Islam in Turkey, backed by the IGMG, attests to this point.

Radical Islamists are particularly categorical in their critique of the entire "system" in Turkey. Unlike moderates, fundamentalists are not only critical of secularism, but for them Kemalism, first and foremost, stands for nationalism. Nationalism, a man-made construct, is seen as the anti-thesis of the natural socio-political unit, which is the *umma* (community of believers). According to the ICCB publication *Ümmet-i Muhammed*, the enemies of Islam include nationalism, capitalism, fascism, democracy, secularism, party system, and Judaism. Not surprisingly, except for the last one, all of these constitute, in varying degrees, the building blocs of the Turkish state.

The relatively "moderate" IGMG, however, has a more ambiguous relationship to nationalism, as the usage of the concept "national" in its name (National Outlook) shows. Indeed, the IGMG is attracted to the idea of Turkey being a significant regional power in the Middle East and *primus inter pares* in the Muslim world.

It should also be repeated here that the partisan Islamic tradition in Turkey has traditionally pursued an economic strategy for the country that has been highly autarchic, based on heavy industrialization, and on the protection of national/domestic sectors.[44] Economic statism (which has generally been losing its rigor) and populism appear to the only Kemalist tenets, with which the Islamists seem to be in agreement.

Although the surface has been scratched here, the goal was to demonstrate that while the dominant secularist paradigm in Turkey continues to overshadow a clear expression of Islamist political projects, examples of such expression are much easier to discern in the diaspora.

NOTES

¹The prototype of the group was first formed in West Berlin in 1974. In 1977, the organization moved to Cologne and acquired legal status from German courts in 1985.

²Expectedly, that material turns out to be the IGMG's organic ties with Turkey. There is a consistent denial of being affiliated with any political party in Turkey. What the IGMG likes to put to the forefront are its activities among migrants from Turkey to help them adjust to the German society and to help them preserve their culture and the practice of their religion.

³Ergun Poyraz, *Refah'in Gercek Yüzü* (Ankara: Poyraz Yayinlari, 1996).

⁴Ruşen Çakir, *Ne Şeriat Ne Demokrasi: Refah Partisini Anlamak* (Istanbul: Metis Yayinlari, 1994), 170, 171.

⁵One such project and perhaps the best publicized one was called *Adil Düzen* (Just Order) by the Welfare Party (RP). Just Order was envisioned as a strongly regulated market economy within which the state had the authoritative monopoly to publicly "certify" the trustworthiness and moral certitude of citizens.

⁶Rainer Hermann, "Political Islam in Turkey" (lecture given on 5 May 1995), Orient Institut der Deutschen Morgenländischen Gesellschaft, Beirut.

⁷The brand of Islam advocated by DIB is criticized by heterodox folk variants because of its highly centralized, formal, and one-sided (Sunni) sponsorship of high Islam that denounces the superstitious and sectarian dimensions of the Islamic culture. One of the biggest issues of contention for Alevis, in this regard, is the budget of DIB that finances mosque construction and the education of *imams*. The Directorate is also criticized by orthodox Sunnis and fundamentalists because it regulates religious matters on behalf of the state.

⁸ Kemalism is based on six pillars, principles, or guidelines: secularism, populism, revolutionism, nationalism, statism, and republicanism.

⁹Ruşen Çakir, *Ne Şeriat Ne Demokrasi: Refah Partisini Anlamak* (Istanbul: Metis Yayinlari, 1994), 170, 171.

¹⁰The *Şeyh-ül-Islam* used to be the spiritual leader of the Islamic world. The *Şeyh-ül-Islam* also had law-giving powers such as the power to issue a *fetwa* (decree) to have the sultan deposed and the power to declare holy war.

¹¹NTV feature on Turks in Germany. The leader of the Islamist party tradition, composed of the Nationalist Order Party (MNP), the Nationalist Safety Party (MSP), and the Welfare Party (RP) is Necmettin Erbakan. The two major Islamist parties, the Felicity Party (SP), following the closing down of the Virtue Party (FP), and the Justice and Development Party (AKP) that were functioning at the time of this writing, are the successors of this tradition starting with the 1970s and sharing power with social democratic governments.

¹²*Hürriyet*, 27 December 1997.

¹³Mosque associations not only provide sites for purposes of *ibadet* (prayer), but they also function as providers of social solidarity through a variety of activities. The difference in the functions of mosques in Europe and in Turkey also constitutes the main difference in the role played by religion in peoples' lives in both settings. Mosques and mosque associations have a much more comprehensive, all-encompassing social function for migrants. Whereas in Turkey mosques have the relatively limited function of serving primarily as places for prayer, mosque associations in Europe have sports clubs, offer vocational programs, a variety of

courses, give services to help migrants cope with host society demands as well as serve as institutions of political education.

[14] *WDR Exklusiv*, 19 August 1994.

[15] Ergun Poyraz, *Refah'in Gerçek Yüzü* (Ankara: Poyraz Yayinlari, 1996), 146.

[16] Kadir Canatan, *Avrupa'da Müslüman Azinliklar* (Istanbul: Insan Yayinlari 1995).

[17] Ibid.

[18] Yasemin Karakaşoğlu and Gerd Nonneman, "Muslims in Germany, With Special Reference to the Turkish-Islamic Community," in *Muslim Communities in the New Europe*, ed. Gerd Nonneman, Tim Niblock, and Bogdan Szajkowski (New York: Ithaca Press, 1996), 241–269.

[19] *Verfassungsschutzbericht*, 1997, 128.

[20] *Verfassungsschutzbericht*, 1997, 130.

[21] The controversy lied in the fact that eight years of mandatory schooling would prevent children from going to Islamic schools at a younger and more impressionable age. These reforms were implemented in 1998, with the backing of the military and the secularist establishment, against strong protests by the Islamists.

[22] *Verfassungsschutzbericht Bayern*, 1998.

[23] Yasemin Karakaşoğlu and Gerd Nonneman, "Muslims in Germany, With Special Reference to the Turkish-Islamic Community," in *Muslim Communities in the New Europe*, ed. Gerd Nonneman et.al, (New York: Ithaca Press, 1996).

[24] Whether the IGMG and partisan Islam in Turkey contribute to the incorporation of religion peacefully into the existing political system and thereby to the taming of the militant elements among the fundamentalist camps or whether they engage in a holy war by using soft power against the system is a question that can be traced to the ongoing philosophical debate about the compatibility of Islam with democracy. While Turkey may benefit from the organizational experiences of Islam in Western democracies, there are flows that suggest that the IGMG also intends to participate in Turkish politics through unconventional methods. At more than one occasion, Turkish authorities have seized trucks headed to Turkey with weapons loaded from mosques in Germany that belong to the IGMG. *Hürriyet*, March 14 1999.

[25] *Milli Gazete*, 24 February 1997.

[26] *Milli Gazete*, 27 September 1997.

[27] Nermin Abadan-Unat, "Ethnic Business, Ethnic Communities, and Ethno-Politics among Turks in Europe," in *Immigration into Western Societies: Problems and Policies*, ed. Emek M. Ucarer and Donald J. Puchala (London and Washington: Pinter, 1997), 245.

[28] The Berlin-based AYPA-TV has gone into the Guinness World Records as the world's smallest television station. The station has been operating for seven years because of the personal motivation and contribution of two people, who do everything from research, to interviewing, recording, editing, and bookkeeping. The entire AYPA-TV staff consists of Ali Yildirim, Turkish, and Claudia Danschke, German. The station's general political orientation is left-of-center and the two employees say that they are watchdogs of the Islamists' activities in Berlin. Their particular focus has been on researching the connections between new associations and the IGMG and warning German authorities about these connections.

²⁹Ali Yildirim, "Kamuoyunu Aldattilar," *The Turkish Times*, 1 March 2000.

³⁰Yasemin Karakaşoğlu and Gerd Nonneman, "Muslims in Germany, With Special Reference to the Turkish-Islamic Community," in *Muslim Communities in the New Europe*, ed. Gerd Nonneman et.al. (New York: Ithaca Press, 1996). Their business enterprises included Tek-Bir GmbH, Selam Video, Cassette, and Music, Ittifak, Islam Tekaful Kurumu (Sparkasse und Versicherungsgesellschaft). MÜSIAD member businesses operate according to Islamic rules of interest-free banking and commerce.

³¹Enis Berberoğlu, "Yeşil Sermayenin 150 Milyar Marklik Avi," *Hurriyet*, 19 February 1999.

³²Ibid.

³³*Dünya*, 12 June 1999.

³⁴"Islami Sermaye Bavulla Bir Milyar Mark Getirmis," *Hürriyet*, 10 June 1999. "Yine Islami Holding Kuryesi Yakalandi" *Hürriyet*, 7 February 1999.

³⁵ Established in 1982 in Berlin and 1984 in Cologne, DITIB encompasses 740 associations and has 110 thousand members across Europe. Since the middle of 1970s, with the participation of the Islamist MSP and the ultranationalist MHP in coalition governments, DIB was run by the representatives of these anti-secular parties. DIB naturally had affected and politicized DITIB, since the DITIB personnel are appointed and sent by DIB.

³⁶Yasemin Karakasoğlu and Gerd Nonneman, "Muslims in Germany, With Special Reference to the Turkish-Islamic Community," in *Muslim Communities in the New Europe*, ed. Gerd Nonneman et al., (New York: Ithaca Press, 1996).

³⁷Specifically, he was the provincial director of religious affairs (*muftu*) in the province of Adana.

³⁸*Süddeutsche Zeitung*, 10/11 April 1999.

³⁹*Hürriyet*, 28 April 1997. These dates are *national*, and therefore secular holidays in Turkey.

⁴⁰This movement is no longer associated with Kurdism.

⁴¹The web site http://www.igmg.de links the visitor to the Office of the Prime Minister of the Republic of Turkey, to the Turkish embassy in Berlin, the Turkish Human Rights Organization (*Mazlumder*), the Fatih Mosque in Mannheim, Germany, the North American National Outlook Organization (KAMGT), and to the State Statistical Institute (DIE).

⁴²Ilhan Bilgu, "Ideolojik Körlük veya Kutsal Devlet Tapinisi," *Milli Görüş* 61,1999.

⁴³Fetullah Gülen is the leader of a spin-off sect from the Cemaat-i Nur. He was successful, for a while, in projecting the image of a moderate and liberal Islamist. He did this by not alienating state elites, by rubbing elbows with journalists and intellectuals, and by adopting a discourse of human rights, civil society, democracy, secularism and so on. Gülen is particularly active in the area of education, with his own schools and dormitories. Gülen has 200 secondary schools in 54 countries, particularly concentrated in the former Soviet republics, but ranging over countries from Afghanistan to Denmark. He is also known for his close relations with the United States. In 1998, videotapes of Gülen's interviews in New York rocked the Turkish public agenda. In these interviews Gülen was discussing various strategies of capturing the Turkish state apparatus and bringing Islam and the Koran to political power. For a

detailed analysis of Gülen and his following see Faik Bulut, *Kim Bu Fetullah Gülen? Dünü, Bugünü, Hedefi* (Cağaloğlu, Istanbul: Ozan Yayincilik, 1998).

[44]Tanil Bora, "Die Gründe und Dynamiken des Nationalistischen Strebens bzw. Aufkommens in der Türkei." In *Türkischer Nationalismus und "Graue Wölfe,"* 4–19. (Berlin: AstA TU, 1996).

XI
Conclusion

BEFORE CONCLUDING THIS DISCUSSION, SOME CAVEATS NEED TO BE SPELLED out. The first caveat is about Turkey's relations with Europe. The role migrant communities play in Turkish politics is in good part framed by Turkey's interaction with the European Union. This may make the generalization of Turkey's experiences onto other cases more difficult. A somewhat specific set of circumstances makes up the contextual framework that enables Turkey to be more sensitive and even vulnerable to Western influences. But this does not have to mean that transnational influences on states are only possible in such contexts. Similar activities of migrants in the United States, from different national, ethnic, and religious backgrounds, toward their lands of origin would demonstrate that case specificity in this sense may not handicap comparable future studies.

A second case-specific caveat is about the choice of Germany as the host environment. One may argue that there are characteristics attributable specifically to Germany, which may facilitate the very emergence of Deutschkei. Those characteristics make the Turkish experience in Germany somewhat different from Turkish experience in more liberal polities, such as in the Netherlands, France, or Sweden. However, further studies should have little difficulty demonstrating similar, although more diffused, patterns of interaction with the homeland on the part of the members of the Turkish diaspora in these latter countries. Sweden is a good example in this respect.

Since this is a *single-case* study, it shares the potential problems generally attributable to research designs that rely on one or a small number of cases. Indeed, in its current form, this study is more a work in political anthropology than in law-generating political science. It discusses a single case in terms of a body of literature pertinent to it. The idea is that general theories might shed some light on the case and the data specific to the case might change or confirm theories. This interplay between general and specific work, between comparative generalizations and configurative data is what Harry Eckstein calls a "theoretical case study."[1] Theoretical case studies interpret specific cases through established generalizations. But they also necessarily imply the strong assumption that the single cases studied are not unique in one or both of two senses: first, that what is the case in the case studied may also be substantially the case elsewhere, and second, that there are general principles which can account for any distinctive characteristics of the case at hand.[2] In other words, whatever specificity the case at hand may have may be explained by general theories that apply to other cases. The key is more research that can build upon this one.

Another point of contention may lie in the argument that when local cultures are transnationalized, they undergo change and that the hybrid culture, which comes out of the process, has neither the land of origin nor the receiving culture as its main reference point. In other words, the Turkish experience in the transnational space may not be Türkei in Deutschland (Turkey in Germany as it is argued here) but rather Deutschkei as a brand new political formation, existing on its own terms.

Çağlar for example talks about the, scholarly or otherwise, problematization of migrants' experience and identity in negative "neither-nor" terms, whereby the migrant is neither a Turk nor a German, neither French nor Algerian. Alternatively, she argues, this "in-between-ness" may be interpreted in positive terms whereby the *creolizing* influences of transnationalism are seen as producers of new cultures.[3]

Indeed, there are numerous examples of creole or *syncretic* cultures that are produced in transnational spaces. When writing about the transnational connectivity between San Agustin, Oaxaca and Poughkeepsie, NewYork, Alison Mountz and Richard Wright call this new transnational locale *[OP]*, short for *Oaxaca-Poughkeepsie*.[4] Ayumi Takenaka writes that Japanese Peruvians across the Pacific created their own ethnic identity as *Nikkei*, distinct from others by exploiting their international ties and resources. In the case of the *Nikkei*, maintaining transnational ties have accentuated migrants' group boundaries both within the sending and the receiving counties.[5] Nina Glick-Schiller and Georges Fouron discuss how Haitian transnational identity represents a unique category and write that "[n]either the category of race nor that of ethnicity as presently formulated can encompass the experience of populations whose existence is defined across national borders."[6]

If it is true, along these lines, that transnational spaces have characteristics significantly different from their original localities, to what degree of confidence can it be claimed that Deutschkei is a good place to look for the politics of Turkey? Does this not problematize the argument presented here?

The answer lies in the already discussed processes of ghettoization in the receiving society and the maintenance of identification with and interest in the homeland, pervasive even in later generations. It should be repeated that there are powerful forces in the diaspora that deliberately hinder integration or even adaptation to the foreign cultures. Therefore, integration into host societies may not be taken for granted. The Turkish transnational space exists not in Germany (because most migrants do not assimilate, adapt, or integrate) and not in Turkey (because they are deterritorialized for either economic or political reasons). Rather, they exist in the transnational space that can best be described as Deutschkei. Deutschkei is neither quite Türkei nor quite Deutschland. Nevertheless, it is much more Turkei than it is Deutschland in its overall disposition, which is maintained over several generations.

THE TURKISH DIASPORA IN THE UNITED STATES

Like other developing countries, Turkey is affected significantly by the United States' economic, foreign, and global policies. Turkey's NATO membership and the long-standing alliance with the United States certainly make this country an important factor in Turkey's "development." In the 1980s and the 1990s, Turks and Turkey have become particularly receptive and responsive to American cultural products, investment, aid, and diplomacy.

It is estimated that there are around 300 thousand Turks and Turkish-Americans in the United States. Unlike migration to Europe, however, Turkish migration to the United States is marked not by blue-collar labor, but rather by the "brain drain" of students and professionals. Most Turkish migrants to America are from urban middle class background, literate, economically well off, and have direct and better access to new technologies, such as personal computers and the Internet, which facilitate transnational connections.

Recent direct flights between New York and Istanbul or Chicago and Istanbul have made travel between the two countries almost easier than traveling within the United States. New grassroots and umbrella organizations like the Assembly of Turkish-American Associations (ATAA) have galvanized, in recent years, a Turkish-American lobby focused primarily, if not exclusively, on counter-balancing Greek and Armenian pressures on the United States Congress to pass legislation critical of Turkey.

Similar to their cousins in Germany, Turks in the United States are just as indexed to political developments in Turkey. The Turkish media are much more sensitive to events in the United States, to the activities of Turks in the United States, and of Turkish-Americans. This picture raises the question whether a Habermasian critical public sphere has a better chance of being formed in the transnational space between the United States and Turkey.

The answer would have to be a cautious no. First, Turkish associational activities in the United States are rather diffuse and not nearly as vibrant as those in Europe. The sheer size of the United States, although circumvented to some extent by new communication and transportation technologies, contributes to this fragmentation. Some groups' presence, like that of Alevis or Kurds, is marginal, mostly confined to the East coast and particularly to New York.

Second, in part because of their socioeconomic background, Turks in the United States generally do not rely on dense networks and could and do operate individually, in their private and professional lives. Not subject to ghettoizing pressures, they mingle with other migrants and the members of the host society freely and develop interests that include Turkey, but are more multidimensional than those of migrants from Turkey settled in Europe.

Finally, apart from the exception of the Islamists (who actually form a *community of believers* in the United States, rather than a collection of groups *qua nations*), because of the relative lack of ghettoization, migrants from Turkey in the United States do not raise existential constitutional questions with respect to the Turkish state. That is, they are generally more inclined to see to the preservation of the existing political system in Turkey. Most politically significant activity among Turkish nationals and Turkish-Americans is directed towards affecting American foreign policy in order to preserve the existing set of relations with respect to Cyprus, the Armenian issue, the Kurdish question, national borders in the Middle East, and so forth. One main exception to this preservationist drive is the support for Turkey's entrance into the European Union.

FINAL REMARKS

Transnationalism promises to be a pervasive and prevalent phenomenon in the future. Indeed, in the literature on migration there is increasing discussion about a new kind of migrant: a so-called "transmigrant," who moves back and forth across borders, creates and lives in transnational entities that are mainly extensions of their countries of origin, and participates politically, economically, and otherwise in *both* sending as well as receiving polities. The focus here was on the extraterritorial dimension of the national public sphere of the origin; namely, the transnational public sphere created by transmigrants.

NOTES

[1] Harry Eckstein, *Division and Cohesion in Democracy: A Study of Norway* (New Jersey: Princeton University Press, 1966).

[2] Ibid.

[3] Ayşe Çağlar, "The Greywolves as Metaphor," in *State and Society in Turkey*, ed. Nukhet Sirman and Andrew Finkel (London: Routledge, 1991), 79–101.

[4] Alison Mountz and Richard A. Wright, "Daily Life in the Transnational Migrant Community of San Agustin, Oaxaca, and Poughkeepsie, New York," *Diaspora* 5 (1996), 403–428.

[5] Ayumi Takenaka, "Transnational Community and its Ethnic Consequences: The Return of Migration and its Transformation of Ethnicity of Japanese Peruvians," *International Migration* 42:9 (June–July 1999).

[6] Nina Glick-Schiller and Georges E. Fouron, "Terrains of Blood and Nation: Haitian Transnational Social Fields," *Ethnic and Racial Studies* 22 (March 1999), 341.

Bibliography

Abadan Unat, Nermin et al., eds. *Turkish Workers in Europe, 1960–1975: A Socioeconomic Reappraisal.* London: Leiden: D.J. Brill, 1976.
———. "Impact of External Migration on Rural Turkey." In *Culture and Economy*, ed. Paul Stirling, 201–216. Cambridgeshire: The Eothen Press, 1993.
———. "Turkey: Late Entrant into Europe's Workforce." In *The Politics of Migration Policies: Settlement and Integration: The First World into the 1990s*, ed. Daniel Kubat, 307–336. New York: Center for Migration Studies, 1993.
Abdullah, Salim M. "Muslims in Germany." In *Muslim Minorities in the West*, ed. Syed Z. Abedin and Ziauddin Sardar. London: Grey Seal, 1995.
———. "Ethnic Business, Ethnic Communities, and Ethno-Politics among Turks in Europe." In *Immigration into Western Societies: Problems and Policies*, ed. Emek M. Ucarer and Donald J. Puchala, 229–255. London and Washington: Pinter, 1997.
Abedin, Syed Z. and Ziauddin Sardar. *Muslim Minorities in the West.* London: Grey Seal, 1995.
Ackermann, Andreas. "Ethnologische Migrationsforschung: Ein Überblick." *Kea* 10 (1997): 1–28.
Adler, Stephen. "Emigration and Development in Algeria: Doubts and Dilemmas." In *Guests Come to Stay: The Effects of European Labor Migration on Sending and Receiving Countries*, ed. Rosemarie Rogers, 263–284. Boulder and London: Westview Press, 1985.
———. *International Migration and Dependence.* Hampshire: Gower Publications, 1977.

———. *The Turkish Conundrum: Emigration, Politics, and Development, 1961–1980.* Geneva: ILO, 1981, 1984.

Ahmed, Ishtiaq. "Exit, Voice, and Citizenship." In *International Migration, Immobility, and Development: A Multidisciplinary Perspective*, eds. Hammar, Tomas, Grete Brochmann, Kristof Tamas and Thomas Faist, 159–185. Oxford: Berg, 1997.

Althusser, Louis. *Lenin and Philosophy and the Other Essays.* London: New Left Books, 1971.

Anderson, Benedict. *Imagined Communities.* London and New York: Verso, 1983.

Andrews, Peter Alford. *Ethnic Groups in the Republic of Turkey.* Wiesbaden: Dr Ludwig Reichert Verlag, 1989.

Apitzsch, Gisela and Norbert Dittmar. "Integration or Repatriation?" *UNESCO Courier* (September 1985).

Appadurai, Arjun. "The Production of Locality." In *Counterworks: Managing the Diversity of Knowledge.* Richard Fardon, ed. 204–225. London: Routledge, 1995.

———. *Modernity at Large: Cultural Dimensions of Globalization.* Minneapolis and London: University of Minnesota Press, 1996.

Appiah, Anthony K. foreword. In Saskia Sassen, *Globalization and its Discontents.* New York: the New Press, 1998.

Appleyard, Reginald T., ed. *The Impact of International Migration on Developing Countries.* Paris: Development Center of the Organization for Economic Co-Operation and Development, 1989.

———. "Migration and Development: A Global Agenda for the Future." *International Migration* 30 (1992): 17–32.

Argun, Betigül Ercan. "Universal Citizenship Rights and Turkey's Kurdish Question." *Journal of Muslim Minority Affairs* 19:1 (April 1999), 85–103.

Asch, Beth J. and Courtland Reichmann, ed. *Emigration and its Effects on the Sending Country.* Rand, 1994.

Aydin, Ahmet. *Kürtler, PKK, ve A. Ocalan.* Ankara: Kiyap, 1992.

Balli, Rafet. *Kürt Dosyasi.* Istanbul: Cem Yayinevi, 1991.

Basch, Linda G., Nina Glick-Schiller, and Christina Blanc-Szanton. *Nations Unbound: Transnational Projects, Post-Colonial Predicaments, and De-Territorialized Nation-States.* Langhorne, PA: Gordin and Breach, 1994.

Bauböck, Rainer. "Migration and Citizenship," *New Community* 81:1 (1991).

Baumann, Gerd and Thijl Sunier, *Post-Migration Ethnicity: De-Essentializing Cohesion, Commitments, and Comparison.* Amsterdam: Het Spinhuis Publishers.

Baydar-Engin, Oya. "Die Kehrseite der Auswanderung—die Rückkehr: Fakten,

Probleme, Forschung, Theorien." In *Türkische Migranten in der Bundesrepublik Deutschland*, ed. Sami Özkara, 288–297. Köln: Önel Verlag, 1990.

Bayer, Yalcin. "Yeter Söz Milletin." *Hürriyet*. January 17, 1999.

———. "Yeter Söz Milletin." *Hürriyet*. January 23, 1999.

———. "Yeter Söz Milletin." *Hürriyet*. February 10, 1999.

———. "Yeter Söz Milletin." *Hürriyet*. February 11, 1999.

Beck, Ulrich. *Was ist Globalisierung?* Edition Zweite Moderne. Frankfurt: Suhrkamp, 1998.

———, ed. *Perspektiven der Weltgesellschaft*. Edition zweite Moderne. Frankfurt: Suhrkamp, 1998.

Bell, Daniel. "The 'Public Sphere,' the State, and the World of Law in Eighteenth Century France." *French Historical Studies* 17 (Fall 1992): 912–934.

Berman, Sheri. "Civil Society and the Collapse of the Weimar Republic." *World Politics* 49 (April 1997): 401–429.

Bieber, Florian. *Ethnic Conflicts in Kosovo and Turkish Kurdistan*. April 1998. Athens: AIM.

Bjorgo, Tore and Rob Witte, eds. *Racist Violence in Europe*. St. Martin's Press, 1997.

Bora, Tanil and Kemal Can. "1980'li Yillarda Faşist Hareket." *Birikim* 10 (February 1990): 37–49.

———. *Devlet, Ocak, Dergah: 12 Eylül'den 1990'lara Ülkücü Hareket*. Istanbul: Iletisim Yayinlari, 1994.

Bora, Tanil. *Milliyetçiliğin Kara Bahari*. Istanbul: Birikim Yayinlari, 1995.

———. "Die Gründe und Dynamiken des Nationalistischen Strebens bzw. Aufkommens in der Türkei." In *Türkischer Nationalismus und "Graue Wolfe,"* 4–19. (Berlin: AstA TU, 1996).

Bourne, R. "Transnational America," *Atlantic Monthly* 118 (1916), 86–97.

Boyd, Monica. "Family and Personal networks in International Migration: recent Developments and New Agendas. *International Migration Review* 23:3 (1989).

Brubaker, Roger. *Citizenship and Nationhood in France and Germany*. Cambridge, Mass.: Harvard University Press, 1992.

Cady, Linell. *Religion, Theology, and American Public Life*. Albany: State University of New York Press, 1993.

Cağlar, Ayşe. *The Prison House of Culture in the Studies of Turks in Germany*. Sozialanthropologische Arbeitspapiere. Freie Universitaet Berlin, Institut for Ethnologie, Schwerpunkt Sozialanthropologie (1990).

———. "The Greywolves as Metaphor." In *State and Society in Turkey*, eds.

Nükhet Sirman and Andrew Finkel, 79–101. London: Routledge, 1991.
———. German Turks in Berlin: Social Exclusion and Strategies for Social Mobility. *New Community* 21:3 (1995), 309–323.
Çakir, Ruşen. *Ne Şeriat, Ne Demokrasi.* Istanbul: Metis Yayinlari, 1994.
Caloun, Craig, ed. *Habermas and the Public Sphere.* Cambridge, Mass.: The MIT Press, 1992.
———. "Civil Society and the Public Sphere." *Public Culture* 5 (1993): 267–280.
Çalişlar, Oral. *Öcalan ve Burkay'la Kürt Sorunu.* Istanbul: Pencere Yayinlari, 1993.
Canatan, Kadir. *Avrupa'da Müslüman Azinliklar.* Istanbul: Insan Yayinlari, 1995.
Canfalonieri, M. "La Rimesse degli emigranti e l'economia delle zone di partenza." *Studi Emigrazione* 16 (March 1979) 5–41.
Casanova, Jose. *Public Religions in the Modern World.* Chicago and London: The University of Chicago Press, 1994.
Castles, Stephen and Mark J. Miller. *The Age of Migration: International Population Movements in the Modern World.* Second Edition. rev. and updated. Houndmills, Basingstoke, Hampshire: Macmillan, 1993, 1998.
Cem, Ismail. "Ottoman-Turkish Interpretation of Islam on Ethnicity." Interview with the *French Daily L'Express*, Ankara: 12/15/1998.
Cerase, F. "Expectations and Reality: A Case Study of Return Migration from the United States to Southern Italy," *International Migration Review* 8, (1974), 245–262.
Chaliand, Gerard and Jean-Pierre Rageau. *The Penguin Atlas of Diasporas.* Penguin Books, 1995.
Chapin, Wesley D. "The Turkish Diaspora in Germany." *Diaspora* 5:2 (1996).
Chepulis, R. "Migration Policies and Return Migration with Particular Reference to Yugoslavia" *Studi Emigrazione* 28 (September 1981), 319–355.
Cinel, Daniel. *The National Integration of Italian Return Migration, 1870–1929,* (1991).
Clifford, James. "Diasporas." *Cultural Anthropology.* 9:3 (1994), 302–338.
Çölaşan, Emin. "Şer Yuvalari." *Hürriyet.* 3/25/1999.
Conner, Walker. "The Impact of Homelands upon Diasporas." In *Modern Diasporas in International Politics.* Gabriel Sheffer, ed. 16–47. London and Sydney: Croom Helm, 1986.
Copeaux, Etienne. *Tarih Ders Kitaplarinda (1931–1993) Türk Tarih Tezinden Türk Islam Sentezine.* Translated by Ali Berktay. Istanbul: Tarih Vakfi Yurt Yayinlari, 1998.

Coşkun, Zeki. *Aleviler, Sünniler, ve Öteki Sivas*. Cağaloğlu, Istanbul: Iletişim Yayinlari, 1995.

Dalman, Metin and Ismail Tabak. *Avrupa'da Insan Ticareti ve PKK*. Istanbul: Türk-Alman Basin Ajansi (DTPA), 1995.

Demir, Vedat. *Türkiye'de Medya ve Özdenetimi*. Istanbul: Iletişim Yayinlari, 1998.

Di Leonardi, Michaela. *The Varieties of Ethnic Experience: Kinship, Class, and Gender among California Italian Americans*. Ithaca, NewYork: Cornell University Press, 1984.

Diaz-Briquets, Sergio cited in Papademetriou, Demetrios G. and Philip L. Martin. eds. 1991. *The Unsettled Relationship: Labor Migration and Economic Development*. Foreword by Diego C. Asencio. New York: Greenwood Press, 1990.

Dressler, Markus. *Vom Ulu Önder zum Mehdi – Zur Darstellung Mustafa Kemal's in den Alevitischen Zeitschriften Cem und Nefes*. Istanbul: Orient-Institut der Deutschen Morgenlandischen Gesellschaft, 1996.

Ebiri, Kutlay. "The Impact of Labor Migration on the Turkish Economy." In *Guests Come to Stay: The Effects of European Labor Migration on Sending and Receiving Countries*, ed. Rosemarie Rogers, 207–231. Boulder and London: Westview Press, 1985.

Eckstein, Harry. *Division and Cohesion in Democracy: A Study of Norway*. Princeton, New Jersey: Princeton University Press, 1966.

Elazar, Daniel, "The Jewish People as the Classic Diaspora: A Political Analysis." In *Modern Diasporas in International Politics*, ed. Gabriel Sheffer, 212–258. London and Sydney: Croom Helm, 1986.

Erbektaş, Sinan. "Die Aleviten in Europa." In *Wie der Phoenix aus der Asche: Renaissance des Alevismus*, eds. Vorhoff, Karin, Barbara Frischmuth, Martin Greve, and Sinan Erbektas, 103–105. Cologne: AABF Publications, 1998.

Ergil, Doğu. *Doğu Sorunu: Teşhisler ve Tespitler*. Özel Araştirma Raporu. TOBB, 1995.

Esman, M.J. "The Political Fallout of International Migration," *Diaspora* 2:1, (1992).

Faist, Thomas. *A Preliminary Analysis of Political-Institutional Aspects of International Migration: Internationationalization, Transnationalization, and Internal Globalization*. Bremen: Center for Social Policy Research, ZeS-Arbeitspapier, Nr. 10/95, (1995).

———. "From Common Questions to Common Concepts." In *International Migration, Immobility, and Development: A Multidisciplinary Perspective*, eds. Hammar, Tomas, Grete Brochmann, Kristof Tamas and Thomas Faist, eds. 247–276. Oxford: Berg, 1997.

———. "The Crucial Meso-Level." In *International Migration, Immobility, and Development: A Multidisciplinary Perspective*, eds. Hammar, Tomas, Grete Brochmann, Kristof Tamas and Thomas Faist, eds. 187–217. Oxford: Berg, 1997.

Fandy, Mamoun. "CyberResistance: Saudi Opposition Between Globalization and Localization." *Comparative Studies in Society and History* 41:1 (1999), 124–147.

Fardon, Richard, ed. *Counterworks: Managing the Diversity of Knowledge.* London: Routledge, 1995.

Fawcett, James T. "Networks, Linkages, and Migration Systems." *International Migration Review* 23 (1989), 671–680.

Feis, Herbert. *Europe: The World's Banker (1870–1894): An Account of European Foreign Investment and the Connection of World Finance with Diplomacy Before the War.* Yale University Press, 1930.

Fierlbeck, Katherine. "The Ambivalent Potential of Cultural Identity." *Canadian Journal of Political Science* 29:1 (1996), 3–22.

Fischer, Alfred Joachim. "Deutsche Emigranten in der Türkei." In *Das Türkische Berlin*, eds. Martin Greve and Tülay Çinar, 10–12. Berlin: Die Auslaenderbeauftragte des Senats, 1998.

Foucault, Michel. *Discipline and Punish: The Birth of the Prison.* Translated by Alan Sheridan. New York: Vintage Books, 1977.

Frank, Andre Gunder. *The Development of Underdevelopment.* Boston, New England: The Free Press, 1966.

Garcia, Maria Christina. "Hardliners v. 'Dialogueros': Cuban Exile Political Groups and United States' Cuba Policy." *Journal of American Ethnic History*. 17:4 (September 1998), 3.

Giddens, Anthony. *The Consequences of Modernity.* Stanford, CA: Stanford University Press, 1990.

Gilroy, Paul. *There Ain't No Black in the Union Jack.* London: Hutchinson, 1987.

Gitmez, Ali and Czarina Wilpert. "A Micro-Society or an Ethnic Community? Social Organization and Ethnicity amongst Turkish Migrants in Berlin." In *Immigrant Associations in Europe*, ed. John Rex, Daniele Joly, and Czarina Wilpert, 86–124. Gower, 1987.

Glick-Schiller, Nina, Linda Basch, and Christina Blanc-Szanton. "Towards a Transnationalziation of Migration: Race, Class, Ethnicity, and Nationalism Reconsidered." *The Annals of the New York Academy of Sciences* 645. New York: New York Academy of Sciences. 1992.

———. "From Immigrant to Transmigrant: Theorizing Transnational Migration." *Anthropological Quarterly* 68 (January 1995): 48–63.

Glick-Schiller, Nina, and Georges E. Fouron. "Terrains of Blood and Nation:

Haitian Transnational Social Fields." *Ethnic and Racial Studies* 22 (March 1999): 340–367.
Gökdere, A. Y. *Yabanci Ülkelere Işgücü Akimi ve Türkiye Ekonomisi Uzerine Etkileri.* Ankara: Türkiye Iş Bankasi, 1978.
Gold, Steven J. "Transnationalism and Vocabularies of Motive in International Migration: The Case of Israelis in the United States." *Sociological Perspectives* 40:3 (Fall 1997), 409–428.
Goldring, Luin P., "Power and Status in Transnational Social Fields." In *Transnationalism From Below*, eds. Michael Peter Smith and Luis Eduardo Guarnizo, 165–195. New Brunswick, 1998.
Gonzalez, Nancie L. and Carolyn S. McCommon. *Conflict, Migration, and the Expression of Ethnicity.* Westview Press, 1989, 1995.
Gourevitch, Peter, "The Second Image Reversed," *International Organization* 32 (Autumn 1978), 881–912.
Greve, Martin and Tülay Çinar, eds. *Das Türkische Berlin.* Berlin: Ausländerbeauftragte des Senats, 1998.
Greve, Martin. "Türken in Berlin." In *Das Türkische Berlin.*, eds. Greve, Martin and Tülay Cinar, 12–18. Berlin: Die Ausländerbeauftragte des Senats, 1998.
Grossman, Lawrence K. *The Electronic Republic: Reshaping Democracy in the Information Age.* New York: Viking Penguin, 1995.
Guarnizo, Luis E. *One Country in Two: Dominican Owned Farms in the United States and the Dominican Republic.* Ph.D. Dissertation, Department of Sociology, The John Hopkins University, 1992.
Habermas, Jürgen. *The Philosophical Discourse of Modernity.* Translated by Frederick G. Lawrence. Cambridge, Masschussetts: The MIT Press, 1992.
———. *The Structural Transformation of the Public Sphere: An Inquiry into a Category of Bourgeois Society.* Translated by Thomas Burger with the assistance of Frederick Lawrence. Cambridge, Mass.: The MIT Press, 1996.
Hammar, Thomas, *Democracy and the Nation-State: Aliens, Denizens, and Citizens in a World of International Migration.* Aldershot, Hants, Englanad: Avebury, Brookfield, Vt., USA: Gower Publishing Co., 1990.
Hammar, Tomas, Grete Brochmann, Kristof Tamas and Thomas Faist, eds. *International Migration, Immobility, and Development: A Multidisciplinary Perspective.* Oxford: Berg, 1997.
Hannerz, Ulf. *Transnational Connection: Culture, People, Places.* London and New York: Routledge, 1996.
Hanioğlu, Şükrü M. *The Young Turks in Opposition.* Oxford and New York: Oxford University Press, 1995.

Hassanpour, Amir. "Satellite Footprints as National Borders: MED-TV and the Extraterritoriality of State Sovereignty." *Journal of Muslim Minority Affairs* 18 (1998): 53–72.

Heper, Metin, ed. *Strong State and Economic Interest Groups: The Post-1980 Turkish Experience.* Berlin and New York: Walter de Gruyter, 1991.

———. "Strong State as a Problem for the Consolidation of Democracy: Turkey and Germany Compared." *Comparative Political Studies* 25/2 (1992), 169–194.

———. *State Tradition in Turkey.* Beverly Hills: The Eothen Press, 1985.

Hermann, Rainer. *Political Islam in Turkey. A Lecture.* May 5, 1995. Beirut: Orient-Institut der Deutschen Morgenlaendischen Gesellschaft, 1997.

Hermele, Kenneth, "The Discourse on Migration and Development." In *International Migration, Immobility, and Development: A Multidisciplinary Perspective*, eds. Tomas Hammar, Grete Brochmann, Kristof Tamas and Thomas Faist eds., 133–159. (Oxford: Berg, 1997).

Herzfeld, Michael, ed. *European Identity and its Conceptual Roots.* Prospect Heights, Illinois: Waveland Press, 1996.

Hirschmann, Albert. *Exit, Voice, and Loyalty: Responses to Decline in Firms, Organizations, and States.* Cambridge, Mass.: Harvard University Press, 1978.

Holub, Robert C. *Jürgen Habermas: Critic in the Public Sphere.* London and New York: Routledge, 1991.

Honekopp, Elmar. *Zur Beruflichen und Sozialen Reintegration Türkischer Arbeitsmigranten im Zeitverlauf.* Nüremberg: Mimeographed, 1990.

Huntington, Samuel. "The Clash of Civilizations," *Foreign Affairs* 72:3 (Summer 1993), 22–48.

Jamin, Mathilde and Aytac Eryilmaz. *Fremde Heimat: Eine Geschichte der Einwanderung.* Essen: DOMIT, 1998.

Johnson, Robert A. "On the Teeter-Totter of Ego.: Interview. *Parabola* (Summer 1997):

———. *Owning your own Shadow: Understanding the Dark Side of the Psyche.* San Fransisco: Harper, 1991.

Jung, Carl Gustav. *Aion: Researches into the Phenomenology of the Self.* Princeton, New Jersey: Princeton University Press, 1968.

Kadioğlu, Ayşe. "Milletini Arayan Devlet." *Türkiye Günlüğü* 33, (March-April 1995), 91–101.

Kahin, Brian and Charles Nesson, eds. *Borders in Cyberspace: Information Policy and the Global Information Infrastructure.* Cambridge, Massachusetts and London: The MIT Press, 1997.

Kaldor, Mary, Barbara Einhorn, and Zdenek Kavan, eds. *Citizenship and Democratic Control in Contemporary Europe.* Cheltenham, England: Brookfield, Vt.: E. Elgar, 1996.

Karakaşoğlu, Yasemin and Gerd Nonneman. "Muslims in Germany, With Special Reference to the Turkish-Islamic Community." In *Muslim Communities in the New Europe,* ed. Gerd Nonneman, Tim Niblock, and Bogdan Szajkowski, New York: Ithaca Press, 1996.

Kearney, M. "The Local and the Global: The Anthropology of Globalization and Transnationalism." *Annual Review of Anthropology* 24 (1995): 547–565.

Keskin, Hakki. *Die Turkei: Vom Osmanischen Reich zum Nationalstaat.* Berlin: Olle & Walter, 1977.

Kress, Gunther. "Ideological Structures in Discourse." In *Handbook of Discourse Analysis,* ed. Teun Van Dijk A., 27–42. London and Orlando: Academic Press, 1985.

Kritz, Mary M, Lin Lean Lim, and Hania Zlotnik, eds. *International Migration Systems: A Global Approach.* Oxford: Clarendon Press, 1992.

Kubat, Daniel, ed. *The Politics of Migration Policies: Settlement and Integration: The First World into the 1990s,* New York: Center for Migration Studies, 1993.

Kumar, Krishan. "Civil Society: An Inquiry into the Usefulness of an Historical Term." *British Journal of Sociology* 44:3 (September 1993), 375–499.

Landolt, Patricia. *Salvadoran Transnationalism: Towards the Redefinition of National Community.* Working Paper 3 18. The Johns Hopkisn University, Program in Comparative and International Development, 2000. http://www.jhu.edu/~soc/pcid/papers/18.htm; Internet.

Lindo, Flip. 1995. Ethnic Myth or Ethnic Might? On the Divergence in Educational Attainment between Portuguese and Turkish Youth in the Netherlands. In *Post-Migration Ethnicity: De-Essentializing Cohesion, Commitments, and Comparison,* eds. Gerd Baumann and Thijl Sunier, 144–164. Amsterdam: Het Spinhuis Publishers.

Luke, Timothy. *From Nationality to Nodality: How the Politics of Being Digital Transforms Globalization.* Ultibase. http://ultibase.rmit.edu.au/Articles/luke2.html; Internet. Oct 7, 1998, 1–22.

Lustick, Ian. *Hegemony and the Riddle of Nationalism: The Dialectics of Political Identity in the Middle East.* Unpublished paper, 1996.

Macfie, A. L. *Profiles in Power: Ataturk.* London and New York: Longman, 1994.

Mahler, Sarah J. "Theoretical and Empirical Contributions Toward a Research Agenda for Transnationalism." In Michael Peter Smith and Luis Eduardo Guarnizo, eds. *Transnationalism From Below,* 64–103. New Brunswick,

New Jersey: Transaction Publishers, 1998.

Mandel, Ruth. "Ethnicity and Identity Among Migrant Workers in West Berlin." In *Conflict, Migration, and the Expression of Ethnicity*, ed. Nancie L. Gonzalez and Carolyn S. McCommon. Westview Press, 1989, 1995

Marcus, George E. and Michael M. Fischer. *Anthropology as Cultural Critique: An Experimental Moment in the Human Sciences.* Second Edition. Chicago and London: The University of Chicago Press, 1986, 1989.

Marcus, George. "Ethnography in/of the World System: The Emergence of Multi-Sited Ethnography," *Annual Review of Anthropology* 24 (1995), 95–117.

Martin, Philip L. *Administering Foreign-Worker Programs: Lessons from Europe.* Lexington, Mass.: Lexington Books, 1982.

———. *The Unfinished Story: Turkish Labour Migration to Western Europe*, Geneva: ILO, 1991.

Massey, Douglas, et. al. "Theories of International Migration: A Review and Appraisal." *Population and Development Review* 19 (September 1993): 431–466.

Mastny, Vojtech and R. Craig Nation, eds. *Turkey Between East and West: New Challenges for a Rising Regional Power.* Boulder Colorado and Oxford: Westview Press, 1996

MED-TV. The Alevis: Expression at Last. http://www.ib.be/med/med-tv/sterka/issue03/alevi.htm.

Melikoff, Irene. *Haci Bektaş: Efsaneden Gerçeğe.* Istanbul: Cumhuriyet Kitaplari, 1998.

Mill, John Stuart. *On Liberty*, Indiana: Hackett Publishing, 1978.

Miller, Mark J. "The Political Impact of Foreign Labor: A Re-Evaluation of the Western European Experience." *International Migration Review* 16:1 (1980), 27–61.

———. *Foreign Workers in Western Europe: An Emerging Political Force.* New York: Praeger Publishers, 1981.

———. "The Challenge of Radical Islam," *Foreign Affairs* 72:4, (September-October 1993).

Mills, Sara. *Discourse: The New Critical Idiom.* London and New York: Routledge, 1997.

Mitchell, Katharyne. "Transnational Discourse: Bringing Geography Back In." *Antipode: A Racial Journal of Geography* 29 (1997), 101–114.

Mountz, Alison and Richard A. Wright. "Daily Life in the Transnational Migrant Community of San Agustin, Oaxaca, and Poughkeepsie, New York." *Diaspora* 5 (1996):

Müftüler-Bac, Meltem. *Turkey's Relations with a Changing Europe.* Manchester

and New York: Manchester University Press, 1997.
Mutlu, Servet. "Ethnic Kurds in Turkey: A Demographic Study." *International Journal of Middle Eastern Studies* 28 (1996), 517–541.
Nathans, Benjamin. "Habermas's 'Public Sphere' in the Era of the French Revolution." In *French Historical Studies* 16 (Spring 1990): 620–646.
Nettl, J. P. "The State as Conceptual Variable." *World Politics* 20:4 (1998), 559–592.
Neuloh, O. "Structural Unemployment in Turkey: Its Relation to Migration." In *Turkish Workers in Europe, 1960–1975: A Socioeconomic Reappraisal*, ed. Nermin Abadan Unat et. al. Leiden: D.J. Brill, 1976.
OECD Telecommunications Database, 1999. http://oecd.org/dsti/sti/it/stats/tcdata99.htm; Internet.
Oltayli, Ilber. *Osmanli Imparatorluğu'nda Alman Nüfuzu*. Istanbul: Iletisim Yayinlari, 1998.
Öncü, Ayşe. "Packaging Islam: Cultural Politics on the Landscape of Turkish Commercial Television." *New Perspectives on Turkey* 10 (Spring 1994): 13–36.
Oran, Baskin. *Atatürk Milliyetçiliği: Resmi Ideoloji Disi bir Inceleme*. (Kemalist Nationalism: An Inquiry Outside of the Official Ideology). Istanbul: Bilgi Yayinevi, 1988.
Özcan, Ertekin. *Türkische Immigrantenorganizationen in der Bundesrepublik Deutschland*. Berlin: Hitit Verlag, 1989.
Özdemir, Cem. *Ich bin ein Inländer. Ein Anatolischer Schwabe im Bundestag*. Munich: DTV Premium,1997.
Özkara, Sami, ed. *Türkische Migranten in der Bundesrepublik Deutschland*. Cologne: Önel Verlag, 1990.
Paine, Suzanne. *Exporting Workers: The Turkish Case*. London: Cambridge University Press, 1974.
Panossian, Razmik. *Nationality and Identity Differences in Homeland-Diaspora Relations*. ADK/Armenisch-Deutsche Korrespondenz, 1999. http://asbarez.com/archives/1999/99051 1rp.htm. May 1999.
Papademetriou, Demetrios G. and Philip L. Martin. eds. *The Unsettled Relationship: Labor Migration and Economic Development*. Foreword by Diego C. Asencio. New York: Greenwood Press, 1991.
Park, Robert E. cited in Andreas Ackermann, "Ethnologische Migrationsforschung: Ein Uberblick." *Kea* 10 (1997): 1–28.
Parla, Taha. *Türkiye'de Siyasi Kültürün Resmi Kaynaklari: Kemalist Tek Parti Ideolojisi ve CHP'nin Alti Ok'u*. Istanbul: Iletisim Yayinlari, 1995.
Penninx, Rinus. "A Critical Review of Theory and Practice: The Case of

Turkey." *International Migration Review*, 16/4 (1982), 781–818.

Piore, Michael J. *Birds of Passage: Migrant Labor and Industrial Societies*. Cambridge: Cambridge University Press, 1979.

Pope, Nicole and Hugh Pope. *Turkey Unveiled: A History of Modern Turkey*. Woodstock and New York: The Overlook Press, 1997.

Portes, Alejandro. "Transnational Communities: Their Emergence and Significance in the Contemporary World System." Working Papers Series, 16 (April 1995). www.jhu.edu/~soc/.ladark/.workingpapers/.16; Intrenet.

———. "Global Villagers: The Rise of Transnational Communities." *American Prospect* 25 (March/April 1996): 74–77.

Poyraz, Ergün. *Refah'in Gerçek Yüzü*. Ankara: Poyraz Yayinlari, 1996.

Pries, Ludger. "Transnationale Soziale Räume." In *Perspektiven der Weltgesellschaft*, ed. Ulrich Beck, 55–87. Edition Zweite Moderne. Frankfurt: Suhrkamp, 1998.

Quenk, Naomi L. *Besides Ourselves: Our Hidden Personality in Everyday Life*. Palo Alto, California: CPP Books, 1993.

Ralle, Bianka. *Modernisierung und Migration am Beispiel der Türkei*. Saarbrucken and Fort Lauderdale: Verlag Breitenbach Publishers, 1981.

Rex, John, Daniele Joly, and Czarina Wilpert. *Immigrant Associations in Europe*. Gower, 1987.

Rheingold, Howard. *The Virtual Community: Homesteading on the Electronic Frontier*. Reading, Mass.: Addison-Wesley Publishing Co., 1993.

Roberts, Bryan R., Reanne Frank, and Fernando Lozano-Ascencio. "Transnational Migrant Communities and Mexican Migration to the US." *Ethnic and Racial Studies* 22 (March 1999): 238–267.

Robertson, Roland. "Glokalisierung: Homogenitaet und Heterogenitaet in Raum und Zeit." In *Perspektiven der Weltgesellschaft*, ed. Ulrich Beck, 192–221. Edition Zweite Moderne. Frankfurt: Suhrkamp, 1998.

Robins, Kevin, *Negotiating Spaces: Media and Cultural Practices in the Turkish Diaspora in Britain, France, and Germany*. 1999.

Rogers, Rosemarie, ed. *Guests Come to Stay: The Effects of European Labor Migration on Sending and Receiving Countries*. Boulder and London: Westview Press, 1985.

Russell, Sharon Stanton. "Remittances from International Migration: A Review in Perspective." *World Development* 14:6 (1986), 677–696.

Safran, William. "Diasporas in Modern Societies: Myths of Homeland and Return." *Diaspora* (Spring 1991): 83–99.

Said, Edward, *Culture and Imperialism*. New York: Alfred A. Knopf, 1993.

Samuels, Andrew et. al, *A Critical Dictionary of Jungian Analysis*. London: Routledge, 1986.

Sassen, Saskia. *Globalization and its Discontents*. New York: the New Press, 1998.
Sayari, Sabri. "Migration Policies of Sending Countries: Perspectives on the Turkish Experience." *Annals of the American Academy of Political and Social Sciences* 485 (May 1986):
Schmitter-Heisler, Barbara. "Sending Countries and the Politics of Emigration and Destination." *International Migration Review* 19 (1983): 469–484.
Schwarz, Klaus. "Ein Rückblick." In *Das Türkische Berlin*, eds. Martin Greve and Tülay Cinar, 7–10. Berlin: Die Ausländerbeauftragte des Senats, 1998.
Seidel, Gill. "Political Discourse Analysis." In *Handbook of Discourse Analysis*, ed. Teun A. Van Dijk, 43–60. London and Orlando: Academic Press, 1985.
Seligman, Adam. *The Idea of Civil Society*. New York: The Free Press, 1992.
Şen, Faruk. *Ankara-Bonn Hatti*. Ankara and Cologne: Onel-Verlag, 1997.
———. "Turkish Communities in Western Europe." In *Turkey Between East and West: New Challenges for a Rising Regional Power*. Vojtech Mastny and R. Craig Nation, eds. 223–267. Boulder Colorado and Oxford: Westview Press, 1996.
———. *Türkische Migranten in Deutschland*. Essen: Zentrum fur Turkeistudien, 1997.
Şen, Faruk, Sedef Koray, Süheyla Kadioğlu, and Johannes Fest, eds. *Migration Movements from Turkey the European Community*. Essen: Center for Turkish Studies, 1993.
Sener, Cemal. *Alevi Sorunu Üstüne Düşünceler*. Istanbul: ANT Yayinlari, 1994.
Sezer, Ahmet Necati. *Die Türkischen Organisationen im Wandel, 1960–1990*. Frankfurt am Main: Gülenç Verlag, 1996.
Shain, Yossi, *Governments-in-Exile in Contemporary World Politics*, New York and London: Routledge, 1991.
———. 1999. *Transnationalism and the American Experience: On Immigration, Nationhood, and Citizenship*. http://migration.unikonstanz.de/english/events/telaviv/shain.html; Internet.
Sharma, Yojana. 1999. *Fear of Violence in the Wake of Kurdish Deaths in Berlin*. http://www.oneworld.org/ips2/feb99/1346037.html
Sheffer, Gabriel, ed. *Modern Diasporas in International Politics*. London and Sydney: Croom Helm, 1986.
Sirman, Nükhet and Andrew Finkel, eds. *State and Society in Turkey*. London: Routledge, 1991.
Smith, Michael Peter and Luis Eduardo Guarnizo, eds. *Transnatioanlism From Below*. New Brunswick, New Jersey: Transaction Publishers, 1998.
Smith, Robert C. *Los Ausentes Siempre Presentes: The Imagining, Making, and Politics of a Transnational Community Between New York City and Ticuana, Puebla*. Manuscript. Institute for Latin American and Iberian Studies,

Columbia University, October 1992.

———. "Mexican Immigrants, the Mexican State and the Practice of Mexican Politics and Membership," *LASA Forum* 24 (Summer 1998), 19–24.

SOPEMI. *Trends in International Migration: Continuous Reporting System on Migration*, Annual Report. Paris: OECD, 1999.

Soysal, Yasemin, *Limits of Citizenship: Migrants and Post-National Membership in Europe.* Chicago: University of Chicago, 1994.

———. "Boundaries and Identity: Immigrants in Europe." In *European Identity and its Conceptual Roots*, ed. Michael Herzfeld. Prospect Heights, Illinois: Waveland Press, 1996.

———. *Changing Parameters of Citizenship and Claims-Making: Organized Islam in European Public Spheres.* EUI Working Paper No. 96/4, 1996.

Stahl, Charles, ed. *International Migration Today.* Volume 2: Emerging Issues. Belgium: UNESCO and University of Western Australia, Center for Migration and Development Studies, 1988.

Stirling, Paul, ed. *Culture and Economy: Changes in Turkish Villages.* Cambridgeshire: The Eothen Press, 1993.

Storr, Anthony. *The Essential Jung.* Princeton, New Jersey: Princeton University Press, 1983.

Stratton, John. "Displacing the Jews: Historicizing the Idea of Diaspora." *Diaspora* 6 (1997):

Sunier, Thijl. 1995. Disconnecting Religion and Ethnicity: Young Turkish Muslims in the Netherlands. In *Post-Migration Ethnicity: De-Essentializing Cohesion, Commitments, and Comparison*, eds. Gerd Baumann and Thijl Sunier, 58–77. Amsterdam: Het Spinhuis Publishers, 1995.

Takenaka, Ayumi. Transnational Community and its Ethnic Consequences: The Return of Migration and its Transformation of Ethnicity of Japanese Peruvians, 42:9 (June-July 1999).

Telci, Gülçin. "Gülçin Yaziyor." *Hürriyet.* January 31, 1999.

The Ministry of Labor and Social Security, The Directorate for Service to Workers Abroad, *The 1998 Report* (Ankara: 1999).

Thomas, W. I. and F. Znaniecki. *The Polish Peasant in Europe and America: Monograph of Immigrant Groups, 1918–1920.*

Tololyan, Khachig. "The Nation-State and its Others: In Lieu of a Preface." *Diaspora* 1 (1991): 3–7.

———. "Rethinking Diaspora(s): Stateless Power in the Transnational Moment." *Diaspora* 5 (1996): 3–36.

The Turkish Constitution of 1982, with 1995 Amendments. Ankara and Istanbul: Alkim Yayinlari, 1996.

Uçarer, Emek M. and Donald J. Puchala. *Immigration into Western Societies:*

Problems and Policies. London and Washington: Pinter, 1997.
Van Bruinessen, Martin. "Shifting National and Ethnic Identities: The Kurds in Turkey and the European Diaspora." *Journal of Muslim Minority Affairs* 18 (1998): 39–52.
———. *Kurds, Turks, and the Alevi Revival in Turkey*, 1999.
Van Dijk, Teun A, ed. *Handbook of Discourse Analysis.* London and Orlando: Academic Press, 1985.
Van Hear, Nicholas. *New Diasporas: The Mass Exodus, Dispersal, and Regrouping of Migrant Communities.* Seattle: University of Washington Press, 1998.
Van Velzen, L. *Peripheral Production in Kayseri, Turkey: A Study of Prospects for Industrialization Arising From Small and Middle Scale Enterprises in a Peripheral Growth Pole.* The Hague: NUFFIC, 1977.
Vertovec, Steven. "Conceiving and Researching Transnationalism." *Ethnic and Racial Studies* 22 (March 1999): 445–462.
———. "Three Meanings of 'Diaspora,' Exemplified Among South Asian Religions. *Diaspora* 6 (1997): 277–299.
Volkan, Vamik and Norman Itzkowitz. *Turks and Greeks: Neighbors in Conflict.* Cambridgeshire, England: The Eothen Press, 1997.
Volkmer, Ingrid. "Universalism and Particularism: The Problem of Cultural Sovereignty and Global Information Flow." In *Borders in Cyberspace: Information Policy and the Global Information Infrastructure*, eds. Brian Kahin and Charles Nesson, 48–84. Cambridge, Massachusetts and London: The MIT Press, 1997.
Vorhoff, Karin, Barbara Frischmuth, Martin Greve, and Sinan Erbektaş. *Wie der Phoenix aus der Asche: Renaissance des Alevismus.* Cologne: AABF Publications, 1998.
Walker, Ruth. 1998. "Flight of Kurds Opens Holes in Europe's Borders." *The Christian Science Monitor.* 1/12/99.The Parliament of Kurdistan in Exile. http://www.ariga.com/peacebiz/peacelnk/kurd.htm#few; Internet.
Wallraff, Gunther. *Ganz Unten.* Cologne: Kiepenheuer & Witsch, 1985.
Weiner, Myron. "Labor Migrations as Incipient Diasporas." In *Modern Diasporas in International Politics*, ed. Gabriel Sheffer, 47–74. London and Syndney: Croom Helm, 1986.
———. *International Migration and Security.* Boulder, Colorado: Westview Press, 1993.
Weissner, Gunnar. "Grundfragen Aktueller Politischer und Militarischer Entwicklungen in den Kurdischen Provinzen der Turkei." *Orient.* 38 (1997), 289.
Werbner, Pnina. *Embodying Charisma: Modernity, Locality, and Performance of Emotions in Sufi Cults.* London and New York: Routledge, 1998.

White, Jenny. "Belonging to a Place: Turks in Unified Berlin." *City and Society.* Annual Review (1996), 15–28.

———. "Turks in the New Germany." *American Anthropologist* 99/4, (December 1997), 754–768.

Wolbert, Barbara. *Der Getötete Pass: Rückkehr in die Türkei. Eine Ethnologische Migrationsstudie.* Berlin: Akademie Verlag, 1995.

———. "Pass und Passagen: Zur Dynamik und Symbolik von Migrationsprozessen am Beispiel der Rückkehr Türkischer Arbeitsmigranten." *Kea* 10 (1997): 49–69.

Wuthnow, Robert. *Communities of Discourse: Ideology and Social Structure in the Reformation, the Enlightenment, and European Socialism.* Cambridge, Mass.: Harvard University Press, 1989.

Yildirim, Ali. "Kamuoyunu Aldattilar: Islam Federasyonu Milli Görüş ve Erbakan'la Yakin Ilişki Içinde." *The Turkish Times,* March 1, 2000.

Yesilgöz, Yücel. "The Turkish State and Racist Violence." In *Racist Violence in Europe.* Tore Bjorgo and Rob Witte, eds. St. Martin's Press, 1997.

Yurderi, Tolga. *Internet Development in Turkey: A Case Study.* Canada: SoftCom Technology Consultancy, 1997.

Zentrum für Türkeistudien. *Türkei-Jahrbuch.* Essen: ZFT, 1998.

Zentrum für Türkeistudien. *Das Ethnische und Religiöse Mosaik der Türkei und Seine Reflexionen auf Deutschland.* Münster: ZFT, 1998.

Author Index

Abadan-Unat, Nermin, 58, 59, 70
Ackermann, Andreas, 68
Ahmed, Ishtiaq, 66
Anderson, Benedict, 21
Appadurai, Arjun, 21

Basch, Linda, 5
Bauböck, Rainer, 5
Berman, Sheri 31, 32
Bieber, Florian, 81, 82
Birand, Mehmet Ali, 89
Blanc-Szanton, Christina, 5
Bora, Tanil, 143, 144

Çağlar, Ayşe, 170
Çalişlar, Oral, 134
Can, Kemal, 143, 144
Casanova, Jose, 29
Çinar, Tülay, 68, 69
Copeaux, Etienne, 85

Dalman, Metin, 124
Dressler, Markus, 115

Eckstein, Harry, 10, 170
Elazar, Daniel, 24, 25
Elekdağ, Şükrü, 90
Ergil, Doğu, 125

Fouron, Georges, 170

Giddens, Anthony, 20
Glick-Schiller, Nina, 5, 170
Greve, Martin, 68, 69
Guarnizo, Luis, 26

Habermas, Jürgen, 21, 29, 30, 43
Hanioğlu, Şükrü, 51
Hassanpour, Amir, 127
Hirschmann, Albert, 72

Itzkowitz, Norman, 86

Jamin, Mathilde, 67
Jung, C.G., 87

Kadioğlu, Ayşe, 83
Karakaşoğlu, Yasemin, 70, 157
Ketenci, Şükran, 42

Landolt, Patricia, 24
Lindo, Flip, 41

Melikoff, Irene, 109
Miller, Mark, 4, 72
Mountz, Allison, 170
Müftüuler-Bac, Meltem, 56

Mumcu, Ugur, 142

Nonneman, Gerd, 70, 157

Oltayli, Ilber, 54
Öncü, Ayşe, 91

Piore, Michael, 58
Portes, Alejandro, 5, 27, 31
Pries, Ludger, 22, 24, 26, 27

Robins, Kevin, 71

Sayari, Sabri, 86
Schmitter-Heisler, Barbara, 71
Schneehorst, Suzanne, 125
Şen, Faruk, 42, 57
Sezer, Duygu, 89

Smith, Robert, 24, 25
Soysal, Yasemin, 75

Tabak, Ismail, 124
Tololyan, Khachig 5,

Van Bruinessen, Martin, 21, 126, 127
Vertovec, Steven, 25, 66
Volkan, Vamik, 86

Weiner, Myron, 72
Weissner, Gunnar, 120
Wright, Richard, 170
Wuthnow, Robert, 30

Yildirim, Ali, 159
Yurderi, Tolga, 94

Subject Index

Abdülhamid II, 52–54
absentee voting, 74
ADA, 39, 40
Akyildiz, Erhan, 93
Alevi Academy of Europe (AAA), 109
Alevi-Bektashi organizations, 112
Alevi associations in Europe, 108
Alevi-Bektashi Cultural Institute, 114
Alevis, 6,8, 66, 67, 73, 84, 89, 101–116, 142, 145, 158, 164, 172
   organization in Western Europe, 44
   conflict with Sunnis, 83, 105, 110, 114
   renaissance of, 87, 92, 93
   and state reformation, 102–104
   and the internet, 114
   and Kemalism, 114–116
   and Ottomans, 104
Alevism, 93, 107
Ali, the prophet, 102, 115
Almancilar, 59
Atınok, Resul, 124
Altayli, Enver, 149
Anatolia, 116
Anwerbestopp, 41
Armenian question, 95, 172
Armenians, 82
ASALA, 83, 133
Asia Minor, 103

Assembly of Turkish-American Associations (ATAA), 171
association agreement of 1963 between Turkey and the European Union, 56
Association of Ataturkist Thought in Europe (AADD), 47
Association of Independent Alevi Youth (BAGD), 107
Association of Kurdish Workers from Kurdistan. *See* KOMKAR
associational indicators of transnational politics, 23
Atatürk, Mustafa Kemal, 52, 115
Ausländerregelklassen, 67
AYPA-TV, 159

Bade, Fritz, 55
Baghdad railway, 54
Bahçeli, Devlet, 150
Balkans, 109
Barzani, Mesud, 135
başbuğ, 142
Batman, Ali, 144
Bavarian Turkish Coordination Council, 48
Bayar, Celal, 55
Baykal, Deniz, 76
Bediüzzaman Said-i Nursi
beka, 87

Bekaa Valley,121, 123
Bektashism, 103, 109
Berlin Turkish Hearth (Berlin Turk Ocagi), 139
Beşiktaş Scientific Society, 52
Big Unity Party (BBP), 74, 143, 144, 149
Brunning, Heinrich, 55
Bulaç, Ali, 156
Buldan, Hasan Ali, 93
Bundesaufsichtsamt fur den Wertpapierhandel, 160
Bündnis90/Grünen, 77
bureaucratic centralization, 84
Burkay, Kemal, 133, 134
Büyük Ülkü Derneği (Greater Ideal Association), 141

caliphate, 47, 109, 121, 161
Can, Halil, 107
Carretta Carretta, 76
CCMP/MHP/MCP/MHP, 149
Çelebi, Musa Serdar, 144, 145, 149
CEM Foundation, 104
Cem, 101, 102, 115
Cemaat-i Nur, 162. *See also* Nurcular
cemevis, 108, 110
Cemiyet-i Nisa (Islamic Womens' Association), 159
cenaze, 148
Center for the Documentation of Migration from Turkey (DOMIT), 42
Center for Turkey Studies, 42, 57
chain migration, 23
  from Turkey to Europe, 41
Christian Democratic Union (CDU), 76
Christian Social Union (CSU), 141
Christians, 82
Ciller, Tansu, 159
Circassians, 110, 145
civil society, 29, 31, 88–90
civil society in Weimar Germany, 31, 32
collective shadow, 86, 87
commercialization of the broadcast media in Turkey, 90–93

Committee of Union and Progress (CUP), 52, 54, 148
Confederation of Alevi Organizations in Europe (AABK), 108
Conference on Security and Cooperation in Europe (CSCE), 56
Constitutional Court (of Turkey), 85, 90, 115, 141
consular indicators (of transnational politics), 23
contextual indicators (of transnational politics), 27
Copenhagen criteria (for European Union membership), 57, 90
Council of Alevi-Bektashi Representatives (ABTM), 112
creolization, 17, 170
cumulative causation, 22
cyberspace, 93–95,
  and Alevis, 114
  and Kurds, 130–133
  and ultranationalists, 147, 148
  and Islamists, 163
Cyprus question, 95, 172

dar-ül harb, 65, 161
dede (in Alevism), 101, 110
Democratic Socialist Party (DSP), 113
Democratic Peace Movement (DBH), 112, 129
Der Spiegel, 133
deterritorialization, 21
  of the local 8
Detroit, Carl, 53
Deutsche Bank, 54
Deutschkei, 6, 32, 42, 44, 46, 48, 57, 66, 70–73, 101, 102, 140, 144, 156, 169–171
  field work in, 11
  consular outreach in, 48
  elections in, 75
Dev-Sol, 8
deyiş, 106
diaspora, 4, 21, 66, 67
Dilipak, Abdurrahman, 156

Subject Index

Directorate for Religious Affairs (DIB), 69, 103, 104, 112, 141, 142, 154, 160, 164
Direzione dell Emigrazione, 25
Doğan, Izzettin, 104
Dominican Republic, 23, 25

Eastern Report of 1995, 125
Ehl-i Beyt Foundation, 163
El Salvador, 24
electoral connections, 74–76
electoral indicators (of transnational politics), 23
electoral tourism, 74–76
Enver Pasha, 53
Erbakan, Mehmet, 155
Erbakan, Necmettin, 153–155, 158
Erdogan, Tayyip, 162
ERNK, 124, 125
etatisme. *See* statism
ethno-industries, 70
European Commission on Human Rights, 56
European Convention for the Prevention of Torture, 56
European Economic Community (EEC), 56
European Human Rights Court, 90
European Mosque Construction and Support (EMUG), 155
European National Outlook Organization (AMGT), 153. *See also* Islamic Community-
National Outlook (IGMG)
European Turk, 145, 146
European Turkish Islamic Union (ATIB), 74, 143–148, 163
European Union, 18, 52, 131, 132
and Turkey, 55–57, 85, 87, 90
EUTELSAT, 90, 124, 162
ezan, 146

Federal Office for the Protection of the Constitution, 157, 159
Federation of Alevi Communities (Alevi Cemaatleri Federasyonu), 110
Federation of Alevi Unions in Europe (AABF), 106, 108, 110, 113
Federation of European Democratic Turkish Idealist Associations (ADUTDF), 74, 139, 141, 142, 144, 145, 147, 148
Federation of Kurdish Associations in Germany (YEK-KOM), 124
Federation of Patriotic Unions, 110
Federation of Turkish Associations of North-Rhine Westphalia, 65
Federation of Workers Associations in Federal Germany (FIDEF), 46
Felicity Party (SP), 158
fetwa, 162
financial indicators (of transnational politics), 23
Firat, Ali, 133
first republicans, 88
Five Year Development Plan 1962–1967, 58
France Liberties Foundation, 121
franc-maconnerie, 109
Freedom and Democracy Party (ODP), 39, 40

Gastarbeiter, 53, 82
Gavras, Costa, 132
Gaziosmanpasa, 104
German Immigration and Naturalization Law, 69, 70
German National Socialist Party (NSPD), 141
German-Turkish Press Agency (DTPA), 124
Germany quota, 158
ghettoization, 44, 70, 126
globalization (and transnationalism), 19, 20
glocalization, 20
Gökalp, Ziya, 148
grassroots transnationalism, 27
gray wolves, 131, 139–141, 144
Greek Orthodox, 82
green capital, 169
Green Party, 76, 77
group differentiation among migrants, 21, 67

Gülçiçek, Ali Riza, 110, 113
Gülen, Fetullah, 164
Güney, Yilmaz, 132

hac, 148, 163
HAKK-TV, 161
Hasan and Huseyin, 102
Hatiboğlu, Ömer Vehbi, 61
hearth of intellectuals, 84
hemşehrilik, 41
Hevi, 1128, 129, 130
humanism, 109
Hürriyet, 93, 113

Inter-Akademi, 148
HBB-TV, 93
ICCB. See Kaplancilar. See also the Turkish Federation of Islamic Communities
idealism (ulkuculuk), 144
idealist hearths, 143, 150
ideational indicators of transnational politics, 27
identification with homeland, 70, 71
IGMG. See Islamic Community-National Outlook
illusion of homogeneity, 81–84, 86
imam, 141
imam-hatip preparation schools, 155
import substitution industrialization (ISI), 60
Immi-Gruen e.V., 77
indexation to homeland politics, 71–73
Instituto Espanol de la Emigracion, 25
internet and Turkey, 93–95
Islamic Community-National Outlook (IGMG), 153, 155, 157, 158, 161, 163, 164
Islamic Television in Germany (TFD), 159
Islamism, 103, 148
Islamists, 6, 66, 57, 74, 142, 153–164, 172,
and Kemalism, 163, 164
and the internet, 63
Islamist-nationalists, 143–145
islamization of Turkish ultranationalism, 143–145
Ismail, Hekimoglu, 156

Islamrat, 155

Jacobinism, 88
Jaeck, Ernst, 53
jannisaries, 109
Jet Pa Holding, 159
jihad, 47
Joint Parliamentary Committee of the European Union, 56
jus sanguinis, 68
jus soli, 69
Justice and Development Party (AKP), 162

kabe, 110
kahve dernekleri (coffeehouse associations), 43
Kapikule, 75, 143
Kaplan, Cemalettin, 161
Kaplan, Metin, 161
Kaplancilar, 47, 161, 164
Karakoc, Refik, 129
Kaya, Yasar, 132
Kemal, Namik, 109
Kemalism, 66, 84, 85, 88, 106, 107, 114–116, 154, 158
Kerbela, 102
Kessler, Gerhardt, 54
Khalistan, 21
Kilic, Ali, 113
Kilim, 144, 145
Kirca, Ali, 92
Kirmanci, 127
    development of, 21
kirmizi koltuk, 92
Kisakürek, Necip Fazil, 156
kizilbash, 105
Kombassan Holding, 159
KOMKAR (Association of Kurdish Workers from Kurdistan), 119, 120, 128, 129, 131, 133
Konya, 159
Kosovar Albanians, 81
    and Kurds, 82
Kosovo, 81, 109
Kreuzberg, 8, 9, 25, 42, 71, 101

Subject Index

description of, 15
kurban, 148
KURD-HA (Kurdish News Agency), 124
Kurdish Conference in Paris, 121
Kurdish Culture and Information Center, 67
Kurdish ethnonationalism, 52, 103, 106, 107
Kurdish Institute in Paris, 94
Kurdish Parliament in Exile (KPE), 123, 125, 130–132
Kurdish question, 85, 89, 131, 132, 172
Kurdistan, 9, 119, 131
virtual, 123
Kurdistan Democracy Party (KDP), 135
Kurdistan Freedom and Democrcay Congress (KADEK), 12, 135
Kurdish identity, 89
Kurds, 3, 4, 6, 18, 66–68, 72, 82, 103, 104, 110, 119–137, 145, 158, 163
in diaspora, 21
and Kosovar Albanians, 81
history of, 84
and revival of ethnic consciousness, 86
and the internet, 130–133
and Kemalism, 133, 134
Laçin, Ziya, 129
laicism, 154. *See also* secularism
Law on Publications and Broadcasting in Languages other than Turkish, 122
laz, 110
leftists in exile, 45, 46
Liberation Army of Turkish Prisoners (ETKO), 142
Libertarian Turkish-German Friendship Council (HUR-TURK), 76

Magic Box, 90
masonic lodges, 109
Mawdudi, 156
MCP, 140, 141
MED-TV, 83, 94, 124, 127, 128
medreses, 162
mehdi, 115
Mehmet Ali Pasha, 53
migrant networks, 22, 23, 87

Middle Eastern Technical University (METU), 94
Milli Gazete, 158, 159
Milli Görüş. *See* Islamic Community-National Outlook (IGMG)
Misak-i Milli, 84, 134
MIT (National Intelligence Agency), 149
Motherland Party (ANAP), 75, 76, 147, 162
Muhammed, the prophet, 102
multiculturalism (in Germany), 69, 116
MÜSIAD, 159
myth of return, 5, 41

naqshbandiyya, 161, 162
National Action Party (MHP), 43, 74, 131, 139, 140–143, 147, 150
National Outlook. See Islamic Community-National Outlook (IGMG)
National Security Council (MGK), 48, 85, 130
Nefes, 115
North American Free Trade Area (NAFTA), 26
neo-Islamism, 84
neo-Kemalism, 115
neo-Ottomanism, 84, 148
netizens, 22
non-electoral forms of political participation, 27
North Atlantic Treaty Organization (NATO), 171
neutral state thesis, 81
newroz, 46, 124
Nikkei, 170
Nurcular, 162

Oaxacan Mixtec, 26
Oaxaca-Poughkeepsie (OP), 170
Ottomans, 51, 52, 57, 103
Ottoman empire, 53, 54, 86, 148
Ottomanism, 86
Ottoman-Turkish bureaucratic centralization
Ottoman-Turkish history, 120

Overseas Chinese Afairs Commission (OCAC), 25

Öcalan, Abdullah, 4, 18, 81, 121–124, 133, 134
   the capture of, 3
   the trial of, 90
Öker, Turgut, 106, 110
Özal, Turgut, 88, 90, 122
Özdemir, Cem, 17, 18, 70, 77
Özgür Politika, 12, 124, 130

pan-Turkism, 53
Parliamentary Assembly of the Council of Europe, 56
Patriotic Union of Kurdistan (PUK), 135
Peace Committee, 46
Peace Party (BP), 108, 113
Persian Gulf War, 122
PKK (Kurdistan Workers Party), 3, 8, 18, 83, 90, 106, 107, 119–125, 130, 132, 150
political exclaves, 71
political exiles, 44, 45
Program for Mexican Communities Abroad (PCME), 26
Puebla Food Corporation, 25
public sphere, 103
   of civil society, 29, 31, 88–90
   expansion of, 86–90
   and Habermas, 29, 30, 90, 172

Radio Bilinguale, 26
Radio Speaking Turkey, 91
Refahyol, 105, 159
Reichenbach, Hans, 95
remittances, 57, 59, 60
Republican People Party (CHP), 76, 113, 115
return migration, 57–59
Reuter, Ernst, 55
Risale-i Nur, 162

S.O.S Rassismus, 110
saz, 106
second republicans, 88, 97

secularism, 154. *See also* laicism
secularization, 84
Securities and Exchange Commission (SPK), 95
Seljuk, 103
semah, 106
Serbia, 81
Serxwebun, 12, 124, 130
Sevres Syndrome, 87
seyh-ül Islam, 155
Sezer, Ahmet Necdet, 90
Shaikhs, Kurdish, 121
sharia, 109, 157, 162
Shariati, Ali, 156
Sivas, 104
siyaset meydani, 92
Social Democratic Federation of Peoples' Associations (HDF), 76
Social Democratic Populist Party (SHP), 91, 121, 122
Socialist Pary of Kurdistan (PSK), 119, 128, 129, 133
Solingen, 44
SPD, 76
Star 1, 90
state appropriation, 6, 153–155
state conservation, 6, 139, 140
state formation, 6, 120, 121
state reformation, 6
   Alevis and, 102–104
State Security Courts (DGMs), 85
statism, 88
Strauss, Franz Josef, 141
Suleymancilar, 162. *See also*VIKZ
Sunnis, 102, 104, 107, 158
syncretic, 170

Talabani, Jalal, 135
tarikat, 154
tekke, 112
transmigrants, 5
transnational critique, 28, 55
transnational public sphere of civil society, 22–31, 88–90
   features of, 10, 11
transnationalism, 51

Subject Index

and political science, 7, 8
and globalization, 19, 20
and the world wide web, 23–27
institutional indicators of, 27, 28
non-institutional indicators of, 31, 32
Treaty of Sevres, 121
TRT, 90
TRT-INT, 93
True Path Party (DYP), 91
Tunahan, Süleyman Hilmi, 162
Türk Cemaati, 141
Türk-Genc (Turkish Student and Youth Association), 141
Türkeş, Alpaslan, 139–143
Turkey Unity Party (TBP), 110
Turkish constitution of 1982, 47, 91
Turkish Coordination Councils, 48
Turkish Daily News (TDN), 128
Turkish Federation of Islamic Communities (ICCB), 142, 145
Turkish-Islamic synthesis, 44, 84, 106, 143, 149
Turkish-Islamic Union of Religious Affairs (DITIB), 48, 160, 161
Turkish Penal Code (Articles 141, 142, 163), 56, 122
Turkish Supreme Electoral Board, 75
Turkism, 148
Turks in the United States, 171, 172

ultranationalists, 6, 66, 67, 74, 139–150
and the internet, 147, 148
and Kemalism, 148–150
Umayyad, 103
umma, 155
ummet-i Muhammed, 164
umre, 148

unconventional indicators (of transnational politics), 27
unifying supraidentity, 84
ülk" ocaklari (idealist hearths), 143, 150
Union of Alevi-Bektashi Organizations (ABKB), 108
Union of Islamic Cultural Centers (VIKZ), 162
United Nations, 46, 56, 121
United States, 171, 172

Verfassungsschutzbericht (1997), 124
Von Bismarck, Otto, 53, 54
Von der Portens, Max, 55
vaiz, 93
Veziroğlu, Ali Haydar, 112, 113
village development cooperatives, 58

WDR/SDR, 124
Welfare Party (RP), 157, 158
worker companies, 58, 63

YAJK, 124
Yazicioğlu, Muhsin, 74, 144, 149
YCK, 124
Yilmaz, Mesut, 75, 76
Yilmaz, Şevki, 158
Yol, 132
Young Turks, 31, 51–53, 109, 148
Yugoslavia, 81
yuksek tansiyon, 93
Yüksel, Ali, 155, 158
Yumakoğullari, Osman, 158
Yurdatapan, Şanar, 44
Zacatecan Confederation, 26
zaviye, 112
zekat, 148